CONVICTED AND CONDEMNED

Convicted and Condemned

The Politics and Policies of Prisoner Reentry

Keesha M. Middlemass

NEW YORK UNIVERSITY PRESS

New York

NEW YORK UNIVERSITY PRESS
New York
www.nyupress.org

References to Internet websites (URLs) were accurate at the time of writing. Neither the author nor New York University Press is responsible for URLs that may have expired or changed since the manuscript was prepared.

ISBN: 978-0-8147-2439-2 (hardback)
ISBN: 978-0-8147-7062-7 (paperback)

For Library of Congress Cataloging-in-Publication data, please contact the Library of Congress.

New York University Press books are printed on acid-free paper, and their binding materials are chosen for strength and durability. We strive to use environmentally responsible suppliers and materials to the greatest extent possible in publishing our books.

Manufactured in the United States of America

10 9 8 7 6 5 4 3 2 1

Also available as an ebook

Dedicated to Zook

He was a word artist extraordinaire,

trusted keeper of keys,

and my friend.

CONTENTS

Preface and Acknowledgments   ix

Introduction: Felons Are Contemporary Outlaws   1

1. Felony Conviction as Social Disability   21

2. Unwelcome Homecoming   51

3. Denying Access to Public Housing   81

4. Education's Failed Promise   109

5. Not Working and Unable to Work   141

   Conclusion: Public Hostility   171

   Methodological Appendix   189

   Notes   199

   Bibliography   239

   Index   269

   About the Author   283

PREFACE AND ACKNOWLEDGMENTS

First and foremost, I am profoundly thankful to the men and women who were willing to share so much of their private lives with me, including their personal successes and struggles. I think about each of them often, and wish them all well. Participants' lived experiences unfolded over quiet conversations and amusing exchanges, and I deeply appreciate their candor and am indebted to them for revealing what it means to be a modern-day felon, how government and public policies undermine their reentry efforts, and what it means to live on the periphery of society. This book is the participants' collective story: Their narratives shape the trajectory of this research in immeasurable ways to offer a distinct viewpoint about what it means to live as a convicted felon. I am grateful for the opportunity to be their narrator and hope that each participant recognizes his or her voice in the text and that my efforts live up to their expectations. Many participated with the goal of helping others: "I want them out there to know that just because we did bad don't mean we can't do good."[1]

I owe a special debt of thanks to three organizations: the Andrew W. Mellon Foundation, the Vera Institute of Justice, and The Ohio State University's inaugural Crime and Justice Summer Research Institute: Broadening Perspectives & Participation. I am beholden to the Mellon Foundation for its financial support, which afforded me the time to write, think, and conduct preliminary research for this project while at the Vera Institute of Justice. Special thanks to Chris Stone and Michael Jacobson for supporting the Postdoctoral Fellowship on Race, Crime, and Justice, which provided the space for intellectual discourse and investigative research at the intersection of race, policy, crime, politics, and prisoner reentry. My residency in New York City set the stage to broaden my examination of prisoner reentry and the socially disabling effects of a felony conviction. The Summer Research Institute at The Ohio State University was a boot camp for academics, offering invaluable interactions with junior and senior scholars, as well as experts in the field of sociology, race, punishment, and criminal justice. Special thanks to Professors Ruth D. Peterson and Lauren J. Krivo for their leadership and professional guidance, and to Professor Emeritus Paul Beck, who shared his knowledge and research insights with me.

I am very appreciative for the steadfast support of friends, colleagues, and contemporary outlaws alike, who offered encouraging words, extended themselves in big and small ways, and communicated a continual belief in my aim of raising the level of social consciousness about the project of a felony conviction. I extend a special thank you to Professor Paul Boxer; I have benefited immensely from our friendship and our conversations about social justice, punishment, and reentry. I am indebted to Warren Thompson for facilitating my access into the world of prisoner reentry, alongside Jerome, David, Priscilla, and Roxanne, who collectively shared their shrewd intelligence about reentry and how a felony constrains people. I am grateful for my friend, mentor, and colleague, the late Professor Manning Marable; he believed in my ideas before they were fully developed, and I will be forever thankful for his confidence in my ability to write a contextualized narrative using first-person accounts of what it means to navigate the social landscape as a felon.

Writing a book requires one to move words across the page, which is a uniquely solitary endeavor that takes form in the company of others; I had ongoing and beneficial conversations with my friends, Professors CalvinJohn Smiley and Keith Reeves. I appreciate my friends, colleagues, and fellow scholars, Professors Wendy Smooth, Julia Jordan-Zachary, D'Andra Orey, Khalil Muhammad, Taja-Nia Henderson, Carla Shedd, Michael Leo Owens, Pearl Ford Dowe, Lisa L. Miller, Zaire Dinzey-Flores, Osagyefo Sekou, and Adolphus Belk, and extend a big thank you to my friends Professors Rosa Aloisi, Sarah Martin, and SarahBeth Kaufman for their encouragement. I appreciate the assistance of student workers Alyssa Alfaro and Susan E. Clark and am grateful for the early support from Professors Leith Mullings, Premilla Nadasen, Cheryl Mwaria, Dana-Ain Davis, Aimee Cox, and Robyn Spencer. Last but not least, I want to extend a special thank you to Professors Charles Menifield, Fredrick Harris, and Jyl Josephson, who each provided indispensable backing and assistance at a critical time in my career.

Thanks to a fabulous circle of friends and family, I lived a semi-balanced life. The engaging diversions included culinary adventures with Crystal Izquierdo and Kim Owens; dinner parties with organic vegetables and distilled spirits with the late Craig "Zook" Davis, Tarmaine "Superman" Hall, Johanna Gonzalez, "Self" Rayford, and Sonia Burnett; time with my sista-friends Nicole Barcliff, Noelle Lusane, Janet Draper West, Iman Hypolite, and Javiela Evangelista; and trips home to visit my parents, Bob and Marilyn Middlemass, my brothers, Dean and Mike, sister-in-law, Jill, nieces, Lauren and Ally, the Adamses, the Jungs, my friend Jenny Dolden, and the Gibson clan.

While writing this book, I read a wide range of texts and had conversations with intellectually curious people in random Brooklyn cafés, restaurants, and international airports: Conversations concerned corruption in Machiavelli's *Prince*; punishment and love in *The Prophets* (A. Heschel); and great works examining obscure mysteries found in ancient texts and secret societies hiding in plain sight. Some of the best conversations swirled around *The Art of War* (Sun Tzu); in an abstract sense, the metaphor of war is an accurate representation of what "tough on crime" politics and policies feel like in real life: Participants described prison as a form of combat, reentry as an ongoing battle, and a felony conviction as a never-ending fight against an inhospitable society. War is also theoretically apt when writing a book, as it is descriptive of the struggle over opposing values and tenets. Every socially conscious author struggles over word choice and wrestles with ideologically biased words and politically laden text to communicate socially fraught issues because words matter. It takes care to convey the experiences of others and to stay true to participants' voices while transmitting participants' authentic lived experiences; therefore, I use their language to describe the world they occupy.

Many thanks to Ilene Kalish, the fabulous staff at NYU Press, and the anonymous reviewers; their insightful recommendations and their constructive criticisms enriched the clarity and focus of analysis in many ways. By highlighting the personal narratives of participants, I reinforce the theoretical framework of social disability, make the disabling effects of a felony conviction obvious, and signal why this study is so important. Max, a participant, explicitly understood: "What you doing is a good thing, no one ever asked before, about all this. No one."[2]

The lived experiences of female and male felons reentering society in Newark, New Jersey, display how the current regime of laws undermines reentry: When this study is extrapolated nationwide, this book tells the story of more than 12,500 women and men returning home every week socially disabled and unable to reenter society successfully, and demonstrates how felons are socially disabled *after* completing their sentence. The current system entails that everyone pays in some form to support the vast tentacles of the criminal justice system, net-widening laws, and socially disabling policies, including taxpayers, future victims, and communities. The ultimate goals of reentering society should be to improve reentry outcomes and reduce the number of future victims, but to accomplish these twin aims and reform the system, a collective effort must acknowledge how current policies work in real time. It is my belief that an overhaul of existing laws should be done with the objective of allowing individuals to do their time, pay their debt to society, and return to the community without their criminal past haunting them, which will protect society from future crime and reduce the number of victims.

My hope is that each reader will be motivated by the amassed evidence and analysis to rethink notions of the carceral state, to acknowledge the racial bias embedded in the system and the way the historic residue of racism, punishment, and the fear of blackness, combined with political rhetoric and public policies, banishes certain people to the margins of society. If anything, I hope each reader is convinced that society's solution to social problems *cannot* be more punishment. Punishment for the sake of punishment makes bad situations worse, and it seems as if the only ostensible rationale for more punishment is political vindictiveness, which creates a retributive system that breeds contempt for the system. Society cannot felonize its way out of the current politically spawned mess. With any luck, those who think punishment is the *only* answer to social ills and who hold tightly to the adage that "felons are felons" and undeserving of a second chance are small in number and empathetic readers far outnumber them. The latter, I hope, will be moved to stand up for social and racial justice wherever they find injustice.

TRIGGER WARNING: Profanity is embedded in the "discursive narratives"[3] of participants throughout the text, and is included in its original form because sometimes respectable vocabulary is insufficient or ineffective at conveying information that expresses one's emotions, verbalizes one's frustrations, and informs others about one's state of mind. Language is powerful, and profanity is a rhetorical tool used for special emphasis about ideas that cannot be captured through polite words. Profanity has its advantages in an otherwise formal text, as there is no better way to communicate: "I'm fucked."[4]

Introduction

Felons Are Contemporary Outlaws

When I entered the world of reentry, I was looked upon as an outsider with no standing. I was atypical, a stranger, a black woman with a PhD who was interested in getting to know the men and women occupying the select and exclusive space of an organization designed to help returning prisoners. Such establishments offer assistance to both men and women reentering society, and those inhabiting such locations are not unusual, except for one thing; almost everyone has a criminal record, including the majority of staff. I recognized that I was an oddity, so in order not to be prematurely rejected, I knew I had to explain my intentions and prove that I was sincere before I would even have an opportunity to narrate the lives of felons reentering and returning to society. Thus, as an interloper, I had to prove that I was credible before I could gain their assent. To do so, I had to build trust and rapport simultaneously; in the beginning, rapport was tenuous, at best, and there was no trust. Prerequisites to accomplishing these twin aims were to be accessible and affable; so, for twenty-nine months, I showed up to the nonprofit, week in and week out, and was present, visible, and engaged, thereby providing multiple opportunities for individuals to question and challenge me about my motives, to recognize that I was dedicated to learning their truth, and to reason on their own that I was trustworthy. The underlying issue, I discovered, was a deeply entrenched wariness of outsiders: I had to prove that I was not trying to trick anyone into saying something that would attract the attention of the police or parole officers and get someone sent back to prison. Once participants realized I was not the police, the effort spent gaining their trust proved valuable; our interactions became a series of exchanges about what it really meant to be a person with a felony on their "face sheet," which is also referred to as a rap sheet, "jacket," or criminal record.[1]

Each day I interacted with adults convicted of a felony, I walked only a few city blocks from a major transportation hub in the largest city in New Jersey to the nonprofit organization. The few city blocks I navigated represented a gulf of difference between those affected by a felony conviction, including their families and the communities they return to, and the elected officials who pass laws that shape the lives of felons upon their return to society. In order to reveal the lived experiences and narratives of those reentering society as felons, I wanted to discover, learn, and observe reentry experiences in real time. To accomplish this goal, I have based this book on ethnographic fieldwork and in-depth interviews, which put me in the middle of a reentry space where I talked to participants and asked them how they felt and what they thought about while reentering society. My goal was to determine how their lived experiences are shaped by their felony conviction, so I set out to learn in what ways the consequences of a felony conviction reach beyond the traditional boundaries of the criminal justice system, enabling me to theorize how a felony conviction operates as a "social disability."

I borrow the term "social disability" from disability studies, which examines the social, political, cultural, and economic factors affecting individuals living with a disability,[2] to argue that felons are treated in a manner analogous to the way those with physical disabilities have been treated. The social model of disability contends that disability is socially constructed and seeks to change society to accommodate people living with disabilities. For instance, persons with restricted physical abilities who require a wheelchair to access or navigate public activities and spaces would be hindered in their mobility without curb ramps or other public modifications. Society changed by providing accommodations to enable people living with disabilities to participate on an equal basis with others in a range of activities. For felons, however, there are few, if any, social accommodations. A felony conviction restricts social interactions and hinders felons' efforts to reintegrate into society because there is no equivalent curb ramp.

The scope of the hostility directed towards felons is represented by this fact: If the criminal justice system did not convict one more person of a felony from this day forward, and socially disabling policies remained in place without change, millions of women and men would still have to figure out how to reenter society essentially on their own.

Participants knew there was no public assistance for people like them: "No one is there for you. You alone."[3]

While I was in the field, it quickly became evident that reentering society after a felony conviction is principally the individual's responsibility, but problems arise before an individual can reenter because one's felony conviction follows one far beyond the criminal court and the prison walls. When felons attempt to reconnect with family, learn how to acclimate to society, try to secure housing, find a job, and complete a host of other important goals, including wrestling with any trauma they may have suffered and accessing health care, the felony conviction hinders them. To reenter the community successfully, individuals must negotiate and accomplish *all* tasks, without fail, and do so by establishing themselves without social services and public benefits. Yet, the socially disabling consequences of a felony make surmounting *all* of the necessary steps to reentering society difficult because those who are returning home are more likely to be homeless, without family support, destitute, lacking social capital, poorly educated, jobless, and experiencing food insecurity. If someone on parole fails at a single task, such as not being able to secure a legal job, he or she can be sent back to prison. When the least prepared fail to reenter successfully, society blames the individual and holds him or her accountable for his or her failure while neglecting to consider "tough on crime" policies that use a felony conviction to create modern-day outlaws. Criminals, except for their criminal behavior, are ordinary people who live relatively normal lives,[4] but, as I will show, once a person is convicted of a felony, the felony *changes* that person and the law *transforms* him or her into a contemporary outlaw. This is the case because a felony conviction is a distinctive form of stigma that brands a person and changes his or her social status into an identity infused with extra-legal meaning. A felony conviction marginalizes a person long after existing laws have been changed or he or she has "maxed out." "Maxing out," a phrase used by criminologists, practitioners, and participants, describes any prisoner who serves his or her entire prison sentence, is released, and is no longer under the control of the Department of Corrections (DOC).[5]

Each participant wanted to max out, but after a prisoner has been released from prison on parole "with papers"[6] or "maxes out," he or she faces an alternative reality because a felony conviction carries with it a form of hostility that is rooted in practices and policies separate from the criminal justice system. In order to illustrate society's hostility towards felons and the need to rewrite policies to remove a felony conviction's undesirable social meaning, I narrate the lived experiences of felons returning home. As prisoner reentry is connected to a number of interrelated issues, such as history, politics, social mores, culture, and race, I also explore the historical development whereby a felony conviction became a stigma due to its unfavorable social construction, examine how "tough on crime" politics sustains punitive practices, analyze existing policies to show how a felony conviction obstructs reintegration, and describe racial animus and how, in particular, blackness was and continues to be equated to criminality.

Race and its historical, social, and political connection to crime are central to making sense of the enduring power of a felony conviction, its relationship to slavery, and the linking of black skin to criminality. Political and societal investment in a felony conviction reaches back to before the founding of the country, but when slavery became the official policy of the U.S. government, it institutionalized race, and being a slave became equivalent to a criminal life sentence for black people.[7] The pattern of racializing crime continued after the institution of slavery was dismantled, when criminal statutes were rewritten to achieve similarly oppressive results. Race is the paradigm in which laws have been written by national and state legislators during various historical periods; each time, amidst social, political, and economic changes, politicians altered the law and whom it targeted for retribution, and used race to erect specific policies, including Jim Crow,[8] the creation of the inner city,[9] the "War on Drugs," and the criminal code.[10] "Race is a uniquely divisive characteristic of American social life" and has been used as an enduring justification to create policies negatively targeting the black community.[11] The historical impact of race continues to weigh on present-day issues involving police tactics, the criminal justice system, punishment, and prisoner reentry.[12]

One lingering racialized issue of importance is the "War on Drugs," which emerged in the 1980s and has been maintained to the present with the support of both Republican and Democratic presidents.[13] When the violence associated with crack cocaine and its open-air drug markets was splashed across national news outlets, an image solidified in society's mind conflating race and drugs as synonymous.[14] Politicians viewed this as an opportunity to build a political platform that appeared to combat drugs and simultaneously to be "tough on crime." The "War on Drugs" is a metaphorical war against an inanimate object,[15] and has expanded to become a set of interlocking policies that target racial minorities[16] while largely ignoring white drug users and dealers. The "War on Drugs" repeated historical patterns of targeting the black community with policing and surveillance tactics disproportionate to its size.[17] Similar laws followed 9/11; as a pretext for ferreting out domestic and international drug kingpins and those deemed "other," police forces were militarized for "war."[18] A continuing casualty in this "war" is anyone convicted of a felony.

A felony conviction is a socially constructed lived experience that extends the past into the future.[19] It is influenced by context, location, different racial-social-historical eras, and politically infused language, but the combination of political and historical decisions, public policies, and the lived experiences of convicted felons has not received sufficient scholarly attention.[20] In order to bring together these related but disparate aspects of what it means to be a contemporary outlaw, I have utilized an interdisciplinary research design incorporating multiple methods. This approach conveys the layered reality of a felony—its racial and historical context and its socially disabling effects—which has distinct post-sentence consequences.

The Research Context

Essex County, New Jersey, which contains the state's largest city, Newark, accounts for 16.3 percent of New Jersey's prison admissions, and 54 percent of prisoners released in New Jersey return there,[21] which signifies that reentry, if one looks closely, unfolds in every corner of the city. Due to the overwhelming social needs of former prisoners returning to Essex County, most of the state's reentry services are located in Newark, and one of the most intimate junctures of reentry is the safe space where those returning to society ask for help. The nonprofit organization where I conducted fieldwork is located in the downtown core of the city and occupies one-half of an upper floor of a nondescript building; the organization's office space is divided into a reception area, two conference rooms, a kitchenette, storage space, a computer lab, and six private offices for staff, volunteers, and interns. The organization has offered reentry services in Newark dating back to the 1970s and has a solid reputation for providing information to adults transitioning home after a criminal conviction, but like several other small nonprofit organizations, it operates with limited financial support. During my fieldwork, its days and hours of operation changed from being open five days a week, seven hours a day, to being open four days a week and then to being open for three days a week for four hours a day.[22] Even with limited hours and services, the dedicated staff kept the threadbare office thriving. All but two staff members had previously been incarcerated, yet all of them were from Newark and were invested in the success of the organization and its mission. Collectively, they cared deeply about changing the trajectory of felons coming home. As one female staff member said,

> I did a year in prison almost thirty years ago and I don't want to see the next generation in Newark have to struggle like I did. That [one year] was enough for me. I ain't going back [to prison]. You have to learn from your mistakes to do things differently, and I learned, but some don't. We here for all of 'em.[23]

Anyone transitioning home from local or county jail or state or federal prison and in need of assistance is welcome at the nonprofit organization and is referred to as a client. Clients arrive due to word of mouth about the services offered, consisting of job placement services; assistance securing a birth certificate, state photo identification, or Social Security card; a variety of workshops and classes; case management to coordinate service providers and government agencies; and free access to the internet. The computer lab is always busy; clients are eager to learn computer skills, apply for jobs on-line, and utilize social networking sites to reconnect with their children and family.

The Meaning of "Participant"

Each client in this study is referred to as a participant. Scholars in different disciplines use a variety of terms to describe the people they study, and the description depends on the orientation of the researcher. Ethnographers use the term "host population" or "ethnographic hosts" to refer to individuals, groups, or cultures investigated, while psychologists use the term "subjects," and sociologists and anthropologists use "populations" or "informants."[24] Although these terms are not universal, they are the dominant ones used by each discipline. The customary word across disciplines is "informants," who are individuals who inform researchers about their world.

I consciously choose *not* to use the term "informant," which has negative political and social connotations for the already marginalized population of participants. Informants, in the context of law enforcement, are people who supply information to the police, and who are often referred to as "narcs," "snitches," "stool pigeons," "bitches," or "rats." On the other hand, "subject" and "human subjects" are clinical and detached terms, and since participants had already been dehumanized by the criminal justice system, I felt that repeating that process would deny each participant his or her humanity. Therefore, I employ the word "participant" to show respect for the lived experiences of each individual who shared his or her world with me. For similar reasons, I purposely choose to use the word "prisoner" or "former prisoner" rather than "inmate."[25] All of the participants had at least one felony conviction, visited the non-profit organization for reentry assistance, and had insider knowledge acquired through their distinctive experiences. As a result, I set out "to treat participants with respect, protect them from harm, and save them from embarrassing [or illegal] exposure."[26] This book was made possible only because of their participation, and each was promised strict confidentiality.[27]

Research Design and Methods

On the basis my previous research,[28] I recognize how a felony conviction is a lived experience impacting individuals over time; therefore, as an integral part of this research, I accept that there are several ways in which someone could reconstitute his or her life with a felony conviction on his or her public record but without access to social and public benefits. By taking this approach, I aim to expand our understanding of how a felony conviction takes on a distinct meaning during the social interactions required to reenter society. Because I consciously consider participants' perceptions of what it means to be a felon, I inevitably had to go beyond survey and secondary data and enter the world of reentry to collect original data. In total, I spent twenty-nine months in the field. From February 2011 to June 2013, I conducted ethnographic fieldwork at a single site where I was both participant *and* observer of prisoner reentry in real time.[29]

"In Situ"

I combined ethnographic data with participation-observations, in-depth interviews, and archival research of publicly accessible documents, which required me to be "in situ."[30] As an outsider, spending a considerable amount of time "in situ" put me in the position to describe reentry where it happens, permitted prolonged participant-observations and interactions over time, allowed me to interpret the culture from which behaviors are formed, granted me the time to establish rapport and gain the trust of participants, and enabled me to collect an array of data.[31] This choice made it possible for me to contextualize micro-level behaviors in the larger social communities and policy environments that participants reentered.

While taking an ethnographic approach, in particular, is rare for Americanists in political science,[32] it is normal for reentry scholars.[33] By utilizing an interdisciplinary, multimethod, ethnographic research design, I captured the layered personal narratives of reentering society as a felon using the "magpie approach."[34] The magpie approach compels researchers to collect and accumulate data from numerous sources and participants across time, and although the magpie approach in situ was time-consuming, it was worthwhile.

Initially, I felt as though I was working on an enormous jigsaw puzzle without a picture to guide me, so to avoid simplifying things or projecting my disposition onto participants' experiences,[35] I learned the language of reentry, considered behaviors from participants' point of view, and treated all gathered data as equally important, even when its usefulness was not immediately apparent.[36] The dedicated time in the field allowed me to identify patterns, categories, and themes[37] from the detailed record of notes that I kept about what I surveyed, heard, and witnessed.[38] As new data was collected, I analyzed it against previously accumulated data,[39] which meant determining whether observed attributes were unique or shared experiences. If the latter, I considered how and whether such characteristics were part of a broader pattern of reentry linked to racial-social-historical precedents or public policies. If it was the former, I attempted to ascertain what was going on, and why, at the individual level. The entire process was repeated numerous times across data, making it possible for me to make sense of disparate data and figure out whether and how seemingly dissimilar data were connected. Collecting data from multiple sources using different methods was time-consuming, but facilitated my writing a detailed analysis and telling a story of prisoner reentry that is socially and culturally situated, holistic, and supported by empirical evidence.

The scholarship on prisoner reentry identifies the key factors that impact the ability of men and women to reenter society successfully, which often overlap with the factors that would reduce recidivism rates;[40] so, "understanding the factors that contribute to ex-offenders' reintegration success and failure is an important avenue for continued research."[41] I believe that the process of reentering society needs to be assessed using data that captures all of its complex disorder and that helps us to understand why a failure to reenter and recidivate is the norm. Therefore, in an effort to understand reentry beyond the customary variables, I examine macro-level public policies and how they construct and reconfigure felons' lives by specifically focusing on participants' micro-level decisions and their lived experiences while returning home.

In the Field: Data-Collection Strategies

Using the mixed-methods approach described above, I focus on participants' narratives to learn the subtleties of reentering society. Observations and personal narratives illustrate the random nature and often contradictory, complicated, and messy experience of reentering urban life,[42] and they capture the breadth and depth of experiences that are used to configure and reconfigure the way one reenters society; demonstrate how a felony conviction operates like a petite penal institution;[43] and provide details on how personal encounters and interactions are applicable to a variety of issues scattered across the phenomena of reentry.[44] Over time, while I was collecting data, a contextualized picture of how a felony conviction is a lived experience *and* a social disability emerged,[45] which provides a unique perspective on how an individual reenters and moves through society as a convicted felon.

The first step of data collection was concerned with ethnography, the purpose of which is to learn from others, break down barriers, and witness cultural configurations.[46] The researcher's role is to develop a deep and thick description of edifying patterns to convey how others perform in public.[47] "Pure ethnography" involves immersing oneself in a particular cultural environment, but research is ethnographic when its principles are applied during data collection and analysis.[48] I employed ethnographic standards by first establishing my presence at the nonprofit organization and discreetly observing interactions among staff, clients, and volunteers in an effort to witness the culture of reentry as an unfolding narrative.[49] Observations provided indispensable situational knowledge about how a felony shapes lived experiences and how its disabling effects influence micro-level behaviors. Ethnography revealed "key participants" who helped me make sense of their world[50] and gave voice to reentry practices and customs that are often neglected or misunderstood in traditional reentry scholarship.[51]

The second strategy involved moving from unobtrusive observations to participant-observations, which created an opportunity to collect critical testimony about participants' felony convictions and the ways in which convictions specifically affected participants. Each individual reenters with divergent levels of social capital, hard resources, skill sets, housing options, psychological needs, abilities, and family support. Therefore, reentry is different for everyone. Participant-observations help to unmask the diversity of reentry experiences and display how a felony conviction is like its own petite penal institution that entangles people in its grip.[52] This was evident when the smell of homelessness scented the air or angry voices filled the room.[53]

On the basis of my continuous attendance at the nonprofit organization, I was able to establish a fragile sense of trust with participants, enough for me to attend a weekly group meeting designed to increase the likelihood of successful reentry. Something akin to a workshop, the weekly meeting was simply referred to as "Group." Group was one of several workshops held at the nonprofit;[54] lasting between one and a half and two hours, Group involved informal conversations developed around a shared experience or news event introduced by the Group's facilitator. Group focused on improving soft skills, such as communication aptitude, the capacity to engage in inconsequential discussions about the weather or sports, and the importance of having a positive attitude while reconnecting with family and reentering society. During each Group, I chronicled participants' narratives as well as my own observations.[55] Attending Group as a participant-observer was labor-intensive, but of great value; the dedicated time afforded me the opportunity to discover the underlying meanings of a felony conviction; learn about the intentions and practices adopted by participants reentering society; discover participants' perspectives on reentering society with limited access to social capital; and apply social disability theory to individual and collective reentry experiences.

Attendees of Group were expected to listen and talk. This expectation seems simple enough, but many prisoners do not talk to a great extent while living in what Erving Goffman, a Canadian-born sociologist and considered one of the most influential sociologists of the twentieth century, refers to as a "total institution."[56] A "total institution" is an enclosed social system that has almost complete control over every aspect of residents' lives, and can include mental hospitals and prisons.[57] When incarcerated, prisoners are cut off from society, and while they are secured in a single location, the totality of their lives unfolds in the limited space.[58] In such a setting, many prisoners purposely adopt a defensive position because a misunderstanding in prison can lead to unpleasant or violent repercussions, so they keep to themselves. A direct consequence is that many of the men, and some of the women, did not engage in "normal" conversations while incarcerated: "This [Group] is important to me, because I'm talking and stuff and I ain't talked this much for a very long time. A real long time, but I need to learn how [to have conversations] again if I'm going to make it out there [in the community]."[59] Group provided participants a safe place to talk, to share their opinions and anxieties about reentering, and to voice their frustrations, which were relatively new experiences for many of them.

Most participants came to the nonprofit emotionally closed off and angry, but it was important to begin to sort out their buried emotions by sharing their feelings about the varied challenges of transitioning home with similarly situated individuals. Group provided an exclusive and critical space for participants to share their fears and the negative effects of being incarcerated, in turn depicting the human tragedy of prison, how it deprives individuals of their humanity, and how it breaks spirits and families. Although it was not a regular event, participants did occasionally share their previously hidden pain about being incarcerated, and how they were coping with angry kids and heartbroken parents, fractured relationships, and their own regrets. After serving fifteen and a half years in state prison, Sylvester said, "I come home after being locked up and I wasn't there, my mom, my kids, their mom, all struggling because of me. Family falls apart; they did time with me out here when I was in there. They not doing well. That's on me."[60]

When talking about their felony conviction and reentering society, participants spoke about wanting to change their criminal mentality to avoid going back to prison and about how they were "making" it and surviving on the outside; these exchanges revealed participants' sense of what makes reentry so hard. Notably, participants knew there was no help coming, innately accepting that there was not a second chance for them: "I've been looking for help, anything really. I need it all, but it ain't there."[61]

Others talked about how coming home was disruptive to their mental well-being:

> I'm still trying to find my balance, you know. Been home months now, and I still wake up and don't know where I am sometimes. That shit can make you delusional, like you not sure you out [of prison] and you still locked up. At night, it's real crazy, 'cuz I can get up and walk around, touching stuff, open the fridge, close the fridge, open it back up, look out the window thinking I can go outside, and go, [and think] wow, stuff like that.[62]

Group helped participants talk about their formerly unacknowledged feelings and permitted others experiencing similar "crazy nights" to know they were not alone. The conversations in Group focused on ways to manage many of the new things they had to contend with; participants talked about how they had to learn to live in prison and reentering society was about learning how to live on the outside, but the hard part was that once they were home, participants quickly found out that what they had been told inside prison about reentry was a myth.[63] "We been lied to."[64]

The third data strategy involved personal interviews. I conducted fifty-three semistructured in-depth interviews with women and men reentering society who were identified as key participants.[65] During each interview, I asked participants a series of questions from an IRB-approved protocol about their life before their felony conviction, their level of knowledge about housing, education, and employment policies related to a felony conviction, how government policies affected them, and their personal reentry experiences.[66] The interview questions were designed to acquire information about participants' views of their felony conviction; how it affected their daily lives; and what it meant as they reentered society.[67] Each of the fifty-three interviews was conducted in a semiprivate office at the nonprofit organization, and ranged between thirteen and ninety-six minutes in length, lasting an average of forty minutes.[68]

The fifty-three interviews situated the personal lives of men and women; gave voice to different experiences at the micro-level;[69] contextualized the culture of reentering society; and strengthened and supported the data collected from the ethnographic fieldwork and the wide-ranging participant-observations. For instance, I wanted to know about their housing situation. Many participants were experiencing homelessness, but to varying degrees. Several were living on the street; others were living in a homeless shelter; a handful were trying to make an intimate relationship work; and some were attempting to cope with sibling angst and loathing so they could sleep in a real bed. These finer details emerged by my directly asking participants where they slept, who was helping them, and what the nature of the relationship was. Participants described their living situations as calm, "cool," unstable, and "crazy."[70] Such details contribute to understanding the differential effects of homelessness and the weak family bonds participants experience upon returning home, but also how the lack of social capital among participants exacerbates negative reentry outcomes.

The fifty-three interviewees were convicted of a variety of felony crimes, with criminal sentences ranging from thirty days to fifty years.[71] The participants skewed towards racial minorities: thirty-nine self-identified as black (73.6 percent), seven as Latino (13.2 percent), four as white (7.5 percent), and three as mixed race (5.7 percent). Of the fifty-three interviewees, forty-seven were men (88.7 percent).[72] In this context, the reentering population reflects who is incarcerated in New Jersey; its incarcerated population is one of the most racially stratified in the United States.[73] Subsequently, the combination of disproportionately high minority confinement, low rates of white incarceration, and a high concentration of prisoners returning to Newark is reflected in the composition of the client population, and therefore the gender, racial, and ethnic makeup of participants reflects the disparities in New Jersey's criminal justice system.

The fourth data collection strategy was archival research. Given my previous research,[74] the majority of narratives resonated as true, but scholars who research deceptive and truthful statements argue that the likelihood of obtaining either is "the level of chance."[75] Lying is a common activity in everyday interactions,[76] so it was necessary to determine the degree of veracity by actively eliciting information from independent sources. While in the field, I realized that participants' chronological retelling of their lives contained gaps, and even though I spent dozens of hours asking questions and intermingling with staff, clients, and participants, an ongoing challenge of collecting data was to differentiate truthful from misleading testimonials. Archival research of publicly accessible records corroborated participants' age (i.e., birth date), legal name, criminal charges, length of sentence, and parole status. Archival research was crucial to fill in missing gaps of time; reduce the unknowns; differentiate between intentional fabrications and shaky memories;[77] validate the interview data, participant-observations, and ethnographic data; and uncover new slices of data about the connection among time served, a felony conviction, social capital and family support, and prisoner reentry success or failure.

How Policies Use a Felony Conviction to Construct Social Disability

The unique primary data links first-person narratives and lived experiences to public policies and the social, historical, and political environments connected to a felony conviction. The interdisciplinary and mixed-methodological approach demonstrates that a felony conviction is qualitatively different from other punishments because the negative ramifications of a felony conviction stretch across policies outside of the traditional boundaries of the criminal justice system, extend the degree of punitiveness beyond the sentencing court, and communicate society's contempt for the individual.[78] A direct result is that felons are socially disabled because the incapacitating effects of a felony are entrenched in public policies that undermine former offenders' ability to reenter society successfully, and are the result of "net-widening" regulations.[79]

Net-widening refers to the expansion of statutorily defined crimes, administrative restrictions, and associated penalties that connect a felony to different types of punishment outside of the criminal justice system.[80] I argue that a felony conviction is a net-widening because once an individual is labeled a felon, administrative sanctions are used in an effort to widen the net so as to socially control men and women released from the DOC, and the net of penal control widens beyond the customary boundaries of the criminal justice system via the use of a felony conviction.[81] Limiting a felon's access to programs and public benefits widens the adverse consequences of a felony conviction and stretches them out from the criminal justice system to create different nets of social control to capture a greater number of people.[82] A felony conviction operates as a net widener because its damaging consequences are embedded in policies that discourage "good behavior," produce social disabilities and negative externalities, such as homelessness, and, I argue, may even encourage criminal conduct by those attempting to reenter society. "Having a record; I'm a felon, it changes everything, and I can't change that. It's your 'overcoat,' an' you have to learn how to wear it at all times."[83] The system is able to socially control and disable an expanding number of people, which results in an increased number of felons being rearrested and sent back to prison.[84]

Net-widening rules place more restrictive sanctions upon felons' bodies, which increases the burden of punishment on the individual felon. As a result, a felony conviction keeps men and women linked to the criminal justice system indefinitely, which begs the question, Is a felon ever allowed to serve his or her time, pay his or her debt, *and* reenter society? If the answer is yes, then any punishment imposed by the criminal courts would be sufficient. If not, then it necessitates asking, How do policies socially disable felons? What public aim is achieved by socially disabling felons after completion of a court-mandated sentence? What civic good is served by the discourse of illegality? Is a felon ever allowed to reenter without the public's hostility shadowing them?

Chapter Outline

This book connects social disability theory, public policies, and the reality of reentering society as a convicted felon to answer the above questions. Chapters 1 and 2 survey the development of criminality by weaving together the interrelated issues of history, politics, racial animus, and the social construction of a felony. Chapters 3–5 apply social disability theory to the lived experiences of being a felon in three policy areas considered the most important for successful reentry outcomes: housing, education, and employment. This study reveals how a felony conviction extends punishment after completion of a criminal sentence, how policies undermine attempts to reenter, and how a felony is its own petite penal institution.[85]

Chapter 1 begins with a synopsis of how felons are socially constructed and targeted, which is the underlying basis for how and why felons are socially disabled via public policies. To shed light on how deep-rooted societal beliefs construct hostility towards felons, I introduce social disability theory and use it to draw an analogy between people living with disabilities and the societal oppression of felons.[86] Second, I explore the historical discourse of a felony, its relationship to criminal punishment, and how a felony conviction was socially constructed to produce public stigma. Then, I consider how politicians are motivated to deny social benefits to convicted felons. Finally, I examine the social construction of race and the racialization of crime, and connect racial animus to a felony. The significance of race cannot be ignored because it connects the past with the present and authenticates the project of a felony as an investment in contemporary practices that cannot be separated from historical race relations. Race matters; there are more black people tangled in the tentacles of the criminal justice system than were enslaved at the beginning of the American Civil War.[87] The linking of blackness to criminality and its connection to punishment means that race is directly tied to the politics and policies of prisoner reentry.[88]

In Chapter 2, I give voice to the difficulties of living while socially disabled by a felony conviction, and rely on participants' point of view to challenge "top-down" policy-oriented prisoner-reentry research that tends to be disconnected from individual lived experiences.[89] This chapter sets the stage for the analysis of the lived experiences of convicted felons in the policy chapters that follow; by analyzing reentry from a "bottom-up" perspective, I show how felons' ability to return to the community is hampered by the way a felony conviction constitutes its own petite penal institution[90] and the way it acts as an extension of the carceral state:[91] "I'm a convicted felon, no way to get around that, whatever I do, that stays."[92] This self-awareness affects the way one plans for the future and instills a survival attitude in the minds of those reentering society.

> It [reentry] becomes a way of life, you know, being told *no all the damn time* [emphasis original]; you have a plan, then [to] be told no, no, no, you get let down, and then you let your kids down. Ain't no reason to try and be good [crime free] when you just goin' get held down, rejected-like, [and] be told no, no, no.[93]

By revealing the hostile reality that convicted felons encounter upon coming home, I am able to detail the range of challenging encounters participants had to confront as they attempted to subsist, an unimaginable undertaking after surviving prison. Furthermore, by featuring specific themes from the data, I am able to construct a discourse of reentry that demonstrates how participants are shadowed by their criminal past and prison experience, menaced by their PTSD-like symptoms, intimidated by the complications of establishing their identity, frustrated by angry family members, and challenged by the difficulty of navigating hostile laws attached to a felony conviction.

Chapter 3 evaluates the expansion of federal housing laws under Democratic and Republican presidents alongside participants' experiences of trying to secure safe housing. Public housing policies and rules are established by the federal government and implemented at the state and local levels. Federal laws grant local public housing authorities the power to implement rules concerning the acceptance of tenants or the rejection of applicants. Rules allow tenants to be evicted if they have an arrest record, even if they have not been convicted of any crime; if they have a felony conviction; or if their guests are convicted of a felony. The creation and implementation of such policies are connected to the "War on Drugs" and politicians' "tough on crime" rhetoric intended to socially disable all felons, but particularly those convicted of drug offenses. This chapter presents participants' perspective on such housing policies, describes their experiences with housing and their options as convicted felons, and challenges the conventional notion that families are willing and able to provide housing for family members reentering society. In a vast majority of instances, participants were experiencing different degrees of homelessness due to a lack of family support and hostile policies that blocked them from accessing public housing.

Chapter 4 delves into education practices inside prison alongside "tough on crime" education policies passed in the 1990s to explore participants' outlook on education and how they evaluate it alongside other equally important concerns, such as employment. Participants unanimously shared that education was important due to its connection with employment, and that without it they were "screwed." However, attending classes is contradictory to meeting the requirements of parole, conflicts with their family's needs, and does not circumvent an employment criminal-history background check used by public and private and small and large companies and organizations.[94] Educational programs have been cut inside prison and felons are denied Pell grants; this means that attending school would require a considerable financial investment, but because a diploma does *not* avert a background check or guarantee a legal job upon completion, many participants said that it made little to no sense to make such a capital investment without a guaranteed outcome. Participants' conclusions are a direct result of hostile policies that deny felons "everything that's good."[95]

Chapter 5 assesses employment and a felony conviction, and how the inability to secure a legal job manifests in economic anxiety, inability to pay towards debt, and food insecurity. Participants talked about their attempts at finding legal employment and how it was the *most* important thing for them to do in order to desist from crime; yet, a strong desire to be employed and the ability to secure a legal job are different issues. Participants shared how hard it was to secure a job because of their felony. The inability to secure legal work undermines successful reentry, while outstanding criminal justice fees and child-support payments in arrears add an additional and overwhelming financial burden. Without work, it is impossible to pay on their debt, or pay for housing, school, food, clothing, and other life necessities. A common refrain is, "I need a job *now*" (emphasis original).[96]

The conclusion analyzes how socially disabling policies targeting convicted felons are connected to the public's hostility but are antithetical to successful prisoner reentry and closely aligned to recidivism. The public's hostility is tied to historical and political connections between race and criminality, which is evident in the way black men and women are viewed by the police. Politicians have the ability and power, if they wanted to, to tone down their political rhetoric and reduce, or even eliminate, the most egregious social disabilities of a felony conviction. This is possible with targeted policy changes; yet, such changes would require a fundamental modification in the politics of punishment, as elected officials would need to reform sentencing laws *and* take prisoner reentry seriously by investing in educational opportunities inside and outside of prison, increasing employment prospects for convicted felons, and providing stable long-term housing to former prisoners.

Current proposed changes to criminal and sentencing laws are a good start, but will not remove the debilitating aspect of a felony conviction post-punishment; therefore, policy changes need to eliminate the use of a felony conviction as a net widener at the back end of the criminal justice system. Upon completion of a criminal sentence, felons should be allowed to reenter and reengage in society, but for that to happen, policies must be changed to assist former prisoners rather than socially disable them. By removing the ability to use a felony conviction to restrict access to social and public benefits, policy changes would diminish the likelihood of felons reverting back to hustling, reduce future crimes, decrease the number of future victims, and lower overall recidivism rates, all of which would increase the general public's safety.

A felony conviction stigmatizes men and women and converts them into contemporary outlaws. If former prisoners are unable to jettison their felony after completing their criminal sentence, including parole, then a felony conviction pursues participants like Nemesis:

I'll never be completely free. Never. That felony will follow me wherever I go. People push you away and [you] have to live a life of no. Being pushed away constantly, I feel ignored like and forgotten, like I'm less than a person: *I'm nothing* [emphasis original] 'cuz I'm a felon. I'm pissed, actually, always struggling and battling out here; it ain't easy. I did my time, 'n I'm always going to be less than because of my [drug] charge. Don't matter what I do to be good. Ain't nobody going to let me be [to reenter].[97]

1

Felony Conviction as Social Disability

If the system don't disappear you, you get out, but to what?
I will forever have to "stay in my lane," ain't no other thing
going to work.
—Field Notes, May 8, 2013

I'm still here breathing. Living. I'm here; but still down 'n
out. Need to learn how to keep my head on straight, you
know, keep my head above water, because it's hard out here.
—Field Notes, February 6, 2013

I am not my record, but I'm a convicted felon and that record says I'm a bad person.
—Darren, August 15, 2011

The majority of individuals convicted of a felony have experienced
prison. Studies indicate that approximately one in one hundred Americans is behind bars.[1] Of the incarcerated population, approximately 95
percent of all prisoners are discharged from the Department of Corrections (DOC).[2] Various national estimates indicate that between
650,000 and 760,000 adults are released from state and federal prisons
each year,[3] which equates to more than 12,500 people reentering society
as felons every week[4] and hundreds of thousands of men and women
convicted of a felony living in various communities across the country.
Parallel to the criminal justice system, contemporaneous public policies
target felons' bodies to convey a sense of permanent criminality: Out
of the hundreds of thousands of prisoners reentering society and those
who have already returned home, all of them are subject to a complex
maze of civil penalties that, while legal, are detrimental to their ability to
successfully reenter society.[5]

Civil penalities

Felons are denied access to social benefits
Socially constructed

This chapter explores how felons are socially constructed and disabled by introducing social disability theory and drawing a parallel between disabled people and the oppression of felons.[6] The section that follows surveys the historical evolution of a felony, its relationship to stigma and criminal punishment, and how politicians use the public's fear to deny felons access to social benefits. Lastly, the chapter explores how race is socially constructed, how crime is racialized, and how public policies converge to connect racial animus to public fear and a felony conviction. The significance of racial history in the United States cannot be overstated due to its connection to the criminal justice system, public fear, and hostile public policies.

The prejudicial weight attached to a felony conviction is similar to the negative social construction of "others."[7] The term "others" refers to socially unacceptable or illegitimate groups within society who are "othered" through the use of socio-demographic characteristics, like social status, race, gender, religion, nationality, or social class, which are used to create symbolic distinctions between groups and can lead to social exclusion of an entire group.[8] Felons are "othered" and excluded from the general social milieu, and as a result of historical policies and the racial history of the United States, there is a strong foundation in place that allows modern policies to target felons, deny them benefits, and force them to live in society's dark corners.

Each of the fifty states and the federal government use a felony conviction to revoke or deny benefits and rights of citizenship, regardless of the crime, irrespective of rehabilitation, and in spite of how much time has passed since the conviction or release from DOC; yet, state-level impositions are the most significant forms of punishment imposed on felons.[9] The punishments differ from state to state, are applied in an ad hoc manner,[10] and are dispersed throughout statutory codes, civil regulations, and bodies of law in such a way as to make them "almost untraceable."[11] Various terms used to describe the policies hidden in statutes include "secret sentences,"[12] "invisible punishments,"[13] "collateral sanctions,"[14] "internal exile,"[15] "civil disabilities,"[16] and "the collateral consequences of a felony conviction."[17] There is no formal mechanism with which to quantify the scope of the consequences of a felony conviction,[18] but the legal stipulations are increasingly recognized as central to criminal justice policy.[19] The restrictions deprive individuals of a variety of public rights, privileges, and benefits, but the totality of consequences that revoke and restrict public benefits *after* arrest, trial, sentencing, incarceration, and parole and probation is unclear[20] and remains profoundly misunderstood.[21] Michael Pinard, a professor of law at the University of Maryland who specializes in prisoner reentry, legal theory, race, and criminal justice issues, argues that the current state of knowledge about the range of invisible and secret punishments is incomplete, at best; he contends that the literature is virtually silent about how federal and state-level policies shape the lived experience of felons.[22] The separateness in the literature limits the ability to explain how multiple issues contribute to why individuals fail at reentry. If we are to uncover the disabling effects of the complex maze of legislative and administrative regulations, as well as "off-book" sanctions that operate as the public's conscience in an underhanded manner to inflict post-prison punishment upon felons' bodies,[23] the "secret sentences"[24] must be exposed.

Civil disabilities, the release of prisoners, and the increased number of felons living in the community are not new criminal justice issues; rather, the challenge, alongside not knowing the extent of "off-book" civil sanctions and disabling consequences of a felony, is calculating the sheer number of felons living in communities across the country, which has grown significantly in the last decade, reaching into the millions, but cannot be specified.[25] The National Employment Law Project estimates that 20 percent of adults have an arrest or conviction record.[26] Some suggest that the percentage is as high as 25 percent.[27]

Civil disabilities and their negative impact are *not* central to the criminal justice process, nor are they included in the punishment imposed by the sentencing courts because a countless number of actors, such as judges, district attorneys, prosecutors, defense attorneys, public defenders, court clerks, the Department of Corrections, and parole and probation, are not legally obligated to explain or account for the disabling consequences of a felony. All felons are treated in the same manner, regardless of their crime, documented rehabilitation, and efforts to "be good," and are socially disabled and denied access to the same public spaces and benefits.[28] The negative social construction, and the assumption that all felons are equally villainous, means that politicians are able to use political rhetoric to reject the notion of rehabilitation and pass policies that deliberately exclude all felons from social benefits. The resulting lifetime of social disability forces individuals to choose the best decision from a number of bad options. For instance, many participants experienced food insecurity: When food is scarce, the goal of securing one's next meal becomes an all-consuming effort that overwhelms other endeavors. If a felon remains permanently socially disabled and suffers from food insecurity, the likelihood that he or she will commit a new crime increases: "If you got nothing, no house, no food, you hungry, really, you got nothing to lose, so you do what you need to [steal], really, to eat, to live."[29]

Once labeled as a felon, the individual carries the burden of that stigma, which is not a byproduct of random historical misfortune; rather, the permanent institutional character of a felony conviction is a politically spawned event.[30] Felons embody the concept of "social dirt,"[31] and are viewed negatively by society, which continues the degradation process started by the criminal justice system and places felons outside of normative social boundaries.[32] Upon returning home, felons desperately want to distance themselves from their criminal status but are unable to do so because a felony conviction prevents one from "being good" under the omnipresent eyes of the law.[33]

Social Disability Theory

Disability studies conceptualizes the body as a central organizing mechanism in society,[34] and to comprehend how a felony conviction became a social disability, it is critical to emphasize the body as the juncture at which the law is inflicted. The traditional concept of disability encompasses bodily function, focusing on impairments that limit life activities and the ways in which different bodies are shaped by a disability.[35] There are three main models of disability—the medical, the social-political, and the individual.[36] The medical model conceptualizes disability as having a medical response or resolution determined by medical professions. A medical determination of a disability is based on clinical criteria that relate to both the nature and the severity of the impairment[37] and emphasizes the intervening variable(s) that led to the disability, such as an accident, age, injury, or birth defect,[38] as well as nondisabling impairments, such as disfigurement, which have a similar negative socializing effect.[39]

Other scholars contend that the act of defining a disability is social and political in nature, arguing that it is social because disability requires a societal response to make environmental modifications for the full participation of people living with disabilities and includes the way the types, rates, and distribution of disability across geography and age of the populace are defined.[40] Describing a disability is also a political process, as disabilities are defined by the dominant political structures of society that uphold cultural values, economic and legal formalities, and the construction of physical and social spaces.[41] The social-political model argues that a disability is based on limitations on one's ability to participate in social activities, perform common public roles, and function in society.[42] The inability to participate in communal social and public activities is attributed to a complex collection of social conditions that have negative connotations for individuals living with disabilities— connotations that are political in nature due to the distribution of benefits and support programs according to the type and nature of a disability.[43] The social-political model adds a dimension to disability that is absent from the medical model but overlooks the way individuals are affected by their specific impairment or disability.[44]

The individual model is grounded in a discrete pathology that conceives disability as an impairment that limits any single person from participating in "normal" collective or social pursuits.[45] The disability, even if resulting from a personal tragedy, impacts the operational, functional, and social ability of an individual.[46] The disability manifests in curtailing an individual's ability to work outside of the home, use public transportation, access public spaces, and utilize standard housing.[47] The degree of an individual's disability determines how the body is represented and viewed by others, and how social attitudes and public and private institutions determine an individual's reality.[48] The individual model of disability makes it a lived experience, treats the disability as a distinct factor for an individual, and addresses how the degree of disability determines society's response to the individual's impairment.[49]

The three models construct disability differently,[50] and each model is based on unnatural breaks on a continuum that has overlapping definitions. Each model does not address whether economic, financial, social, and sexual opportunities are constrained by the disability or how some disabling limitations devalue individuals and isolate them from public interactions.[51] As a result, the context of disability, its subsequent visibility and physical severity, and the need for intermediaries and assistance for individuals living with a disability to perform socially[52] mean different things for different people; however, a common link across all disabilities is that individuals experience episodes of being "out of society" and unwelcomed in some spaces inhabited by able bodies.[53]

Some models of disability describe how individuals living with a disability experience feelings of "otherness,"[54] and an analogy can be drawn with individuals convicted of a felony, who are constructed as "other" by society and experience episodes of being "out of society."[55] Negative social constructions have implications for each group's respective lived experience. A lack of empathy makes each group appear less human.[56] Erving Goffman, the Canadian-born sociologist who has influenced generations of scholars, argues that a disability has degrading elements that create social stigma,[57] as if the disabled individual is quasi-human.[58] The hyper-individualization of a disability and a felony conviction is symbolic of how the two distinct groups are fashioned as unrepresentative of humanity[59] and stigmatized on the basis of fear, myth, and society's misunderstanding about identity and social categories.[60] The lack of understanding makes it easier to exclude "others" from society, resulting in a form of segregation that limits access to social capital and material possessions, and involves higher levels of debt and restricted economic opportunities.[61] Disability can determine the social standing of individuals; if adults living with a disability can be placed outside of society to become invisible when public accommodations are unavailable, a felony conviction is similar because without societal adjustments, a felon's body can be placed outside of society, too.

A Felony Conviction as a Disability

Felons are *legally* disabled[62] and incapacitated,[63] which limits their ability to engage with and in society.[64] Once someone is convicted of a felony, his or her conviction carries an unexamined power over his or her body. When felons exit prison, society stigmatizes, discredits, and fears them, which results in a societal exclusion that is more complete than for adults living with a disability. For instance, when a sidewalk ends without a curb ramp, a wheelchair-bound person may be able to find a way around the barrier and then, if he or she has the resources, lobby for public accommodations in the form of a curb ramp, but when felons reenter society there are no equivalent curb ramps, public accommodations, or resources to lobby government officials, so felons are excluded from acceptable social boundaries today and in the future.

The disabling effects of a felony permanently consign former offenders to the category of "otherness." By publicly marking felons as vile bodies, politicians create net-widening policies to keep this subpopulation disconnected from the social-political economy.[65] The result is that felons are treated harshly after serving time and the civil disabilities become their own form of punishment imposed through statutory devices and administrative agencies[66] that curtail an individual's right to participate in society.[67] A felony conviction is a legal impediment that deems an individual incompetent and ineffectual.[68] Felons cannot enter into legally binding contracts, and they lose a host of other rights, including the right to vote, serve on a jury, hold elected office, or be appointed to public positions; bear arms; serve in the U.S. armed forces; live in public housing or visit family there; and receive financial aid for educational programs.[69] The retributive character of post-punishment civil penalties is ingrained into legal and social definitions; a felony conviction "functions as social dirt,"[70] becomes a life-long disability,[71] and creates an unnatural state of existence.

The challenge of being a convicted felon is that it automatically forfeits an individual's right to be rehabilitated; even if someone is rehabilitated through a comprehensive metamorphosis, lifestyle changes, and family support, these endeavors will not transform a felon into a legally able-bodied nonfelon in the eyes of the law. As one social worker said, "Establishing that one is rehabilitated is real difficult when they got that [felony] charge on their record. No way to unring that bell. None."[72] As a result, a felony functions as a permanent social disability and forces felons to live in what I call the "gray area."[73] The gray area refers to the liminal space and time between participants' leaving prison and reentering society,[74] but before it is known whether that participant has successfully reentered or will fail to reenter. Most participants lived in constant motion and engaged in an intricate dance that was not quite legal,[75] and they were always one step away from going back to "doing what I know in the streets."[76]

The ultimate goal of each participant was to not return to prison, even if it meant living in the gray area until "whenever," as they repeatedly said, "I'm not going back" and "I'm doing what is necessary to stay out." Tyrone lives in the gray area: "I'd rather be homeless and living on the streets than go back [to prison]."[77] Being homeless and living on the streets is considered "success" in the eyes of many reentry scholars because Tyrone has not been rearrested or reincarcerated.[78] But, to make "not going back to prison" a reality entails participants renegotiating society's rules and relearning how to be in the world as a contemporary outlaw.

Theoretically, the process of reentering is easy: get a job, find a place to live, stay out of trouble, and desist from crime. However, rarely does this "simple process" unfold in an orderly sequence of steps when one is homeless, hungry, and marked by a felony,[79] and traditional reentry studies seldom incorporate the experiences of men and women reentering society while adjusting to its pace, living in the gray area between success and failure, and unable to access public benefits.[80] Instead of an orderly process, the reality of reentry resembles a series of forward, backward, and sometimes sideways steps.

The first few months home after serving time in prison are nerve-racking and full of unease as promised housing can fall through or a relative changes his or her mind about the level of support he or she is able to offer. With or without family support, felons are full of anxiety due to the numerous changes in society (e.g., technology) they must confront and they struggle to overcome the socially disabling effects of a felony conviction. Tyrone and others like him do not have the ability to control their own destiny; policies structure many social interactions while denying felons the ability to secure resources needed to reenter successfully. As a result, many elude the law by learning to survive in the gray area; participants learned to improvise and create ways to live without social benefits while tackling, without money, issues that had to be addressed, like securing weather-appropriate clothes[81] and adjusting to the pace of society.

"Inside, everything is slow so when I first got out, I had to adjust myself."[82] Upon reentering society, a felon's life is largely reconfigured because when the word "felon" is attached to an individual's body, society views that person as a debased human being whose corrupt soul has no agency. Yet, participants are multidimensional individuals with agency and the ability to think about their circumstances. Their existence encompasses more than a single word, but because of the word's social residue, felons experience the world differently due to "the oppressor's language"[83] being used to create social disability.

One participant explained how his felony affects him: "My conviction, it haunts me. Been going on twenty years; I can't get past it. It haunts me, I'm telling you." Danny expressed his feelings about the historical residue of his conviction: He served less than one year in jail two decades ago, and his past shapes and "haunts" his present. He has tried to advance his economic well-being, and despite his resourcefulness, continues to feel the sting of his conviction. In an attempt to move beyond his economic insecurity and conviction, he has moved with the purpose of securing employment, gained professional training and certificates, tried different career paths, and earned valuable but low-paying work experience, all to no avail. "Can't get away from it, regardless of what I do or where I go, there it is; really, it's disturbing."[84]

Danny's past is his present; he struggles in the gray area while trying to move beyond his felony. When it appears he is making forward progress, he finds himself three steps back, and then slipping further backwards, a familiar experience for many attempting to overcome their past. A felony socially removes individuals "from everything that is good."[85] Participants unable to move beyond their past to live in the present tend not to plan for the future. "The future is all hope, and I ain't got much of that, so I'm just living, surviving really."[86] Hostile policies targeting felons' bodies makes a felony a "felt value" that comes with extra-legal meaning for those living under a felony conviction's historical burden[87] and its "special ensemble" of culture, history, experiences, and agency[88] that denotes the character of all felons as deserving to be banished from the community.

The Historical Evolution of the Word "Felon"

According to Michel Foucault, the foundational discourse around a felony conviction includes hierarchies of power, systems of ideology, language, religious doctrine, legal principles, and the social context between individuals and institutions.[89] History abounds with the belief that criminal souls are corrupted and should be condemned due to the prevailing societal notions of wickedness.[90] The presuppositions behind a felony conviction bind the individual felon to a predefined existence because the word "felon" is embedded in institutional practices that become cultural norms;[91] as a result, the individual is met with intense social and public hostility.

The original connection among crime, punishment, and the loss of rights is found in medieval beliefs that the punishment should fit the crime,[92] and this idea found its way into the Magna Carta, written in 1215 and known as the Great Charter of Freedoms or as England's Bill of Rights. The proportionality tradition is the belief that in efforts to address disputes between families and clans, punishment should relate to the crime. Examples of proportionality are also found in the King James Bible.[93] The idea of proportionality became the basis of the system for dispute resolutions in the feudal system.

The feudal relationship was based on land and property, and a breach of obligations resulted in the forfeiture of material goods.[94] If a vassal (e.g., tenant) expressed disloyalty to a lord by committing an act that destroyed the "trusted" relationship with the lord, the tenant's lands reverted to the lord and any remaining goods were forfeited to the king.[95] Feudal punishment was designed to reform the offender in the eyes of God, make the community whole, and provide a system of stability to decrease the prospect of future disputes.[96] The feudal doctrine and forfeiture of goods were reshaped into the common law, wherein the convicted was deemed infamous and was deprived of social rights for committing debased crimes.[97] Punishment treated the condemned as if he had died a natural death:[98] He had his lands and chattel confiscated; could not receive gifts, enter into contracts, transfer property, make speeches, hold political office, or attend public assemblies; was deemed incompetent to act as a witness because of moral defect;[99] and in an effort to end the corrupt bloodline, his wife was deemed a widow and his children orphans.[100] Prevailing beliefs banished the civilly dead for violating the social contract and cultural mores, and they were exiled from the kingdom to become outlaws.[101]

Social norms influenced how crimes were defined by judges. Judge-based rulings constructed nine crimes deemed the epitome of evil, including murder, manslaughter, arson, burglary, robbery, rape, sodomy,

mayhem, and larceny. The nine crimes became known as the "traditional nine," and societal customs expected punishment to be ignomini-
ous and leave a lasting stigma on the criminal's body, and involved ear
cropping, cutting off of a hand, slitting of the nostrils, branding, public
whipping, pillorying,[102] confinement to hard labor, or death at the gallows.[103] The quality of punishment was designed to be a felt experience
of degradation and humiliation that also exposed the entire family to
public derision and shame.[104]

English settlers transported this system to America and implemented
British common law throughout the original thirteen colonies.[105] Upon
becoming states, former colonies maintained the British common law,
and offenders convicted of one of the traditional nine crimes experienced punishment that included loss of life, limb, land, or goods;[106]
however, the convergence of English common law principles with the
social and political order of the United States at the turn of the nine-
teenth century created a unique American criminal justice system that
reflected the country's federal system. Early American policymakers
chose between numerous meanings of infamous crime and ignomini-
ous punishment, felony, and civil death; taking note of colonial criminal
laws and British common law, states such as Pennsylvania, Virginia, and
New York created separate statutory crimes with corresponding punishments.[107] Other states tailored their criminal code so crimes "fit" the
political and cultural customs of the state.[108] When new states were admitted to the union, they tended to adopt existing laws and then added
their own.[109] With the development of separate criminal codes in each
state, the definition of felonious behavior and infamy varied and led to a
multiplicity of crimes and corresponding punishments.[110]

In the early 1800s, the burgeoning new laws were unwieldy, and the
civil and criminal codes did not reflect current penal philosophy and
practices. For instance, with the initiation of the penitentiary and the
modernization of society, civil laws and the penal code needed to be
streamlined. By the 1820s, reformers' objective was to make sense of the
cumbersome American legal system by codifying civil laws and state
penal codes to create a logical order of crimes and corresponding punishments. Two leading legal scholars and jurists at the time, William
Blackstone and Edward Livingston, were instrumental in influencing
the reorganization of the American legal system.[111] Taken with the orga-

nizational and legal debate between Blackstone and Livingston,[112] state reformers in New York took the lead in tackling crimes deemed illogical or no longer valid and their corresponding punishments,[113] fashioned an imprisonment clause to incorporate the emerging prison system, and kept the death penalty in place for serious crimes. However, because the term "felon" or "felony" was used for a variety of crimes in the criminal code, New York created a definition that recognized the "common understanding" of "felony" that did not require extensive rewriting of existing statutes.[114] New York's streamlined criminal laws became *The 1829 Revised Statutes of the State of New York*, which created an organized body of law using the scientific method of titles and definitions that described the type of punishment for each crime. The resulting code broadly construed infamous crimes to be punishable by imprisonment in the state penitentiary or by death, formed the foundation of the modern American penal code,[115] and developed a uniquely American definition of a felony.

Penal philosophy at the time, inspired by the Quakers, advocated that the prison was designed to correct criminal minds; it was believed that a "regulated correctional environment," solitary sleeping cells, discipline, enforced solitude, and group labor could "restore" defective minds.[116] Reformers argued that corrupt and depraved minds could be altered in the state penitentiary, but a sentence of one year or more was necessary for the reforms to take hold.[117] Time sentenced became the dividing line between a felony and a misdemeanor, and reformers and legal theory converged to create two levels of crimes: local jails for minor crimes or misdemeanors with sentences of less than one year and the state penitentiary for felonious and infamous crimes with sentences of more than a year.[118] The United States Supreme Court affirmed this notion of punishment for infamous crimes in 1885.[119]

Today, crimes continue to be differentiated into the same two-tier system, reflecting the punitive differences in the statutorily defined severity connected to a criminal offense.[120] The criminal code also mirrors historical, religious, ideological, and political views about which criminals are imprisoned for life or sentenced to death, and which criminals are estimated to be redeemable. Except for auto theft, controlled substances, and violence against women and children, contemporary crimes replicate the traditional nine,[121] and have only expanded because politicians define similar criminal behavior differently; for instance, there are more than ten definitions for taking a human life.[122] The multiple definitions of homicide are due to the politicization of crime. Politicians take positions, claim credit, and advertise their activities in the hope of being reelected,[123] and then go on to make public statements designed to make them appear "tough on crime" and pass legislation for the benefit of their political constituencies.[124] A common political tactic is to define new punishments and rely on a common understanding of a felony to signal to voters that the public's safety is protected because "bad people" will be punished to the fullest extent of the law.[125] Scholars argue that the imagination of legislators, who are incentivized to be "tough on crime," determines how crimes are defined and the degree of punitiveness associated with the corresponding punishment.[126]

When it comes to felons, prohibiting them from public benefits is a winning political strategy, and legislators use the law to buttress the notion that all felons are depraved, strengthening the "loosely coupled institutions"[127] that transform disabled felons into contemporary outlaws. People convicted of a felony are rarely able to escape the pejorative label, and politicians face no negative electoral repercussions for being "tough on crime" or passing and implementing punitive policies. Legislators rely on duplicitous judgments to make felons permanently debased,[128] and the media emphasize the negative qualities of all felons and present people of color as criminal;[129] combined, these actions ensure that the blanket assessment of an individual's character becomes destiny.[130]

Public Fear, Media, and Politics

In the 1980s, the media's racial bias contributed to hardening the public's fear of urban violence, and propelled a political frenzy that drove a discourse that was wholly separate from the issue of resources and reality.[131] Congress increased the federal government's expenditures to fight a new war, the "War on Drugs," and in doing so set in place novel policy approaches to fight crime, though Congress knew little about criminal law and its implementation, and had no concern for the inevitable costs.[132] States spent billions of dollars to arm the police and build up the prison system while encouraging the maximization of prison capacity without anticipating the release of prisoners. As politicians continually pushed a "tough on crime" agenda, the prison system grew unabated, and politicians argued that the cost was the price to be paid to fight crime, punish those found guilty, and address public safety concerns.[133]

With the media's constant display of violent criminals on nightly news,[134] the public wants to be secure from crime and the threat of crime. The rhetoric on talk radio and broadcast news induces an emotional response against the unknown demon criminal,[135] and legislators harness the public's fear to justify passing punitive laws to assuage that fear. It is rare for legislators to think about the negative externalities of those laws; instead of crafting a rational response to criminal acts, legislation is passed to fortify the public's certainty that it can be protected from becoming crime victims by policy mechanisms that demonize and marginalize criminals. With the media's near-constant fixation on violent crimes, politicians respond with "tough on crime" rhetoric that becomes political leverage to garner the public's support for reelection, and the cycle repeats itself. The politics of fear and the media's racialized representation of crime coalesce to create ripe legislative environments and moral panics;[136] an abhorrent crime is committed and is broadcast nationally, so politicians rush to pass punitive laws addressing the dreadful criminal act,[137] and with the public's support, the second and third generation of such bills mutate to become more punitive[138] as the public clamors for the passage of wider and stronger nets to capture and punish those who harm white people.[139]

One clear example is the media's single-minded obsession with sensational crimes involving white children (e.g., Adam Walsh, 1981; Polly Klaas, 1993; Megan Kanka, 1994, leading to the creation of Megan's Law; and JonBenét Ramsey, 1996).[140] Another example is the epidemic of "missing white woman syndrome,"[141] which describes the wall-to-wall national media coverage of criminal acts against white upper-class women (e.g., Laci Peterson, 2002; Lori Hacking, 2004; and Natalee Holloway, 2005). The names of black women and children, who went missing, sometimes within weeks of a missing white woman or child, received almost no national media attention and only limited local media coverage (e.g., Tamika Huston, 2004; LaToyia Figueroa, 2005; Nailah Franklin, 2007; Phylicia Moore, 2007; and Stepha Henry, 2008). Unsurprisingly, moral panics do not occur when a black child or black woman is murdered or goes missing.[142]

The media's attention and public outrage at the violence inflicted upon white women and children, in particular, constructs a narrative that random violence against them is normal and reinforces whites' fear of being murdered, sexually assaulted, or car-jacked by a "scary" black man. Such racial differences are used and exploited during moral panics, which is when legislators ignore more frequent property and white-collar crimes and neglect to consider private intimate crime, such as domestic abuse, sexual assault, and family violence,[143] unless the death of a "missing white woman" is caused by an intimate partner (e.g., Laci Peterson, 2002) or connected to a politician (e.g., Chandra Levy, 2001). Yet, violent crime is quite rare.[144] The media's focus on projecting images that are misrepresentative of actual crime makes it seem as if mayhem and violence against whites by blacks is ordinary.[145] By emphasizing violence directed at white women or children while ignoring violence directed at black women and children, the media constructs a perfect white victim and "black monster," reinforcing whites' negativity towards blacks, which has existed for centuries.[146] Racial bias is common as news outlets routinely display black and brown suspects' faces while white suspects' pictures are rarely shown or their graduation picture is shown rather than their mug shot.[147] This racial bias is further reinforced when the media depicts white murderers or rapists in a positive light in comparison to black victims who are demonized or disparaged on the nightly news, particularly if they are killed by a white person.[148] Such rituals grounded in racial bias are "customary" and sustain whites' fear of black people as criminal.[149]

The media's use of race to project images of who is criminal and who is deserving of compassion becomes a powerful tool to reinforce racial conflict.[150] The media's image of criminality is a means to buttress the stereotypical trope of crime coalescing around two images. The first is of a single angry, armed white man, or lone wolf, who is not labeled a criminal monster, even though white men are now the recurrent face of domestic terrorist attacks.[151] The second image is of a black man, a violent image that is etched into the minds of whites to create a "black monster" prowling neighborhoods looking for white victims; subsequently, the creation of "black monsters" allows society to create unworthy "others" to justify categorizing *all* black men as being disreputable, undeserving, and to be feared.[152] Although the monstrous image varies, the most notorious examples of the politics of criminality include "Willie Horton" and the "White Hands" political commercials.[153]

During the 1988 Democratic presidential primary race, then Senator Al Gore attacked Governor Michael Dukakis, the eventual Democratic nominee, for his support of a furlough program in Massachusetts, but did not name anyone. Republicans took note of Gore's attack, and during their opposition research found Willie Horton. Horton was convicted of murder and sentenced to life without parole for crimes he committed in 1974. In June 1986, Horton was released from prison to a furlough program; out on a pass, he never returned. Less than a year later, and while AWOL, in April 1987, Horton raped a woman, assaulted and pistol-whipped her fiancé, and committed armed robbery. The case of Willie Horton was a political wet dream for Republicans: a black rapist, white victims, and a bleeding-heart Democrat to blame.[154]

In the presidential election between Governor Dukakis and then Vice President George H. W. Bush, Republicans turned the story of Willie Horton into a commercial that forever altered politicians' calculations about crime.[155] The ad embodied white America's fears and was akin to propaganda that the White Citizens Councils have used to recruit new members; the ad detailed an unknown "scary black man" to emphasize what happens when politicians, like Dukakis, are "soft on crime." Bush effectively used Willie Horton to attack Dukakis while cementing his "tough on crime" position, reinforcing the widely held stereotype that black men are criminal and should be locked up, and that Bush was the right man to do the job. After the success of "Willie Horton," white politicians have used the crime issue as an outlet to encapsulate white public outrage and to address white economic insecurity rather than broader societal issues.

Two years after "Willie Horton," in the 1990 U.S. Senate race in North Carolina, Senator Jesse Helms, a white sitting U.S. senator, went up for reelection against Harvey Gantt, the first black mayor of Charlotte. The Helms campaign released "White Hands," a controversial ad that featured an angry white man opening up a job rejection letter. The camera focuses on the man's hands as he crumples up the letter while the voiceover says, "You needed that job, and you were the best qualified. But they had to give it to a minority because of a racial quota. Is that really fair?" The political commercial was a deliberate attempt to engage in the most racially divisive political issues of the time: white economic anxiety, affirmative action, and racial quotas.[156] The commercial made black Americans the enemy of white Americans. Gantt lost.

Scholars identify "Willie Horton" as *the* case that shifted the intersection among politics, race, and crime policy. Before "Willie Horton," the criminal justice system incorporated rehabilitative programs, leniency, and clemency, but after the ad, which was one of many issues that contributed to Dukakis's defeat, politicians' use of racial animus became an acceptable tactic employed for the purpose of passing laws mandating life sentences for a wide assortment of crimes,[157] and cutting the heart out of rehabilitation programs inside and outside of prison.[158] Such political tactics are not historical artifacts; during the 2014 midterm congressional elections, Republicans resurrected "Willie Horton" in "Nikko"[159] to harness white voters' fear and reinforce the idea that black people are innately dangerous and that specific politicians will be "tough on crime."

Elected officials, with a strong incentive to avoid being labeled "soft on crime," persist in passing punitive bills that extend coercive power onto felons' bodies permanently, without regard to the financial costs or effectiveness of being "tough on crime."[160] The costs are staggering: In 2010, states spent $48.5 billion on corrections.[161] Several states are moving forward to amend their incarceration policies for nonviolent drug crimes; for instance, to prevent their prison populations from growing further, Idaho and Mississippi have restructured their systems to focus on violent career criminals and high-risk offenders.[162] Although reducing the incarceration rate is a good start, such reform efforts to reduce the cost of being "tough on crime" are inconsistent, only address the front end of the system, and ignore the back-end use of a felony conviction outside of the criminal justice system.

Politicians tend to take tentative steps because criminal justice reform efforts are politically fragile and can be easily undermined when an event becomes front-page news. In New Jersey, for example, two individuals out of prison on an early-release program were allegedly involved in two murders on the same weekend in different cities, and the media and politicians went crazy.[163] The media reported that a furious Governor Chris Christie argued that a prisoners' parole review should *never* be automatic and that statutes taking discretion away from the New Jersey Parole Board needed to be changed. Christie contended that automatic mandatory parole was not an effective way to manage the release of prisoners; instead, Christie wanted the New Jersey Parole Board to determine who is suitable to be *considered* for parole: those deemed eligible for review would go through a comprehensive threat assessment to determine whether they should rejoin society on parole.

State officials in New Jersey, in a bipartisan effort, agreed that the early-release program was a threat to public safety, so through a tangled set of political maneuvers, the law was altered, and a retroactive gubernatorial veto was sustained. Christie argued that the New Jersey Parole Board has the expertise and should have the discretion to determine when prisoners should be considered for parole, and that "this common sense standard balanced the administrative needs of the corrections systems with the rehabilitative goals of incarceration."[164] A direct result of Christie's retroactive veto is that it undid statutory parole review, replaced it with a politically motivated arbitrary process forcing current prisoners to serve a longer portion of their prison sentence, and reincarcerated hundreds of parolees who had to serve a proportion of their remaining prison sentence before they would again be eligible for parole, despite adhering to the rules and regulations of parole, not committing a new crime, and starting to rebuild their lives.

The two murders and Governor Christie's retroactive veto took place while I was in the field. Participants kept abreast of the news, and they understood that political calculations were involved with crime policies and that they would have to renegotiate the new expectations as the political terrain shifted and resettled.[165] Although I asked each interviewee the same set of questions, during one particular interview a participant brought the topic up about how the public and political context had changed, and Christie's veto became part of our discussion.

> I saw on TV that they snatched [vetoed] that program that was helping people like me, because two guys fucked up. Someone else had to mess up and now everyone has to pay, spending longer and longer time inside [prison]. Everyone doesn't think the same. Those two guys screwed everybody coming out behind 'em. They just fucked it all up for all of us even worse than it already is.[166]

In the months following Christie's veto, parole officers were more dil-
igent in their checks at the nonprofit organization, and they restricted
freedoms previously earned for those who were not reincarcerated. More
than a year after the veto, state and federal parole officers continued to
drop by unannounced to monitor their parolees, making sure everyone
was aware of their omnipresence and power to revoke someone's parole
and send him or her back to prison. Each time, I found their presence
disconcerting, but one time was particularly unsettling; Emmanuel saw
my discomfort, and after the officers left he causally waved it off with a
hand gesture, explaining, "That's nothing; you okay 'cuz they ain't checking on you."[167] The changing nature of policies and political calculations
is part of the "special ensemble" that makes a felony conviction a felt
experience.[168] Plus, the public's disposition and the media's determination of who is a criminal, with or without a conviction, is grounded in
the inextricable fear of black skin.[169]

The Social Construction of Race

The criminal justice system makes race a felt experience; race is the
single most confounding problem in America,[170] is a public force that
retains its strength in cultural beliefs and social status,[171] and is infused
with meaning in social interactions, public institutions, and economic
and political structures.[172] Race, as a classification system, endures in
the public's mind,[173] is not fixed in time,[174] and retains its power because
"[r]ace is an unscientific, societally constructed taxonomy that is based
on an ideology that views some human population groups as inherently
superior to others on the basis of external physical characteristics or
geographic origin."[175]

"Race" appeared in the English language in the early 1500s; "racis" referred to categories of people of common lineage but not fixed biology
or phenotype,[176] but was not initially connected to human taxonomy.[177]
Carolus Linnaeus is credited with the first taxonomy of race in *Systema
Naturae*; in 1758, he mapped "four races" of humans—Americanus, Eu-
ropaues, Asiaticus, and Afer—into geographic regions of conventional
cartography.[178] Linnaeus's system subjectively attributed behaviors,
characteristics, virtues, and physical features to each geographically
located group:[179] Americans were regarded as copper-colored, erect,

straight-haired, and regulated; Europeans were considered fair, brawny, flowing-haired, and governed by laws; Asiatics were marked as sooty, haughty, rigid, black-haired, and governed by opinions; and Afers were judged to be crafty, indolent, negligent, black skinned, frizzy-haired, and governed by caprice.[180] Linnaeus's model ascribed to the "four races" his own prejudiced impressions about what each group looked like and their corresponding temperament, which reinforces the notion that race is a technique arbitrarily constructed to distinguish between groups.[181]

Blumenbach, a student of Linnaeus, added a fifth group to the taxonomy, the Malay.[182] By moving to a five-race scheme, Blumenbach radically changed the geographically based model of humans into a ranked system of hierarchical worth based upon his belief in a Caucasian ideal,[183] causing a fundamental shift in the social construction of race.[184] Blumenbach's five-group taxonomy reflected both geography and his perceived view of beauty, and he ranked the worth of each racial group in relationship to his white archetypal standard.[185] By subjectively choosing to place Caucasian first as "the most handsome and becoming,"[186] Blumenbach supported the creation of biased racial categories that explicitly placed the cultural, physical, and social status of whites higher while degrading the intellectual, cultural, and physical attributes of all other groups.[187] The skewed hierarchy of races is "one of the most fateful transitions in the history of Western science [and the racial hierarchy] has had more practical impact, almost entirely negative, upon our collective lives" than other findings in Western science.[188] This prejudiced ranking of value based on whiteness[189] has fostered social grief ever since; racial categories have become a menace[190] used to codify and express information,[191] and a form of shorthand about certain individuals that endures over time.[192] Despite the fact that racial categories were based on arbitrary and prejudiced ideals, racial taxonomies were wrapped in the cloak of legitimate science, and then used by elites to promote civil, social, political, legal, and economic rules for the purposes of degrading racial minorities:[193] Racialized groups defined as inferior to whites were colonized, enslaved, or imprisoned,[194] and white physical characteristics were elevated over all others to justify the granting of favors to the preferred group.[195]

Race, Slavery, and the Color Line

Race matters:[196] "Being black means you guilty of something in lots of people's eyes."[197] This simple statement takes one participant's everyday lived experience and reduces the lengthy and hostile racial history of the United States into a few words. The idea that race and skin color denote criminal behavior is deeply rooted in the ideology of white supremacy, and operates as an organizing principle that evolved in accordance with the proximity of the color line.[198] The color line, although metaphorical, was designed via slavery and Jim Crow to create an unnatural but distinct line separating blacks from whites.[199] The color line represented white power elites' political, economic, and social investment in creating and enforcing cultural norms that maintained white supremacy and racialized criminality.[200]

The historical black-white color line emerged in the original thirteen colonies, was implemented by the legal system, and was supported by plantation owners, who had a persistent challenge of preventing slaves from escaping to the north while wealthy northerners wanted to stop indentured servants from running away. In order to decrease the number of slaves escaping and indentured servants joining them, colonial governments encouraged the racializing of criminal behavior by presuming guilt for blacks, enslaved and not enslaved,[201] and regulating indentured servants' movements so that they could not gain their freedom until their bonded debt was paid off.[202] The goal was to enhance penalties for blacks but not punish white criminals, regardless of their social status, to the same extent as racial minorities.[203]

For instance, Pennsylvania attached race to particular criminal behaviors and punishment; the state viewed crimes committed by blacks as worse than similar crimes committed by whites, especially where white women were concerned, and devalued black women completely. Pennsylvania passed harsher penalties for black men convicted of raping white women than for white men convicted of the same crime.[204] Black men were sentenced to death for rape and to castration for attempted rape of a white woman. White men who committed the same crime against a white woman were fined, whipped, or imprisoned for a year for the first offense and imprisoned for life for a second conviction.[205]

The criminal code did *not* consider the act of raping or attempting to rape a black woman as unlawful.

Virginia, settled earlier than other states, had one of the largest enslaved black populations and had more experience legislating policies advantageous to whites and injurious to blacks, including criminalizing blackness.[206] Virginia linked blackness to criminality and stamped the mark of the law on all people of African ancestry[207] by enhancing the penalties of statutory crimes for "being black," such as a tax imposed on free black women; if the tax was not paid, black women were enslaved until the tax was paid off.[208] By making "free" blacks criminals, the law affirmed whites' beliefs in white supremacy and fortified the notion that all blacks were "naturally criminal."[209]

Under these conditions, punishment meted out to blacks was harsh compared to the penalties meted out to whites[210] and reinforced racial differences that protected white economic and political privileges.[211] For instance, despite northern states passing laws designed to control Indian, Negro, or mulatto slaves and indentured servants, when racialized policing became insufficient to control indentured and free blacks in the North, society was organized on the basis of skin color: white indentured servants were freed, black indentured servants were enslaved, and as a result the enslaved population became entirely black,[212] which reflected the racist hierarchy grounded in the belief that Africans and their descendants were heathens and unfit for freedom.[213] Although there were small communities of free blacks living throughout the colonies, white plantation owners' requirement for free labor[214] while maintaining white supremacy[215] necessitated enslaving as many blacks as possible.[216]

Racist ideology strengthened whites' beliefs about the innate deviance, reduced intellectual ability, and heathenish emotional and behavioral attributes inextricably linked to blackness.[217] The "scientific" social construction of race supported whites' "logic" about their superiority, thus justifying slavery. Black slaves, whites believed, benefited from being tamed because they were thought to be "childlike and irresponsible, inefficient [and] lazy."[218] Whites also argued that without the presence of slave masters, blacks were liable to act out innate savagery. Such contrary thinking—that blacks were thought to be childlike *and* cold-blooded savages—was based on whites' fear of the black population, which posed a legitimate threat to white hegemony.[219] The racist fear of blackness led to the creation of harsh laws legislating the color line, and racial differences were integrated into criminal law, including the crime of "being black."

The original "tough on crime" politicians were in South Carolina; they used the politics of race and the fear of blackness to keep as many blacks as possible in servitude, enslaved or jailed.[220] The criminal justice system in South Carolina, even by the standards of the eighteenth century, was barbaric and inhumane,[221] and slave patrols captured any black person who was not enslaved. The free black population was demonized as inherently more dangerous than the enslaved population because they were not under the control of a slave master. The white ruling class feared the free black population, and under the guise of maintaining public order, South Carolina responded by revising its criminal code to accommodate whites' fear of blackness, and incarcerated or enslaved as many free blacks as possible in order to support whites' ingrained belief about blacks' inherent dangerous nature, even for the crime of "being black."[222] Blacks were thought of as slave or criminal, with the only difference being that one was owned and the other was "free," and the state was expected to act as master to control free blacks to protect white interests.[223] Once all blacks were presumed to be criminals or slaves, then any black person who could *not* prove his or her nonslave status was committing a crime. The laws punishing blacks displayed a lax system of penalties towards whites, and the double standard, wherein whites were shown undue leniency while blacks received excessive penalties for minor and major infractions, led to increased violence between the races.[224]

Harsh laws and the slave code did not create a docile slave population; laws based in violent retribution created the exact opposite conditions. Violence was a daily part of being a slave, and white violence towards slaves was acceptable as a means to ensure that the enslaved population did not interfere with their own enslavement while slaves who were rebellious and defiant to their own enslavement were punished harshly. Brutality by slave owners was designed to keep slaves compliant, and whites met any slave upheaval with cruel rejoinders towards those who revolted;[225] if any slave ran away and was subsequently caught, he or she was punished by whipping, castration, cutting off of ears, branding on the cheek, or hamstringing.[226] At times, the violence ended in a slave's death, but because slaves were "property" that did the back-breaking work that built and sustained white slave owners' wealth, death was utilized only for individual slaves deemed most likely to attempt to overthrow the peculiar institution of slavery, such as those found guilty of running away, talking about rebellion, or causing a mutiny.[227] The control of blacks was a response to what was always present but left unsaid: whites' fear of the large and growing black enslaved and free population.[228]

The slave code developed into a system of bondage and inhumane punishment that was purposely constructed to keep the black popula-tion enslaved, and was a key contributor to violence in the South.[229] Black enslavement served three purposes. First, it gave whites, regardless of their economic station, a higher status within society in comparison to Africans and their descendants; as a result, poor whites were granted a role in society as a consequence of *not* being black.[230] Second, such laws institutionalized race.[231] Institutionalized racism allowed new Eu-ropean arrivals, who were not slave plantation owners, to form a class of their own in which political, economic, and social rights were granted automatically, making all whites, even new immigrants, subordinate to no one.[232] Third, racially based laws created a system that amalgamated race with crime and attributed criminality to blackness.

The Criminal Justice System

In theory, the criminal justice system is race neutral, and punishment, in principle, is applied equally to people regardless of the crime, the race, ethnicity, religion, or gender of the victim, or the identity of those con-victed, sentenced, and incarcerated. In practice, race neutrality does not exist; racism permeates the criminal justice system at each stage, includ-ing policing, arrest, conviction, and incarceration. The implementation of policies captures a disproportionate number of racial minorities. The Pew Center on the States estimates that one in eleven black men and women are under correctional control. The Bureau of Justice Statistics reveals that black men far outnumber white and Latino male prisoners, and black women far outnumber white women and Latina prisoners; black women are nearly four times as likely to be in prison as white women, and almost two and a half times as likely as Latinas.[233] In some urban communities, more than half of the men and a quarter of the women have a criminal record, and up to 30 percent will churn in and out of prison.[234]

Racial differences in the identity of those policed, convicted, and incarcerated mean that racial bias exists in the determination of who becomes a felon. Due to the fact that a felony conviction operates as a net widener, felons are socially disabled across race, time, and urban spaces. This reality tends to ignore the direct connection of certain policies to the social, political, and institutional history of the enslavement of black people.[235] The residue of race continues to be one of the most volatile points of friction within the legal system,[236] and although race is not explicitly expressed when crime policy and sentencing decisions are made, racial disparities are not due to chance.[237]

In the immediate aftermath of the Civil War, former slaves presented a particular conundrum requiring constitutional amendments and supporting laws to turn former property into citizens; this unique challenge involved granting former "property" constitutional and individual rights of citizenship,[238] but the question of how to do this was very much unresolved. Whites, determined to maintain the color line so as to protect their political power and economic status, resurrected a system that automatically privileged whiteness; known as Black Codes, they were a set of laws designed to return blacks to their pre–Civil War status by restricting freed blacks' mobility and employment options. Black Codes were important because white domination without free black labor was impossible. Black Codes, such as pig laws, were in place from 1865–1866, but when southern politicians regained control of state governments, they revived antebellum racist laws denigrating blacks as inferior and rejecting them as alien.[239] Although the new laws were similar to the Black Codes, they were reenacted as Jim Crow laws.[240]

In an American adaptation of medieval laws, in the 1890s and early 1900s, states applied the notion of infamous crimes to black skin by injecting race into the "new" criminal justice system. Southern governments passed laws in an attempt to control, marginalize, and target black people, and the racialized differences were implemented in the administration of justice; blacks were the recipients of more punitive sentences while whites were indifferent to criminality in their own community.[241] The criminal justice system perpetuated racial inequalities through the creation of "black crimes," which were crimes whites believed blacks were more likely to commit than whites, such as larceny, receiving stolen property, forgery, wife beating, bribery, living in adultery, and vagrancy.[242] The law was applied unequally, and criminal penalties perpetuated white supremacy, as white offenders were often found not guilty of an offense or their criminality was dismissed as righteous while blacks who committed crimes were always found guilty and received harsh punishments.[243]

Southern states tailored their criminal laws to disenfranchise blacks.[244] Whites believed that a felony conviction designed to disenfranchise potential voters was the most effective method to protect white supremacy and consolidate political, social, and economic power into the hands of whites.[245] A felony conviction provided the means to make newly freed slaves and their descendants unable to vote, serve on juries, or serve as a witness in a court of law,[246] but more importantly, the mass incarceration of blacks reenslaved the black population and provided free labor to southern land owners. Convict leasing was an agreement between prison wardens and former plantation owners wherein former slaves and their "free" descendants were leased out to work for nominal fees, an arrangement that simulated slave labor.[247]

By 1920, southern state legislators added other felony crimes they believed black men were more likely to commit;[248] except for white-on-white murder, white criminality often went unpunished.[249] But, by criminalizing additional behaviors that whites believed blacks were more likely to commit, such as theft, burglary, arson, obtaining goods under false pretenses, perjury, embezzlement, and bigamy, whites ensured that blacks were convicted of a felony and disenfranchised because of their conviction.[250] The first generation of blacks born after slavery were removed from the voting rolls and mainstream economy, and in areas in the Deep South "uppity blacks," who challenged white power or were found to be in violation of social mores, were lynched or incarcerated.[251]

As a result of worsening southern social and economic conditions, blacks fled by the thousands to the urban centers of the Midwest and Northeast, where demand for labor in steel mills, packing plants, factories, and on the railroads was high. The Great Migration transformed northern urban centers,[252] which served two functions: to "harness and exploit the labor of African Americans while cloistering their tainted bodies [in a] sociospatial formation" that confined large numbers of blacks to designated urban spaces far from white communities.[253] Urban core communities absorbed the migration of southern blacks and the massive changes in industry,[254] but in the 1960s, social relations and the economy shifted; for the first time in the nation's history, black labor was not in demand.[255] The loss of economic viability for black urban residents is linked to the rehardening of the color line; by the early 1970s, in the shadow of racial and social advancements, the prison industrial complex emerged. Prisons became the locale for the next generation of black men to be marginalized to the lowest political, economic, and social status.[256]

Police tactics and policies transformed the prison population from majority white to majority minority;[257] the historical residue of race, the social construction of blackness as "other" outside normative society, the political calculations about black skin and crime, and whites' fear of blackness are not arbitrary. The racial history of a felony conviction in the United States is intimately tied to the dehumanization of blacks, and was an integral part of white racist ideology; by examining blackness and its connection to criminality, it is possible to see how the laws of the past exist in the present. Scholars find that "being black" leads to punitive criminal sentencing outcomes; recent criminal justice data shows that blacks are punished and incarcerated at higher rates than whites,[258] even when charged with the exact same crime.[259] Participants' lived experience bears this out, as they saw first-hand how the criminal justice system treats black and white offenders separately and unequally.[260]

> I think all [of] us that got caught up in the Drug War was for a reason. I mean, it's all black guys inside [prison], so what that tell you? They wanted us locked up, like in slave times, that's what. It ain't like whites ain't do crime, they just ain't inside with us.[261]

Participants recognize that skin color plays an enormous role in incarceration rates and in determining who is *not* incarcerated.

Due to racial bias and the social construction of blackness, criminality is equated to skin color, which explains the racial empathy gap and racial disparities in the criminal justice system.[262] "When [white] people see black men, they think crime, and that cognitive link is so strong that some people will create 'proof' to justify the association."[263] Racial bias appears during criminal sentencing. Whites are more likely to support punitive policies even though they are less likely to be victims of crime; more likely to overestimate the proportion of crime committed by people of color; and more likely to associate blackness with criminality.[264] A 2014 report laid bare the extent of racial bias in the criminal justice system, and the troubling association whites make between blackness and criminality.[265] Racial bias extends to the way white adults treat black children as young as ten; black girls and boys are perceived as guilty of doing something wrong while white boys are granted the benefit of youthful innocence.[266] The racial empathy gap, racial bias, and the disparate treatment of blacks create a unique danger for each black individual, including putting black people at greater risk of being shot by the police;[267] targeted in the courts and charged with excessive crimes; discriminated against at trial and during the sentencing phase; incarcerated at higher rates; and hounded when they reenter society due to postconviction policies aimed at felons.[268]

The politicization and racialization of urban residents were combined with the decline of the vitality of cities; deindustrialization, white flight, the rapid decline of the tax base, and destitute residents contributed to the decay of northern urban areas. "The ghetto," a pejorative term describing urban spaces where underserved and poor people live,[269] became a reality as economic opportunities dried up; previously thriving cities deteriorated and institutional abandonment increased, except in the area of policing.[270] New surveillance tactics and the "War on Drugs" policed the "surplus [black] population devoid of market utility."[271]

The "War on Drugs"

President Nixon declared a "War on Drugs" in 1971; since then, except for President Carter, who called for the decriminalization of marijuana, presidents of both political parties have waged this war without cessation, directed billions of dollars to battle "public enemy number one," and maintained the Drug Enforcement Agency (DEA).[272] The "War on Drugs" escalated in the 1980s; as drug usage rates soared, drugs were judged to be the cause of the unraveling moral fiber of the nation. The political response to crime[273] was to enshrine historical myths and falsehoods about race and criminality in the minds of whites;[274] legislators used whites' anxiety about rising crime rates and fear of blackness to justify overhauling the criminal justice system. Numerous federal and state laws reformed sentencing policies for drug offenses and offenses related to the drug trade, introduced new surveillance techniques, militarized the police, enhanced mandatory minimum prison sentences, and implemented "truth in sentencing" and "three strikes you're out" statutes in order to be "tough on crime" and criminals. The cumulative policies created a new method with which to police, control, and punish racial minorities[275] that relied heavily on long sentences of incapacitation, increased the number of people incarcerated,[276] and sent thousands of nonviolent drug offenders to prison for staggering amounts of time.[277]

The "War on Drugs" initially targeted crack cocaine, and its criminalization echoed policies created in the 1880s targeting former slaves.[278] In a manner similar to the way southern legislators criminalized particular behaviors, legislators in the 1980s and 1990s differentiated punishments for crack and powder cocaine. The creation of two classes of criminal drug offenses for two different groups of people who used powder cocaine (whites) and crack cocaine (blacks) was motivated by race;[279] crack and powder cocaine are derived from the same coca plant, and have no pharmacological differences.[280] The main differences between crack and powder cocaine are found in the appearance of each drug, the way it is used, where it is consumed, and its physiological and psychological effects. Powder cocaine is a crystalline-like powder that is "cut" with sugar, cornstarch, or flour to reduce its purity prior to its distribution, and is snorted. On the other hand, crack cocaine is "cooked" with ammonia or baking soda to convert the powder into small "rocks" prior to distribution. Crack cocaine can be smoked or injected. When the "rocks" are put in a glass pipe and heated, they make a cracking or popping sound, hence the name "crack," and users inhale the smoke. When the "rocks" are mixed with water and "cooked" with a small amount of heat, such as from a lighter, then the liquid can be injected.[281] Although whites are more likely to snort, inject, or smoke cocaine in powder or crack form, a disproportionate number of blacks have been incarcerated for crack cocaine offenses and serve long prison sentences under mandatory drug sentencing laws.[282] Federal mandatory minimum sentences are the primary cause for the racial disparities between prison sentences for black and white drug defendants.[283]

In the 1980s, crack cocaine was disproportionately used and distributed in open-air drug markets while powder cocaine was primarily dealt and used in private homes, businesses, and nightclubs, where it is harder to police. Initially, violence associated with crack cocaine and its distribution in open-air drug markets took place primarily in urban communities.[284] The media's attention to the crack cocaine epidemic led to a strong response from politicians, who criminalized the behaviors related to its use. President Reagan signed into law a policy that applied different penalties for individuals committing similar crimes; if someone possessed one gram of crack cocaine, he or she received the equivalent punishment as another person in possession of one hundred grams of powder cocaine.[285] The 100-to-1 disparity made racial disparities in punishment skyrocket;[286] the disparity is now 18-to-1, but the law still treats crack cocaine users and dealers harshly in comparison to white powder cocaine users and dealers, who are often directed to drug rehabilitation programs, and if these programs are completed successfully, white cocaine users can avoid a felony conviction and prison sentence.[287] The racialized approach to fighting the "War on Drugs" changed the way drugs were policed and offenders were incarcerated, resulting in an explosion in the imprisonment rate in the United States, which outpaces that of all other comparable countries.[288]

Incarceration serves many roles in the United States, as the prison is used as a form of social control to neutralize offenders and sequester them from society; as a form of punishment; and as a type of political message sent to voters.[289] The United States is overly dependent on a criminal justice system infused with racial bias to address societal challenges, the perceived threat of crime, whites' fear of blackness, and, to a large extent, poverty.[290] When former prisoners return to society, the history and social context of race and the stigma of a felony conviction follow them home, and they are blocked from accessing social, political, and economic rights as a result, which means they must figure out how to reenter society largely on their own.

2

Unwelcome Homecoming

Inside [prison] you learn to survive, not to live, not care about stuff, it's all about respect and surviving. Prison teaches you to survive, so you teach yourself to survive, you change yourself to survive, everything is about surviving. There's nothing else. Nothing. Then you get out, and survive. Same shit, really.
—Bishop, April 2, 2012

After surviving prison, thousands of women and men are discharged to the community with "gate money," the balance on their commissary account, and "dress out" clothes sent by family prior to the prisoners' release or the same clothes that they were wearing when they were arrested.[1] If the prisoner's clothes were thrown in the trash, which often happens, and family did not send "dress out" clothes, then institutional clothes are provided: Clifford loathed his prison-issued "dress out" wardrobe of two white t-shirts and boxer shorts, two pair of prison blue jeans, and a pair of prison soft-soled tennis shoes.[2]

The way Clifford feels about his wardrobe and the way his clothes affect his reentry experiences tend to be absent from traditional reentry scholarship,[3] which supports a standard measure of reentry in terms of either successful reentry or a failure to reenter, as measured by rearrest, reconviction, or reincarceration. Within this framework, reentry scholars are predisposed to focus on individuals' ability to adhere to a set of quantified variables with the expectation that returning felons will desist from criminal activity and succeed at reentry,[4] which means that individual responsibility takes precedence and each person is responsible for his or her own success. I argue that these expectations are unreasonable, not simply to criticize previous scholars' work but to expand the dialogue about what prisoner reentry looks like at the micro-level. For instance, when one talks to former prisoners while they reenter society, it becomes immediately clear that their lived experiences do not fit within the customary dichotomous boundaries of reentry. More often than not, individuals exiting prison lack social capital and family support, have no immediate legal means to earn money, and are unable to access public benefits.

When felons' voices are integrated into the analysis, their narratives offer an opportunity to put on display the unexamined structural and institutional constraints embedded in hostile policies, expose the unique challenges felons face upon coming home, capture the nuances of reentry, and raise interesting and unanswered questions about what felons think about while reentering to tell a different story of how individuals navigate the gray area between success and failure.[5] I urge scholars to move beyond the familiar arguments about the success or failure of prisoner reentry and work to incorporate former prisoners' narratives into their analyses. To date, such narratives have carried little weight, and yet formerly incarcerated prisoners' voices serve as a potent force that exposes the reality of how the oppressive penal chain extends punishment beyond the criminal justice system to keep its hold over felons' bodies. This chapter focuses on the voices of individual felons reentering society in Newark, New Jersey, to chart unmapped territory and provide insights into what it means to be considered a menace to society.[6]

Living in a Total Institution

When a prisoner enters the total institution of prison for the first time, the induction is the first instance of the prison forcing its power upon hundreds of bodies by subjugating prisoners to a host of practices to ensure conformity to the prison's rules and its institutional structures.[7] To start the process of removing one's sense of humanity through a degradation ritual,[8] prison guards and administrators try to destroy an individual's self-image by removing his or her dignity through a series of humiliations that systematically break down a person to his or her lowest low. Through role dispossession, prison personnel aim to damage a person's sense of self so that he or she will become numb, which makes prisoners easier to control. The process transforms individuals' identities into those of captive personas, strips them of their name and replaces it with a number, and exerts total control over prisoners' bodies.

Then they are locked in a cage, and their unique individuality is transformed officially into that of prisoner.[9]

Once incarcerated in a total institution, prisoners are cut off from normal societal interactions, as their entire life unfolds within the limited carceral space.[10] The confined space of a total institution produces a repressive society that forces prisoners to adopt a set of behaviors geared towards a form of endurance. Participants spoke of enduring prison as a strategy to withstand the dominated and hemmed-in space where there is no holiday from the eyes of all-watching guards, the brutal conditions, and the restraining spaces where all social interactions and communication unfold.[11] In this limited space, the number of prisoners "wildin' out," as participants called it, is increasing and is a normal part of surviving prison.[12] "Wildin' out" is common slang referring to a prisoner acting irrationally, as if he or she has little or no sense, has lost his or her mind, or has nothing left to lose and so acts out for attention. Increased incidents of inmates "wildin' out" complicate the already stressful world of prison and is a consequence of overincarcerating drug-addicted and mentally ill inmates;[13] approximately 16 percent of the prison population is mentally ill.[14] Prison is also a place of daily slanders, anger, pain, isolation, dehumanization, numbing predictability, mean-natured guards, and bad food.[15] Participants endured prison in order to survive it, and their conviction(s) played a considerable role in where they were incarcerated.

One's Criminal Resume

A key factor in determining where someone is incarcerated is that person's "jacket," a file composed of information pertaining to his or her criminal history and reports from each prison facility where the person has been incarcerated. The exact information included in the "jacket" varies across jurisdictions but often contains the following: arrest record, type of conviction, orders of commitment, detention and length of imprisonment, demographic information, and transfers between prisons. A prison jacket also includes the prisoner's psychological profile and classification (e.g., risk assessment; violent, nonviolent, or sexual offender; mandated administrative segregation; custody and security levels); health and medical records, including mental health records; an analysis and narrative about the individual as a prisoner (e.g., ability to adjust, compliance with prison rules, behavior); infractions and write-ups, if any, for violating prison rules, and disciplinary actions taken; propensity to fight; records of a prisoner's complaints and the prison's response; social ties inside prison (e.g., current and former cell mates, associates, codefendants, if any, and information as to whether any family member has been or is incarcerated); gang involvement; list of preapproved visitors, external contacts, and their relationship to the prisoner (e.g., reputable family, approved friends, legal representatives); information pertaining to reintegration efforts (e.g., participation in corrective or rehabilitative programs); and a list of the prisoner's belongings and personal effects that have been confiscated because they are banned from the carceral space.[16]

When all of the information is compiled in one place, the report offers a stark view of the person. The language is blunt and desensitized and diminishes the prisoner to a set of observations and generalities derived from court records, psychological evaluations, and reports by prison administrators, which form the basis of the criminal justice system's view of an individual. Theoretically, one's jacket is used by the New Jersey Department of Corrections as a tool to manage prisoners according to type of criminal charge and classification level (e.g., maximum, medium, or minimum security); control the movement of bodies between prisons according to time left to serve and date of eligibility for parole; determine health care and/or psychological needs and the location or availability of corresponding treatment; allocate staff; deliver prison services, including rehabilitative, educational, and vocational programs; determine ability to address special needs, such as a physical disability or religious dietary needs; and locate an open bed. The information is used to calculate where prisoners are incarcerated. However, the availability of educational curricula and services a prisoner would benefit from, such as GED courses or psychological treatment, are rarely integrated into the official calculation in deciding where to incarcerate someone. Of assessments, participants said that they "don't matter, ain't shit."[17] Only one thing matters:

> Yeah, DOC always says they do an assessment for this and that, shit, we all been assessed, for days, we've been watched and evaluated, classified, medicated, and ranked, all so they can determine the best place for us to do our

time, but really, it's all about an open bed. None of us have been matched to programs or needs, and sure ain't none of us been rehabbed. But we, *all of us*, got matched to a bed [emphasis original], 'cuz it's all about the beds.[18]

Despite the thorough assessment by the criminal justice system, prisoners are placed where there is an open bed at the individual's classification level, and according to their experiences, those two categories trump everything else.

If one has a "long jacket," it represents an extensive criminal record and reflects the fact that one has been arrested and convicted numerous times. A "thick jacket" indicates that one has served time in prison and has been assessed by prison officials; local jails may conduct a superficial evaluation, if they do one.[19] When the issue of jackets came up, participants admitted what kind of jacket they had, long or thick, but did not reveal its details; the majority of participants preferred to keep their jackets private because of its personal nature. I was told that it was "a big fucking deal" if a participant allowed me to read his or her jacket.[20] Socrates explained,

> Your papers, your jacket, that give you cred [credibility], but it can backfire on you, too. Not everyone needs to see your jacket. It's all about you, stuff you don't even know about [yourself], so I say just keep that quiet, keep your own shit quiet. Don't share nothing because that will come back to you in a bad way. People don't need to know all they [prisons and DOC] got on you, or see some weakness in you they can get you on later.[21]

While I was in the field, Tyrone allowed me to review his file, which was more than a half-inch thick. He said it was "alright, definitely not the worst file. Some of these guys got thick files, real thick."[22] I was told that some participants had more than one-inch-thick jackets.[23] From the perspective of others, an individual's jacket determines whether someone gets respect, even if no one ever sees it. Al shared that one's jacket is like a criminal resume and is related to the general thinking about the hierarchy of criminal behavior as it relates to one's charge and reentry:

> The more violent the charge, the harder it is [to reenter]. Like murder, attempted [murder], aggravated assault, certain charges aren't going to

work out here. Nope, just ain't. DUI, that's okay, but sex charges, nah, that ain't going to work, neither. Better to deal drugs, sometimes, but drugs is like the boogey man.[24]

Participants' views of different types of criminal charges, violence inside and outside of prison, guns and gun violence, and gangs varied, but all understood the danger of a gun charge.

> You gotta know the rules. Different levels of rules for different stuff. You play with guns, know the rules. Gang affiliation, know what it means. You got a charge, you should know the rules and [what's in] your jacket if you goin' do some dirt, 'cuz that'll come back at you.[25]

In a quiet voice, Tyrone explained how one's jacket and the rules altered the analysis of "doing dirt," which refers to committing a variety of crimes for money: "You tied to a gun, or gangs, your time goes up." Tyrone was sentenced to fifty years on a second gun charge, and shared his thoughts on violence: "It's the violence and if you wildin' out, [that] scares people off. Violence inside [scares people out here], the violence out here, that gets you put away, but you violent inside, you can survive."[26] After serving more than twenty-two years of his fifty-year sentence, and transitioning home on parole, he expanded on his thoughts about guns now that he was walking the streets and not wanting to go back to prison:

> Guns are all over the place now. Youngin's are like little animals, it's crazy. They will just take you out. And with a [gun] charge, you cannot intervene. I need to just walk away. Cannot defend myself, can't have a defensive manner. Eyes open. Always gotta to be "on." Hands open. Always got an escape route. It's a jungle in there [prison] *and out here* [on the streets of Newark, emphasis original]. Gotta stay watching and looking at everyone, and "just say no to guns."[27]

Everyone who came of age in the 1980s laughed: Nancy Reagan's "Just Say No to Drugs" campaign was now a slogan for guns.

Those with more violent criminal convictions will "get huge respect" from other prisoners, but respect can also be earned for surviving the

"Belly of the Beast," officially known as Rahway State Prison, a notoriously violent prison. Also, coming out of South Woods, a state prison known to incarcerate the hardest gang members, earns lots of respect from others, too. The more violent one's conviction, the more likely it is that one served time in Rahway or South Woods; several participants had served time in both. Men with long prison sentences would serve part of their sentence in one state prison, get transferred to another, and then in many instances get transferred back to the prison where they started off years before. One participant served more than a decade at one of the most notorious federal prisons, "Bloody Beaumont," officially called "the United States Penitentiary, Beaumont, Texas," and got huge respect for coming out alive. Women incarcerated in New Jersey serve their sentence in Edna Mahan Correctional Facility for Women, the only prison in New Jersey for women.

Living in a Cage

Participants learned how to "live" in a total institution while sharing a cell that is approximately sixty square feet,[28] which meant they had to move at a slow pace, make their bodies compressed through restricted movements, and keep their hands visible so as to not attract undue attention. While in my presence, participants spoke in general terms about being incarcerated, rarely breaking the unwritten code against discussing the specifics of being locked up;[29] however, when participants talked about the generalities or common experiences of being incarcerated, it meant that they had started the process of dealing with their emotions about being locked in a cage and treated like an animal. "Inside, you live in a cage, that's the only way to describe it," Tyrone stated.[30] Leon confirmed that being incarcerated is the same as being treated like an animal: "They [guards] want you to feel like nothing, less than an animal. Nothing good comes of it, being locked up. Nothing good."[31] For women, it was no different: "You get locked up and treated like an animal. Get looked down on, like you are nobody," shared Janaye. She went on to say,

> Um, I just tried to get past the time. I would write letters and stuff, you know, and read books and stuff. But of course in prison, in jail, you

treated like an animal. I felt like an animal. You gotta get up when they tell you to get up. You eat when they tell you to eat. Go to sleep when they tell you to sleep. Nothing is allowed, you can't be human inside because they treat you like an animal, so you feel like an animal. You just do.[32]

Darren elaborated on how it feels to be locked up: "You lose your senses locked up. You just gonna wanna growl, it's me against the guards so you, like, you do something, anything, to be something, really somewhere, else. Basically, that's how I look at it."[33]

Prison conditions produce dysfunctional behaviors and odd social interactions that ultimately become normalized while one is serving time in prison. Prisoners learn how to "jail," which refers to acquiring the skills needed to survive prison; these behaviors make little sense on the outside but they make perfect sense inside. Plus, the increased presence of drug-addicted and mentally ill inmates intensifies the level of "craziness" inside a total institution, so participants tried to resist falling into that madness.[34] "I learned how to jail. I know how to do time. I know how to survive prison. That's what prison showed me. Oh, and not go crazy."[35]

Others talked about inmates institutionalized to the ways of prison:

Some people get comfortable, it's crazy, they start calling their cell their "house"; it ain't no fuckin' house. *It. Is. A. Cage* [emphasis original]. A box with bars, it is a cell, you ain't control nothing. That's not my house. You get comfortable, then you ain't looking for an exit [to be released from prison]. You must think it's good in there, and some have to think that way to make it. Fuck that, not me.[36]

One way in which some participants kept their humanity was through family visits. Family visits are viewed as an important component to maintaining family ties and staying connected to the outside. However, prison visits can be financially draining for a family and emotionally taxing for a prisoner. For families, it is expensive to support a loved one in prison—costs include keeping money on the prisoner's commissary account for food, postage, paper, pens, envelopes, some clothing items (e.g., warm socks), toiletries (e.g., soap, toothpaste, toilet paper), as well as the high cost of collect phone calls—but a personal visit is the most expensive, and prisoners are frequently incarcerated a great distance from where their family lives.[37] In addition to the expense of travel, the visit can be stressful and traumatizing, especially for children.[38] Visitors go through a security process that can include drug-sniffing dogs, physical pat-downs, and body searches; children are searched like adults.[39] There are strict rules about what visitors can wear, physical contact with their loved one, and what can be taken inside prison; the prison visit is an artificial social interaction that unfolds in a regulated environment located inside the prison, and visitors are subject to comparable surveillance and control mechanisms imposed on prisoners within the carceral space.[40]

For prisoners, a visit is good, but it comes with its own unique challenges. Prior to a scheduled visit, a prisoner must change his or her mindset from the defensive, suspicious posture needed to survive to one that is hopeful. This switch can be stressful as the prisoner wants to and attempts to hide the damaging effects of prison from loved ones.

> Visits are always good, no doubt about that; visits make you feel normal. The problem is before [the visit] you real careful not to get written up [for a rules violation that would automatically cancel visitation rights], and after the visit, you want to go, you know, get up and leave with your family and you can't, and that brings you down, back to the reality of where you are, and that's prison. You try to keep that reality shut down [by holding the emotions in check], but when your family gets up to leave and you are locked up, it's like it [getting locked up] happens all over again. You get messed up in your head when you have to get strip searched [after a visit], go back to your cell, being treated like an animal. That's the real hard part.[41]

Participants spoke about the dual existence they experienced in relation to visits—son, brother, husband, uncle, or father *and* prisoner. This double consciousness[42] provoked feelings that wavered between passivity and rage. "Guards think we stupid" and presume compliance and subservient behavior before and after visits, but participants explained their behaviors differently. "Inside, we expected to be good, but that don't work when you getting yelled at, disrespected. You can't be a man, a real man, inside [prison] because the guards got all the power and you nothing."[43] So, the practice of following prison rules before a visit and adapting back to the rules after a family visit is a form of survival and is imperative if the prisoner is to avoid sanctions or evade getting into a fight with a jealous prisoner who may never have visitors. Prisoners learn to conceal their inner turmoil by conforming to the rules. "After [a visit], you sit down, and you just mad."[44]

Post-Traumatic Stress Disorder

PTSD[45] is normally linked to injuries sustained in war, terrorist attacks, or political violence (e.g., 9/11, the Boston Marathon bombing), sexual or physical abuse (e.g., rape, dating or domestic violence), community violence (e.g., police shooting of unarmed residents), natural disasters (e.g., hurricane, earthquake), violent death of a loved one (e.g., suicide), serious injury (e.g., dog attack, burns), or a traumatic personal ordeal.[46] Incarceration is an ongoing traumatic event, and because nonviolent and violent criminals are serving longer prison sentences, overcrowding is normal and creates an environment that breeds arbitrary violence that dramatically increases the scope and severity of trauma inside; the constant threat of violence inside prison results in relentless paranoia. Prisoners systematically face psychological injuries, suffer emotional distress, and are isolated while "doubled up" in small cells.[47] The physical and mental injuries[48] and the human damage inflicted and experienced in prison result in post-traumatic stress disorder.[49] The turmoil and mental harm comes home with each former prisoner.

PTSD is a set of cascading emotional, psychological, and/or physical responses triggered by multiple events or a single event.[50] One form of trauma participants experienced was "lost" time.[51] Inside prison, every day is indistinguishable from any other day, but upon reentering, participants had to grapple with having lost years or decades of their lives, with having missed their kids growing up, and with the way incarceration has placed a substantial financial and emotional burden on their family. But inside a total institution, the predominant types of injuries sustained by prisoners are physical and prolonged mental harm; to survive prison, individuals become emotionally and physically numb to the dysfunction of living in a same-sex environment.

In a same-sex environment, gender roles are distorted because gender has a public dimension[52] that is embedded in societal interactions.[53] For instance, within regular social exchanges, gender is portrayed as a particular sex category based on a set of practices that are codified as feminine or masculine behaviors.[54] In a same-sex environment, however, customary gender behaviors, gender expression, and "doing gender" can no longer be practiced or assessed according to traditional gender roles. A total institution engenders dysfunction, and in the absence of gender differences in an all-male institution, masculinity is exaggerated. Hypermasculinity ensues as men attempt to be "the man" among men.[55]

Hyper-masculinity in men's prisons manifests itself in a toxic "constellation of socially regressive male traits that serve to foster domination, the devaluation of women, homophobia, and wanton violence."[56] One form of hyper-masculinity is fighting and using violence to forge a reputation as someone not to be messed with. Mason, who served time in "Bloody Beaumont," bragged that he was "8 and 0," having won all eight of the fights he instigated.[57] Mason explained that he utilized violence to avoid violence. Instigating "controlled fights" with other prisoners allowed him to circumvent random fights.[58] Mason knew that prison was plagued with prisoners looking to take their aggression out on others, so by deliberately fighting, he established a reputation as a brawler, providing him the opportunity to transition into the role of negotiator. His image as a fighter protected him from having others use violence against him, including sexual violence.

"Prison is like a jungle. Only the strongest survive, everyone else is a victim."[59] Sexual violence in a male prison is used to dominate and degrade others who are construed as weak or feminine; by victimizing weaker men, a man can appear tough.[60] Xavier used violence to survive prison by adopting predatory behavior as a way to protect himself and not be sexually violated. "I had two choices—I can be a predator or the prey—and I ain't no faggot."[61] Tyrone simplified the choice: "When you go in, you can be an easy mark or do the marking."[62]

In women's prisons, female prisoners suffer the same deprivation of liberty, goods, and services as men, but the prison experience is different.[63] The subculture in women's prisons is distinctive due to the way women relate to one another.[64] Female prisoners create "pseudo-families"[65] in which women take on traditional family roles, such as mother, father, sister, child, and grandparent.[66] Research shows that intimate relationships tend to exist for three reasons; economic manipulation, companionship, or sex.[67]

Some women may choose to enter a same-sex romantic relationship as a way to cope with and survive prison.[68] Estimates vary as to the percentage of heterosexual female prisoners who enter same-sex relationships while incarcerated, and studies demonstrate that such partnerships tend to form around friendships and support systems.[69] Intimate relationships in a pseudo-family constitute a way to self-organize within the prison population in such a way as to enter the social system, expand the ability to acquire resources, and gain access to the benefits of the system.[70] Not all "pseudo-family" relationships are sexual in nature, and can cross racial boundaries, but do operate as a form of emotional and economic support, as well as protection.[71] Although violence may not be as much of a factor, female prisoners are known to engage in financial coercion, sexual intimidation, and assault.[72] The creation of a "pseudo-family" can protect individuals from strong-arm tactics used by other prisoners. Building alliances within a same-sex environment is one response women have to being incarcerated, but these relationships are fragile due to high levels of mistrust, loneliness, and the lack of close social relationships on the outside.[73]

Prisoners experience a loss of control over their lives, and there are no unwounded souls in prison;[74] once an individual is exposed to different and extreme degrees of sexual and violent trauma, paranoia, distrust, and obsessive personal surveillance tactics inside prison, the collective experiences can manifest in PTSD. Negative awareness and thoughts developed in prison can create maladaptive behaviors and can result in PTSD-like symptoms[75] or what I argue is prison-induced PTSD. Although there is no definitive study of this phenomenon, I believe that one of the most prevalent psychiatric results of incarceration is PTSD, which impairs daily functioning, well-being, recovery, and reentry.[76] Prison trauma cannot be untangled from an individual's sense of self, and whatever trauma is experienced, prisoners are damaged. "Going to prison is like going to war; we just ain't got the guns and tanks, that's all that's different because I felt doing time was like going to war."[77]

Socrates contextualized the impact on one's psyche of incarceration, hyper-vigilance, and perpetual suspicion, and explained how returning prisoners deal with their angst and trauma:

When you are away [in prison], you have to deal with all kinds of shit inside that you ain't never think about before. Because there are all kinds of predators inside: sexual, physical, mental. Someone is going to want to mess with you in some way, but no one says anything. We hold it all in to survive; a lot of guys are unable to feel, or actually they learn how not to feel. And we come back, and instead of dealing with the shit in our lives, we just smoke weed, do our stuff, you know, be in the streets, and never deal with the pain we feelin'. Never.[78]

Former prisoners learn how to bury their emotions in prison as a strategy to outlast their sentence.

Every day, you just keep on grinding, holding it all in [emotions], avoiding shit, trying to survive, and not thinking about hope. Hope is something in short supply. You never see any goodness, real hard to find, so hard you think it's fake, so you don't trust it or 'em [kind people].[79]

The reentry process requires former prisoners to contain their emotions and swallow their trauma in an effort to conform to the rules of society, but the mechanisms learned to survive prison become ingrained, and are exhausting.

The fear inside, it's normal, it's constant, you holding on; it's tiring, exhausting, to the point that when I came home, all I wanted to do was sleep. I hadn't had a good night's sleep in like twenty-five years. I wanted to sleep, rest, and be in a room all by myself.[80]

The First Day Home

"On the first day home, it feels so good it hurts."[81] After one has been locked in a cage with a cell mate not of one's choosing, eating the same food, following an identical routine, wearing matching uniforms, and only interacting with prisoners of the same sex for years, the first days home are full of befuddling noises, traffic, fast talkers, kids, and people of all kinds. A great deal of energy is spent making the mental and physical transition from prisoner to free man or woman; just as one had to adapt to living in a cell, one has to adjust to living on the outside. For instance, when most participants were incarcerated, they used coins to ride the bus, but public transportation is now automated and requires a bus card:

> I got real nervous coming down here [to the nonprofit organization] the first few times, the cars buzzing by, not knowing where to get on or off the bus, and using a [bus] card but not knowing how to, you feel stupid, because everything is moving so fast and I stood on the corner not knowing stuff and not knowing who to ask. Was scared to ask, looking stupid is not a good feeling, you know?[82]

During the first few weeks home, former prisoners are "free" to stand on a street corner, and then a car whizzes by, nearly clipping them, forcing them to jump back; for former prisoners, this is an anxiety-provoking event. As participants transitioned from the trauma of prison[83] to a vexing community, they talked about their nerves when first walking the city's streets:

> It can be humiliating, you standing there on the street, people driving by, it's embarrassing-like because you ain't done nothing but you feel guilty of something because you don't know nothing. Everything is real different, and you just mad-like because you don't know stuff. Your nerves are shot.[84]

In practical terms, the mindset required to survive prison must be replaced with behaviors that conform to societal norms. Learning how to adjust to an unfamiliar environment while catching up to the speed of society, dealing with the technological changes that took place while incarcerated, and getting used to the sounds, smells, and colors of the outside world, which can cause headaches, panic attacks, and disorientation, is challenging. One may not have the tools to adapt or the ability to make decisions one hasn't had to make for years; reentry is painful: "I was getting agitated, all the stuff I'm trying to do, some days [having to make a lot of decisions], it can get to be too much. I'm still calming down, at least trying to."[85]

While incarcerated, men and women do not have the ability to make decisions and therefore can become overwhelmed when first home. Participants experienced different types of trauma inside prison, and upon reentering society, have access to varying degrees of resources, social capital, housing, and family support; as a result, some need a lot more time than others to adjust to the pace of society. Some participants had anxiety attacks, and some would lash out in anger due to being frustrated and emasculated by their felony conviction; to cope, some resorted to using the skills they learned to survive prison. Yet, when prisoners are released and return home, they are expected to turn off prison behaviors, put their prison experiences behind them, and "fit in" so they can transition home successfully.[86] But, the world they are reentering is unpredictable and not how they remembered it, so participants revert to what they know in an attempt to survive: "Reentering is about keeping your head on a swivel. Ya gotta keep your head on a swivel, I'm telling ya, because you don't know what's coming, where it's coming from. Always got to stay on alert. Always."[87]

Osborn elaborated on the tactics he used renegotiating society as a felon, what he was thinking about, and what he had to do to *not* go back to prison.

> It's dangerous riding the bus. Gotta stay in my lane. Youngins wildin' out, no respect. Big guns, bad shots. Gotta pay attention all the time, ya can't relax, ever. With the charge, you lose regardless of what was what. I just gotta keep walking, keep it moving, eyes straight forward, say nothing, because if not, and something pops off, I will go back if I don't.[88]

What Osborn refers to is that if there is an altercation at the store or on the bus, as a felon, he can be arrested and sent back to prison while things get sorted out, if they get sorted out, even if he had nothing to do with the original dispute. Other participants shared a similar way of thinking:

> Everyone needs to avoid bad influences, keep positive people in your life, but that can be hard when you go back [to the neighborhood] and people know you and your history. I've been off the block and cut off from all that's out here, so you know, I need to keep that in mind, like being your own look-out all the time.[89]

Felons cannot be hyper-sensitive to big or small affronts, which is the opposite of what they learned in prison; inside, a verbal insult can lead to a fight or worse, but on the outside, former prisoners have to turn off their alert system and walk away because a misunderstanding on the street or at home can lead back to prison. Yet, former prisoners are not a light switch and cannot turn off habits learned to survive prison; they don't know how to *not* be on "high alert" and turn off their survival tactics to conform to societal expectations. Participants were constantly stressed and anxious, which was partially related to their diminished position in society.

Stuart demonstrates a level of consciousness about his diminished position, and how his status informs his reentry decisions:

> If I'd have known there'd be so much scrambling around, going place to place for stuff but leaving with nothing, I don't know; really, reentry, it's all just a scam trying to make something positive out of the situation with nothing. [I'm] trying to at least be positive, but for what? Ain't nothing out here for me.[90]

Although not every participant felt the same as Stuart, many had a hard time trying to reconcile their prison experience with their current status. Sylvester attempted to explain how participants felt while they were stuck between prison and society while reentering society:

> Taking shit is an art form inside [prison]. After you done your bid you living with your mother, grandmother, somebody taking care of you, somebody, you hope, because you ain't got shit. And guess the fuck what? That's progress. Ain't shit, but that's a step up [from a prison cell]. Still, all the shit 'n stuff, it takes all I got to get through another day, but that's what I gotta do.[91]

Many participants carried around a resigned sense that they were unprepared to deal with reality, and that things on the outside had changed, and changed in ways that they did not yet fully comprehend.

> It's all about coping, that's what reentry is really all about. You cope with things you don't even really comprehend. It's all stress; it's real stressful to overcome all the adversity [to reenter successfully]. We all just coping, some are trying to cope, and some cope better than some, you know, just

putting things to the side and keep it moving, but some, some can't walk away. Me, I can't be thin-skinned out here. I have to deal [with people] and stay somewhat connected, keep my feet on the ground, you know, but keep moving. Can't get stuck.[92]

Participants told stories of their fear of going back to prison when they returned to the scene of the crime that led to their initial removal from the community and remembered their angst when they were originally incarcerated and locked in a cage. Their angst is then replicated upon their return home while walking around their old neighborhood. Participants recalled how this was an anxiety-provoking event, like undergoing an out-of-body experience, and they dreaded turning the next corner for fear of having to confront more societal changes.[93] Released prisoners are like displaced people, and lost in the reentry scholarship is that those who served long prison sentences return as strangers to a strange land, to a place with which they had had a previous connection but that is now unrecognizable. They are older, their parents might have died, and siblings have likely moved, so there are fewer family members to help them transition home.

Bradford, who was incarcerated for twenty-five years, returned to a city that he no longer recognized. His parents had died while he was incarcerated, and his extended family was scattered to places unknown. He entered society with no family support, no legal work experience, and limited educational attainment. To further add to his challenges, Bradford was extremely shy and withdrawn. Although it appeared that he listened to the conversations swirling around him, he never contributed, and was apprehensive when meeting strangers. When a new person entered the room, if Bradford could not physically leave, he would "hide" behind gregarious people or withdraw in place. On many occasions, I witnessed him recoil and then retreat into a shell of his own making. Bradford literally became smaller in place, as if he was trying to become invisible; for him, being outside of prison was frightening, and this fear became discernible by his visible social wariness around unfamiliar people.

While in the field, Bradford and I had a handful of stilted conversations; each time I started a conversation with him, he would look down at the floor, say as little as possible, and at the first possible moment retreat quickly to avoid further conversation. He was not rude; rather, he was anxious, guarded, and desperately awkward, and did not know how to talk to me, so he shared little. When he did speak, his words were hesitant, and he was uncertain about his future. Without family to support him and with no permanent place to live, Bradford was visibly lost. My sense was that he was terrified; the last time I spoke to him, he shared that in a few weeks he would be forced to leave his halfway house and fend for himself, but Bradford did not know where he was going to go or where he was going to live, and had no idea how he was going to support himself.

Prison did not prepare Bradford to reenter; he developed observable social distress, and never established a routine that allowed him to abide by the rules of parole while building a foundation, and with no support or long-term assistance, he was reentering with nothing. A couple of weeks after our last interaction, he failed a random drug test, violating his parole, and was reincarcerated.[94] After being incarcerated for twenty-five years, Bradford was comfortable with the ways of prison; he was institutionalized. He left Newark in 1987 and returned in 2012 to a dramatically different society. When Bradford is next released from prison, he will max out,[95] so the next time he reenters he will have less support, he will have no access to transitional housing, his skill set will not have improved, and his language skills may have regressed.

Although Bradford was unable to express his feelings about the hostile world he was entering, Savannah eloquently described her experience, how the label "felon" holds so much power over her life, and how she is socially disabled by the single word.

> Reentry is verbally and physically abusive. The name, the word, is the stupidest word on earth. Most people are entering, not (re)entering. People cannot reenter a community they've never been a part of. Integration and productivity is not where they are, not where they are going to be anytime soon. There are so many challenges to get "there" [to the point of being able to reenter] and stay there [successfully reenter]. Entering, it's what we are doing, trying to do, at least, because that's what I'm doing. [Reentry,] it's all based on words; "reentry," "felon," that being the hardest [of all words] to overcome. It [the word "felon"] takes everything away from you, so you on your own, ready or not, *you are on your own* [emphasis original].[96]

One of the hardest things for contemporary outlaws to overcome is that their past is always present: "I'm tired of running from the truth, my past. Time to just move forward, own it and get beyond it, but how you do that? We got nothing, mad, and shit ain't gettin' better."[97] The "shit" from inside follows each felon home to manifest in various forms of maladaptive behavior.[98]

Bailey had been locked up for two decades, and his greatest challenge coming home was acclimating:

> It is hard to adjust. I know how to do time, and going back [to prison] is not an option, I can't, but the hardest thing is adjusting so I don't go back. I've been home seventy-three days, and it's still hard to believe.[99]

Despite the fact that Bailey had maxed out,[100] he counted each day, just as he had while incarcerated; it was his way of coping. Learning how to stop counting days is difficult; some inmates are institutionalized to counting days and being counted. Prisoners are counted every day so many times that life revolves around the count:[101]

> You get used to the daily count. Now I get nervous when that time of day comes, when I'm supposed to be counted, my body knows what time it is, [it] comes to attention-like. I get nervous, but then it [that feeling] passes. Based on the count, being counted, I was counted every day for eighteen years, I know when I am supposed to be counted, so it's hard to drop [that pattern of] being counted.[102]

Other former prisoners had to face different challenges upon their return home. Alton, at forty-three years old, had served twenty years, seventeen of them consecutively, in state prison and appeared to be adjusting well. During his interview, he was wearing clothes and shoes that were appropriate for the weather, and had a cell phone he was proud of, showing me its features and pointing to his blue-tooth ear piece. His appearance made obvious that he had the support of his family; however, as the interview progressed, he shared how the first few weeks out of prison were genuinely tough and how even months later he was still dealing with different types of setbacks and frustrations. "Every day, still, I'm encountering these small challenges that I didn't expect, didn't even know about, and it can get tough. You just try and not let it get you down. Try and get past it, but man, it's hard." [103]

He got car sick on the ride home from prison; for the previous seventeen years, Alton had not been in a moving vehicle, and his stomach could not handle the rocking-jostling movement of the car on the pothole-filled roads of New Jersey. "I had to ask my mom to pull over so I could get some air." Even after several months home, he was still getting car sick. "It's embarrassing; you can't even sit in a car without wanting to puke, [and] needing to sometimes."

Car sickness is only one challenge that tends to be ignored in the reentry experience after time served in prison; another is sensory overload. When his family took him out for his first meal at a restaurant in almost two decades, Alton walked in, sat down, but had to immediately get back up:

> In prison, it's all drab and dull, one color, everything is grayish, and the sounds of prison become like a dull background noise you get used to, you just do. But that restaurant: the smells, sound, noise, color. All of it was way too much. I had to step outside and gather myself. All the colors and noise made me dizzy. [It was] all way too much. I had to take deep gulps of air because I thought I was going to be sick.[104]

Alton was experiencing sensory overload, a common occurrence for those reentering after being incarcerated; although it often dissipates over time once someone is back in society, for some it never completely disappears.[105]

For many participants, the first meal home was memorable, as they described with fondness the texture of food and variety of options; eating from stoneware or a decorative dinner plate after years of eating off a plastic or metal tray; using silverware that included a sharp knife, fork, and spoon;[106] table linens; drinking as much as they wanted; and the luxury of eating slowly instead of wolfing their food down. Participants shared how they were institutionalized to eat a certain way while incarcerated, shoveling food into their mouths, barely chewing, and quickly swallowing because their meals were timed due to overcrowding and the prisons' need to feed everyone on a set schedule for every meal. Typical were the following two participants' recollections of eating home-cooked food for the first time in years:

My moms put on a spread for me, and that food tasted so good. It was like it melted in my mouth, and I just sat there happy, with this big goofy smile on my face. I think I forgot what food was suppose to taste like.

Yeah, I remember too, my first *real* meal in I don't know how long, that food was so good, like *wow* good. My family brought their best stuff, and I didn't have to put nothing on it, no salt, pepper or ketchup to hide any nasty taste. It was finger-licking good.[107]

Loren's family was so happy when he came home after serving twenty-five years in state prison that they hosted a party in his honor. His entire extended family, friends, and neighbors were invited, and everyone brought food. The food was piled high, and many tables were covered with bowls and plates holding a variety of cuisine: "two types of chicken wings, hot dogs, hamburgers and all the fixings, steak, casserole, lasagna, seasoned vegetables, chili, desserts, cake, ice cream, cupcakes, pudding, candy, all sorts of things to drink, everything. It was a feast fit for a king."[108] Food is a shared experience, and everyone understands the importance of good-tasting food, but more importantly, food is a way for families to bond; when family members fix their best recipes, it is their way of saying, "We love you and missed you." Through food, families communicate their feelings, which were often left unsaid when their loved one was "away" in prison.

From Property to Citizen: Identification and Paperwork

Each participant's transition home differs; some struggle with technology, others struggle with family relationships. A universal experience was that once they were home, when participants finally stopped counting days and their bodies no longer came to attention to be counted, their mental transition home caught up to their physical transition home. Once participants knew that being home was real, that they could go outside to feel the sunshine on their face or look at the stars and not get sent back to prison, they began to exhale and start to deal with and attempt to overcome other challenges, like recreating their identity. How do *you* prove who you are? The common way is through government-issued picture identification like a passport or driver's license. Those who have been incarcerated, however, have a state-issued picture ID with "The Property of the Department of Corrections" stamped on it. An integral part of reentering society is recreating one's legal identity, but without DOC's stamp on it.

Participants had a mix of jackets reflecting a variety of conviction types and criminal and imprisonment histories, but despite the personal nature of one's jacket, many newly home former prisoners initially carry their files around because they contain all of their formal records of identity, and may be the only "official" record with their legal name. Participants wanted to reestablish their legal identity, but when one does not have access to the internet or have an email address, the state agency in question has to process a paper request, and the form must be mailed to the recipient and then mailed back to the agency. Individuals have to provide supporting documentation concerning their identity, but many of those returning home only have a manila envelope full of papers; they have no birth certificate, Social Security card, or other official identification with which to get a state ID. The lack of identification is the defining characteristic that separates those who have been "home" and those who have just returned. Prisoners are the property of the DOC, and when initially released, they remain DOC property while on parole or probation. Former prisoners are only "free" from the control of DOC when they complete their entire sentence and max out.

Transitioning home from prison is legally analogous to the conversion undertaken by slaves transformed from property to citizens, and is reminiscent of historical practices that created boundaries between property and citizen, and the struggle of former slaves creating a formal identity that did not include permission from their former slave master. During fieldwork, I observed women and men pulling out their paperwork, including sentencing papers, court documents, discharge papers, certificates, and prison records, to prove who they were so as to recraft their legal identity. When I witnessed participants pulling documents out of a dog-eared manila envelope, I thought of two things. First, it was as if those returning home were unsure of their identity, which makes sense; they had been stripped of their name and referred to as a number by the DOC. Second, it reminded me of historical accounts of slaves carrying passes when they traveled from one plantation to another to prove whom they belonged to, or of "free" blacks who had to carry identity passes proving they were "free." If confronted by a white man, blacks had to show their slave or "free" pass. If a slave was caught without a proper pass, he or she was detained, sold, or lynched on the spot.[109] If a "free" black did not have papers, he or she could be sold into slavery.[110] Former prisoners are not slaves, and cannot be sold or lynched, but they are socially disabled, and their lack of identity harkens back to slavery, the Black Codes, and Jim Crow.[111]

Huxley described the difficulties that unfolded when he tried to secure a picture ID, could not get the appropriate copies of his records, and did not have the money to pay to expedite the process, all of which are common challenges:

> My job referral has been sitting on someone's desk for probably four weeks now. They wouldn't hire me because my ID was expired, and I needed to get a new one, then when I went to motor vehicle, they said my birth certificate was too old, they couldn't use it, so I had to go get another one at City Hall. City Hall wouldn't give it to me because I didn't have a "good" ID [it had expired], and I had no money to get me a new one. It took me, like all this time, the last four weeks, and I got nothing. [Sighs.] I've been trying to do stuff and I couldn't 'cuz I didn't have an ID and didn't have the forms and money to get one.[112]

Huxley's experience demonstrates how the lack of funds needed to complete a necessary transaction, like securing a certified copy of one's birth certificate, can take weeks. Along the way, some get delayed and are unable to accomplish the task. The challenge faced by Huxley and others can be easily fixed: DOC has each prisoner's legal name, birth date, height, eye color, weight, and picture. The piece of missing information is an address, but someone's identity is not attached to a zip code. The New Jersey DOC could assist the transition home by issuing a state ID with pertinent information and picture but *without* the "Property of the Department of Corrections" stamped on it, and could replace "DOC" with "The State of New Jersey." The New Jersey DOC is a legitimate state agency, so this would require an administrative modification.

Some of those returning home have identification problems because of poor past choices. Maurice, a former drug user, avoided using his legal name whenever he was arrested due to a litany of indiscretions, charges, and outstanding bench warrants. The fear of using his real name resulted in a snowball effect of negative legal ramifications, but once he got clean and off drugs, his past poor choices made securing legal identification difficult. Maurice explained:

If the police ask me for ID now, you know this is the first time in forty-three years I got an ID with *my* name on it. [Maurice puffed out his chest and thumped it.] My name. Seriously. See, when I got here [to the non-profit], I was known as the man with like eleven names, eight Social Security numbers, and ain't none of them mine. None of them were mine. I know the drugs had me so fucked up, so bad, my brother, the next to oldest one, I told you he died when he was like thirty-four, this was in 2004, and a month later, well a week later really, I got locked up and I used his name so I could get out because I knew I had warrants under my name, and his name was clean. And, when they locked me up for like eight days, you know where you sit in the county jail for days and you come back in front of the judge and if you ain't got no other charges or warrants, they let you go. So, when the judge was getting ready to cut me loose, the clerk was at the doors, and yelled out, "Your honor, we need to talk to you." The judge is like, "Ain't got nothing to say, he's leaving." And the clerk, like, she come all the way into the courtroom then, and she's got a manila envelope, waving it, and she says, "Hold on your honor." I forgot her name, but he [the judge] asked her, "What's the problem?" And [the clerk] said, "I don't know who this man is but that's not Michael Anders because I got his death certificate right here." And she pulled out a piece of paper, waving it, and I thought I was going to faint, I swear. I got caught, just like that, and the judge slammed that thingy, you know the gavel, on the other thing, and said, "Cuff him." Man, I had to stay in county [jail] until they verified my real identity, because I wasn't tellin' 'em nothing. [Maurice mimed "zipping" his lips together, and then, with a big smile on his face, continued.] And, well, see that's what drugs do to you, lets you think that you can get away with anything.[113]

Maurice chose not to get legal identification because

[t]he thing is, I didn't want to get it [his own ID], not back then because then to get it, I would have to prove who I am, but if I don't get it, and if I tell you my name is Michael and you search me, and find ID that says something else, they [the cops] going to say, "No, your name is really Maurice." I knew they'd turn around and say, "You going to jail first of all for lying to a cop," on top of the charge you got for whatever you was doing that you weren't suppose to be doing when they stopped you. So, you know, I had to keep incognito. [He starts chuckling.]

For a long time, Maurice lived off the grid, using numerous aliases and Social Security numbers to avoid having his past charges catch up to him and having to deal with reality.

I haven't had a license [with my name on it] since I was in high school because my name was tainted. I always had a warrant for doing something. I couldn't get three seconds clean, and now I got three years. You know how good that feel? That's another thing, I refuse to give that up, being clean: I worked too hard to do that, to get clean and stay clean, and now I can walk around as me. I don't have to look over my shoulder.

Maurice paused, and then a fit of giggles filled the room because he was drug free and had photo identification as himself. "See, now I can be like, 'Hi I'm Maurice, nice to meet you.'"[114] Maurice beamed a big smile; he was so proud of himself.

Securing legal photo identification is a challenge for many former prisoners, but securing legal photo identification was easy in comparison to dealing with stressful family relations. Upon returning home, participants had to deal with family members who had picked up the pieces after they were incarcerated and had carried the financial and emotional burden of caring for them while they were away.[115] Family could be welcoming, but eventually tensions arose around money.

Family and Finances

When former prisoners return home, the financial circumstances of their family and extended family play an outsized role in determining how hard it will be for them to reenter society. Although such a situation was rare, when a participant returned to a financially stable family that was able to provide housing, clothing, food, and, in one case, a job, and everything else an individual needs to restart his or her life, the participant would come to the nonprofit organization for a few weeks for social support and then drift away and not return. For participants whose family had few financial resources and were unable to help in a meaningful way, tension would emerge around the financial status of the family.

The depths of a family's financial struggles usually only come to light when there is no money to buy new clothes,[116] and there is no extra cash to provide for other necessities. This is the first time that many male participants find out how their loved ones, particularly their mothers, the mothers of their children, and their kids, struggled financially while they were in prison.[117]

> My girl, she sometimes just needs to vent and get stuff off her chest about me, she mad, frustrated about how hard it was for her and the kids when I was away. I can't do nothing about that, so I try and take her anger and not react. A lot of guys go in [to prison] as a child and come out as a man. That was me. I went in and came out as a man, but I don't really know what that looks like, to be a man in the house, take care of stuff. I need to learn how to be a man, be a dad, have to build up that trust, learn, you know, how to communicate, and really not react to anything. She hurtin' too, 'cuz of me, and I have to stand up and deal.[118]

When participants find out how they've hurt their family and caused financial hardships while they were locked up, they are hurt and angry. Learning that there is little money available to help is like receiving a punch in the gut and is hard to face, and they are angry because this problem was hidden from them while they were incarcerated. Although there was little, if anything, that anyone could do while incarcerated to contribute to the household's finances, as men, participants felt it was their right to know. The combination of anger and hurt could turn into resentment as some participants wondered what else had been kept from them. The combination of hurt feelings and a sense of being isolated can be a major emotional hurdle to overcome because participants had to swallow their ego, and could only blame themselves for their family's financial state.

Over a series of conversations in Group, several male participants shared their perspective on what made reentering difficult as it related to their families, finances, and their role as provider. When they were unable to buy new clothes and had to seek out charitable organizations to put together a wardrobe, participants understood that they had nothing and, more significantly, realized how dependent they were on others. Men in Group struggled with being dependent on anyone, but in many cases they were dependent on a group of women, such as their mothers, aunts, sisters, the mothers of their children, wives, daughters, and girlfriends. Often, the women in participants' lives provided the financial support and made decisions regarding how the house was run, but male participants viewed this as "all wrong" because they wanted to reassert their manliness.[119] Unable to "be a man," many male participants experienced a sense of hopelessness and uselessness that pervaded their psyche and made them question their sense of self and what it meant to be a man.[120]

"Being a man" was very important to the men in Group, and to them this meant taking care of the bills, paying for their kids' clothes and school supplies, making decisions, and helping their woman look good by buying her clothes and jewelry and paying for her hair appointments.[121] Prior to being incarcerated, many of the men took care of all of the financial responsibilities for their immediate family and extended family. Their "job" may have consisted of selling drugs, robbing people, banks, or cash centers, or committing burglaries, but their criminal behavior was acceptable because the end result was being a good provider who took care of his family and financial responsibilities. The fact that some men engage in criminal activity to take care of their families is in line with the dominant social order, which expects a man to be the breadwinner. The external factors attached to money, such as the perception of being a good provider, cause them to want to signal that there is enough money in the household to afford a certain lifestyle. Yet, participants knew that if they wanted to remain out of prison they could not reengage in criminal activity, regardless of how much they wanted to reassert their role as provider. However, material goods and image can overshadow the internal desire to avoid returning to prison. This struggle between "being a man" and staying out of prison was a regular theme in Group, and part of participants' struggle was due to pressure from their family.[122]

Men described that after being home for a few weeks, the newness of their presence quickly dissipated, and family members began to demand that their loved one "step up and take care of things."[123] At that point, participants had to make a choice: take on a nonprovider role in the family or claim their former status as breadwinner. Participants would make calculations about what they had to do to stay out of prison and what was required to create a source of income.[124] No matter how committed a man might be to *not* going back to prison, he might decide to reengage in criminal behavior to earn some "quick cash" to escape the condemnation of his family. Some men were uncomfortable, even remorseful, about not contributing to their family's well-being while their women "held them down" while they were incarcerated by keeping money on their commissary account and making their life inside marginally better.[125] Upon returning home, though, other men resented that women were taking care of everything and controlled the money. Tyrone explained why that was the case: "Because we [men] are gone. The women are left alone to take care of the kids, you, them, and everything. Men are doing time and women [are] doing what they have to do when we [were] gone."[126] This "hard truth" was difficult to accept.

Former male prisoners talked about how "being a man" was determined by a man's ability to provide for himself and his family and reclaim his traditional role as head of the household, but men returning home from prison tend to be jobless, living at home with their mom or in a homeless shelter, wearing hand-me-down clothes donated by strangers, and being dependent on a woman or women. Male participants hated being dependent, and some clung to their previous roles as provider so tightly that they started to look for ways to make money in the streets. The inability to assert their manliness and maintain their role as provider after spending time in prison was often a significant stumbling block to successfully reentering society.

Transitioning home can be especially hard after spending time in an environment that encouraged hyper-masculinity. Some men want to reclaim their sense of identity immediately upon returning to society by "being a man."[127] Other men were able to renegotiate their family dynamics and learn how to create a new identity that was separate from their former "criminal job" and role as provider. Some struggled to find a new identity and operated in the gray area until they decided to leave "the life" behind.[128] Others talked about "being good" and "staying in my lane,"[129] but I was never sure if they were just telling me that or if they meant it. Some participants would say the "right" thing but it became obvious that they were "doing dirt" when word got back to the nonprofit organization that they were back inside prison.

Home, Surviving

While living in a total institution, prisoners have no autonomy; they are told what to do, how to do it, and when to do it every day. Therefore, the process of transitioning home is challenging as former prisoners must largely manage their own transition from a highly regulated environment of mundane predictability to an unknown environment where they have to make their own choices. This is a tough transition; the ultimate goal of surviving prison is to get out, but coming home and learning how to navigate a new world is daunting. Participants shared how they lost their sense of balance, and when their assumptions about the world are shattered, their survival skills kick in.

> Being locked up is one thing, okay, I did my time [and was punished] for my wrong, but now what? That's all I think about, now what the fuck do I do? Ain't no one with any kinda power thinks about [us] after they lock us up. No one.[130]

As a result of policymakers not thinking about the back end of the criminal justice system (i.e., reentry) while restricting parole eligibility, prisoners are making decisions that are changing reentry. Many make the conscious decision while imprisoned to serve their entire sentence and remain incarcerated until they max out.[131] As more states mandate that prisoners serve at least 85 percent of their sentence, prisoners are calculating that they can easily do the rest of their "short" time to avoid parole. This means that more prisoners are serving their entire sentence and leaving prison "without paper";[132] upon exiting, they are immediately released from the custody of DOC and do not have to report to parole nor live under parole's restrictions.[133] Maxing out means that there are limited programs and resources, but serving an entire sentence is not necessarily discouraged by DOC. States have cut their parole and probation supervision budgets or outsourced parole and the management of halfway houses to private companies in order to "save" money; states are implicitly encouraging the practice of having fewer people on parole, and participants understood this because, despite their criminal activity, former prisoners can be rational actors.[134]

Participants' lived experiences demonstrate that leaving prison and returning to society is full of contradictions; most participants believe that government does not care about them and reentry outcomes are "worse than shooting dice."[135] It is time to recognize that: "Ain't no rehabilitation going on [inside prison]. It is rough inside, violent rough, on a whole 'nother level kinda rough."[136] Prison is not rehabilitating prisoners, if it ever did, so once home, participants knew they were on their own, and their existence was summed up succinctly by Sonja: "I'm fucked. Basically, we're all fucked."[137]

3

Denying Access to Public Housing

I am homeless, a grown man, and I ain't got a place to sleep.
I'm fifty years old, but have to go more backwards because
all I can do is go and live in the shelters, where drugs and
stuff makes it rough. The housing situation for people like
me [with a felony] is not there to help nobody. The charge
just brings you down, and makes you want to go back to doing what you were doing [illegal activity], because really, to
tell you the truth, I can't do nothing legal with that [felony]
charge [on my record]. All I want is to stay clean [off drugs],
and get a safe place to stay so I can live. I need that to have a
chance [to reenter], and I don't. I got nothing with my name
on it. I'm nothing, a nobody.
—Gavin, April 11, 2012

Gavin's experience reentering is the norm for men and women with
felony convictions. Some wrestle with drug and/or alcohol dependency,
and some do not, but all of the participants in my study were struggling after surviving prison without access to housing, a particularly
hard socially disabling effect of a felony conviction. Public housing is
one of the few sources of housing for the poor, but under President Bill
Clinton, policies preventing convicted felons from accessing public
housing were implemented, and as a result, felons are homeless and living wherever they can. This chapter begins by exploring participants'
experiences when attempting to secure housing, which is followed by
an examination of federal housing policies. The latter part of the chapter then combines the two to analyze participants' lived experiences
alongside federal housing policies; by taking into account why housing
is so important to the returning population and why it is so difficult
for convicted felons to secure housing, this analysis details the negative
ramifications of reentering society without a permanent place to live.

Xavier lives with his grandmother: "I live off a ninety-three-year-old woman, my grandmother, eat her food, watch her TV, sleep in her house. I ain't got shit."[1] If not for his grandmother's support, he'd be living on the streets and experiencing food insecurity, and would revert back to his criminal ways in order to eat and have a place to sleep.[2] He knows he cannot stay at his grandmother's forever, and though she has not given him a deadline to get out, he knows that day will come, so if nothing changes, he will be homeless and living on the streets.

For women who are denied public housing due to a felony conviction, particularly women with minor children, the lack of available housing puts them and their kids in a precarious situation, which threatens a woman's ability to reenter successfully. When a woman does not have access to stable and safe housing, the desire to have a roof over her head trumps her own personal safety, as the available housing may depend on maintaining an intimate relationship that is prone to violence. Some women with children may endure a volatile relationship so their kids have a place to stay instead of being on the streets and homeless. Janaye, who is taking care of her two minor children while facing extreme poverty, puts her physical well-being in peril and her reentry success in jeopardy because she must rely on someone else for a place to sleep.

> Well, you know, I'm living with my kids' father, but it's like, really shaky, bad shaky, really bad. We fight, real fights, you know, but I try to make nice to keep the peace. [She falls silent, drops her chin to her chest, and stares down at the table for several moments, inhaling deeply before continuing.] It ain't good, the stress, the fighting, and all, everything is stressful, [and] I get anxious, so I'm working on getting my own place, with my kids, so, that's, you know, that's what I'm trying, doing, what I need to do for me and my kids, but I'm struggling. It's hard out here, with no cash money. He has a job, so we eat, you know, but money, it's all about getting some money together. It's all I think about, how can I get some money, because I have none, and I really, I need some help, with housing and stuff, to make it and stay out [of trouble].[3]

Being poor and denied access to public housing entails making tough decisions. Sonja shakes her head when I ask her about housing and her housing options:

Housing is terrible, for people like me, with a charge. 'Cuz I have nothing and I got that [drug] charge, so it's harder. I'm homeless, living in a
shelter, it's tough, can't see my kids, and you got threats all around, it's
[the shelter] just like being inside [prison], always gotta watch your back.
Your stuff get taken [stolen], living there [the shelter], it's a problem, you
always having to start over again with nothing, you know, they [the shel-
ters] don't help, they the real problem.[4]

The experiences of Gavin, Xavier, Janaye, and Sonja are representative
of what hundreds of individuals convicted of a felony experience upon
their return to Newark, New Jersey, and other cities across the country;
their struggle to secure safe, long-term housing is not unique.

It is also important to note how reentry has changed over the last two
decades and how these changes make securing housing all the more difficult. Prisoners are serving longer periods of time, and while they are
incarcerated, their families fracture and scatter to new locations; parents
die; and some relatives are so disgusted that they refuse to offer their
relative housing, while some families pretend their loved one does not
exist.[5] There are a host of other reasons for former prisoners' homelessness, including the realities that family members may be financially
strapped and lack the resources to house and feed another adult; may
live in homes without a spare bedroom; are emotionally worn out from
providing support while their loved one was incarcerated and are not
willing to "hold them down" any longer; and may have new in-laws who
have married into the family and do not want their recently freed relative living in their house. Additionally—and this is often lost amid the
financial, emotional, and family relationship challenges of reentry—
some former prisoners may carry feelings of shame so deep that they
don't want to live with their mother, depend upon their grown children,
or rely on other family members for housing.[6]

The prison system explicitly assumes and presupposes that family
will step in and care for released prisoners by offering housing, but this
speculative thinking on the part of the DOC and its agents is wholly
incorrect. Most released prisoners return to the community homeless
and experience different degrees of homelessness because of a lack of
family support. Sonja explains why she can't live with her family: "Me,
I'm a criminal, and because of that my family don't deal with me. They

pretty much act like I don't exist anymore. Family, they stay away from me, so I got no choice, I'm staying away from them."[7] Many participants are disconnected from their families. "I am a failure, just am, a failure, and no good to them. My brothers, all of them doing good, got jobs, their own families. Me, I'm almost forty, homeless; I got nothing so I'm no good to them."[8]

Former prisoners who cannot stay with family, for whatever reason, end up homeless because of hostile policies; when someone is no longer confined by the DOC and is released from prison or a halfway house, the DOC, its agents, and participants know that the vast majority of convicted felons will be denied public housing. As a result, upon their return to the community, participants adopt unhealthy coping tactics in response to public policies while they attempt to reconnect with society with limited, if any, family help. Although the level of family support and social capital are unique to each felon, some returning participants had a family member offer them a place to live without a time limit, but were unable to meet, or unwilling to put up with, the intrusive rules mandated by parole: "No one else going to put up with that shit, [parole] looking through their stuff. I'm a felon, they do that [to me], but to my people, 'fuck that' they [family members] say."[9] Another participant had a willing family member offer housing and resources but the family member lived outside of the parolee's jurisdiction, so that person's home was deemed ineligible and the returning family member ended up living on the street.[10]

Rich, a twenty-year-old black man, shared how his felony changed the way his family looks at him, and what that shift in energy signifies for him and his housing options:

> RICH: I went away for like twenty-eight months, and that first night back I went to my moms, but my stepfather, well, he don't want me there. I can feel it. The energy is different, hell, everything is different. You can feel it. No one say anything about it, my time away, but I can feel it, the difference, it's all around.
>
> KM: What do you think that energy is? Where is it coming from?
>
> RICH: Me, I've changed, my charge. Being locked up does that, changes you, and that energy, it's probably their disappointment in me. Me getting locked up, not being at home, not there to help my mom out,

and then coming back, and he [stepfather] didn't expect me to come
back [home]. Not sure where he thought I was going, where I was
supposed to go, but I'm there, well, for now.

KM: You have been home for a little while now. What do you think are
his main concerns or objections?

RICH: Because everything has changed. Just everything. He doesn't
want me around because of my conviction. He don't trust me, and
my mom looks at me funny now, too, so that's probably a big part.

KM: Can you tell me about some of the specific changes?

RICH: It's just like everything, like everything died. I ain't holding up,
you know, to what they want, not meeting their expectations. I ain't
on the same path as I was, and the way it was, like life and everything, was looking good before I left [went to prison], and now I
come home and everything ain't looking too good.

KM: So, you have changed since being locked up, and they have
changed while you were locked up?

RICH: Yeah. I think when I left, everything, everybody just changed
their ways, their minds, what they think about me, for sure. I was
hoping to, you know, go to college, get on my feet, but I might have
to leave [their house] before that, you know, before I can get myself
together. And if that happens, I don't have no place to live. I know
I'm not welcome at my mom's house no more. Probably, well, no
doubt, it's just a matter of time before they say, "get out" and I'll have
to go. Where? I don't know. The shelter, I guess.[11]

Huxley, a thirty-three-year-old man who claimed with a broad smile,
"I'm everyone. I got black, white, Native American, I got it all flowing
through my veins," explained that due to family tensions, his housing
situation was unstable and unpredictable:

Well, the big picture, the neighborhood was unstable, people getting
shot, and I know the folks on the block, which ain't good. [So,] my sister
moved, and I moved in, but we bumped heads, so I moved in with my
son's mother. And well, hmm. . . . It's a place to stay, but it's not real good.
Just a little stable. So, I stay with her and then I may stay at my mom's, really, wherever I can put my stuff, and I've been at the shelter for stretches
of time, too.[12]

Other participants unable to secure safe and reliable housing bury their hopelessness in drugs and/or alcohol, and then return to a life of crime to support their habit. Alyssa, a forty-six-year-old black woman who is married but separated from her husband, has completed an associate's degree, and has management and supervisory work experience at several big box stores, is an example of someone in need of stable housing, but because of her drug addiction and drug conviction, she is constantly "working" to find stable housing to get off and stay off drugs. "My family wants me to get clean and stay clean before I can move back, and I'm just not there yet. Not yet. Maybe one day, but I need a place to live to do that [to get clean] and [to be able to] stay there." She admitted that her choices were the reason for the treatment by her family; they were tired of being codependent to her drug use and felt her absence was in the best interests of her kids, to protect them. Her estrangement from her family was hard. "That hurts, not seeing my kids, but it's best for them, me not being around. I understand what he did and why, but it still hurts, you know."

Alyssa knew that the estrangement was temporary, and that if she could get clean and stay clean she could return home: "I can get clean, on my own, I have, for a month or so, and then I lose my housing and I'm back to square one." With long-term housing and a drug rehabilitation and maintenance program, Alyssa would have a good chance of getting clean and remaining drug free, for she knew she could return to her family once she was successful. Socially disabled by her inability to acquire housing, however, she knew that her cycle of drug dependency would continue; she'd secure short-term housing, get clean, lose her housing at a fragile stage in recovery, become homeless, fall off the wagon, and start using again. This cycle repeated itself. Alyssa admitted she'd been clean several times, but her family wanted six months of her being clean before she came home: "Temporary housing ain't there for six months, more like one [month], if you lucky."[13]

In the 1990s, President Bill Clinton's push for exclusionary public housing rules that used a felony conviction to deny individuals public housing carried over into the private housing industry:[14] The negative societal repercussions of a large homeless population include threats to the public's safety, chronic public intoxication, panhandling, chronic health issues, and victimization of the homeless,[15] and it adversely complicates reentry for those convicted of a felony. Participants openly talked of sleeping at the train station, on the street, in a park, or at the drug house while contemplating going back to the streets to "make bank." Through the exploration of germane public housing policies, the analysis makes obvious that when participants could not find a bed to sleep in, they expended a disproportionate amount of time in an attempt to secure housing and overcome the socially disabling results of hostile housing policies.

The Importance of Housing

Housing and neighborhood development have been on the national agenda for decades[16] and are important components of society; many socioeconomic and positive community-level factors are related to housing.[17] Reliable housing reduces exposure to emotional, mental, and physical stress,[18] and provides stability and access to jobs.[19] Stable housing sustains a workforce that supports economic, social, and political interests, and is an indicator of socioeconomic success.[20] Residential and housing effects increase opportunities to improve one's life chances[21] and positively affect the creation of networks in neighborhoods, social behavioral traits, and social capital.[22]

Homelessness leads to detrimental health outcomes, and growing evidence indicates that periods of unstable housing mixed with episodes of homelessness increase stress levels.[23] Housing instability includes frequent and unplanned moves, evictions, and foreclosure, and can lead to outright homelessness.[24] A common definition of homelessness is the lack of a fixed nighttime residence. The Department of Housing and Urban Development (HUD) defines two types of homeless: sheltered and unsheltered. The sheltered homeless live in temporary or emergency housing while the unsheltered live in places not meant for a person to live, such as in abandoned buildings, cars, or parks, or on the streets. Americans who are homeless, sheltered or unsheltered, and in need of permanent housing tend to have the lowest rate of income, and have only one viable housing option—federally subsidized housing—from which felons are outlawed.[25]

A (Short) Political and Social History of Federal Housing Policy

Multiple programs operate under the direction of the U.S. Department of Housing and Urban Development (HUD), including initiatives to build high-rise and garden-style apartments, mixed-income residential units, and public-private developments designed to address housing shortages for low-income residents.[26] The federal-state-local-private partnerships are designed to build and support housing units to meet the demand for affordable housing and offer housing options for economically poor families.[27] Public housing refers to government programs for low-income families whose income does not exceed 80 percent of the median income for the jurisdiction.[28] Affordable housing developments, on the other hand, are designed for mixed-income (middle-and low-income) tenants. Public housing and affordable housing programs target different populations to achieve diverse political, policy, economic, and social goals. The terms are often used interchangeably; here, however, the focus is on public housing programs and policies designed for individuals with significantly less income than the median income.

Federal housing assistance emerged during the New Deal,[29] when the federal government acknowledged that there was a housing crisis in the United States; with the passage of the Housing Act of 1937, the federal government created public and Native American housing programs for low- and middle-income residents. In every decade since the 1937 act, the politics of housing has revolved around the question of who should benefit and bear the costs of housing, and political divisions over how to make such decisions emerged at the end of President Truman's term. Following the 1952 presidential election, President Eisenhower (1953–1961) and the Republicans' national platform espoused supply-side economics to invest money in businesses, contending that economic prosperity "trickles down," boosts the economy, and achieves multiple objectives.[30] Eisenhower stressed that housing was connected to good citizenship, economic stability, and social well-being, but he advocated for tax cuts for businesses so that the private sector would take a larger role in providing housing for low-income residents. Democrats, in direct opposition, argued that without federal intervention and support, the private market could not and would not provide housing for low-income residents because of the prohibitive costs of land, material, and labor. Eisenhower ignored Democrats' arguments, but due to a loud and steady opposition who saw the federal government as too involved in what many argued was a private market issue, Eisenhower expanded the role of public-private partnerships. The public-private model became politically necessary to stave off criticism, and by directing public funds towards private companies, Eisenhower was able to push programs that subsidized private developers' building public housing.[31] The resulting policies embraced the Republicans' unwavering belief in supply-side economics, and backed public investment in private industry: Public-private partnerships in the 1950s produced more low-income housing units than any other housing initiative.[32]

Due to the importance of housing, President Kennedy advocated for a cabinet-level department, and although his initial proposal failed, President Johnson was successful in reorganizing federal housing policies into a cabinet-level department, and made the government's role in public housing permanent. HUD centralized and reorganized the administration of housing programs by focusing on alleviating the nation's limited housing options in urban areas.[33] Congress supported Johnson's efforts by declaring that urban life was a critical domestic challenge, programs for urban residents were inadequate, and urban low-income residents persistently had to deal with housing shortages.[34] To implement housing programs, Congress granted legislative power to Public Housing Authorities (PHAs) to determine what was best for their locality, manage their local housing units and programs,[35] and enforce federal, state, and local public housing laws; in return, the federal government grants financial subsidies to PHAs to build public and affordable housing.[36]

The reorganization of housing policies was followed by a flurry of legislative activity in 1968, when Congress passed the Housing and Urban Development Act,[37] the Fair Housing Act,[38] and the National Housing Act.[39] The 1968 acts were designed to address multiple issues related to creating healthy urban communities; providing financial support to reduce the cost of housing for low-income families; integrating existing HUD programs; and spurring low- and moderate-income home ownership through private development.[40] Some argue that these programs incited white flight to the suburbs while others argue that the programs were ineffective and expensive.[41] Private entities and conservative voices claimed that competing against federally funded developments was an unfair business practice, and public housing created concentrations of poverty, perpetuated slums that housing laws were supposed to eliminate, increased racial segregation, and fostered a cycle of dependency between the poor and public benefits.[42] When coupled with financial scandals connected to poorly designed public housing projects in the 1960s,[43] the negative rhetoric smoothed the way for Richard Nixon to change the federal government's role in providing public housing for the poor.

Upon being elected in 1968, President Nixon elevated the importance of the private sector in building public housing.[44] Nixon was able to dismantle federal public housing programs by side-stepping the Democratic Congress; through executive policy actions, the government's financial role in the housing industry was restricted or suspended; a moratorium was placed on new public housing construction; future funding streams were cut off; and preplanning and feasibility studies for the construction of subsidized housing were suspended, blocking all future projects.[45] Nixon was able to permanently embed Republican ideals into public housing laws through the Housing and Community Development Act of 1974, known as Section 8.[46]

The 1974 act incorporated changes advocated by the Republican Party, including removing some federal rules to grant flexibility to localities; allowing local and state governments the power to alter existing programs and to set their own housing priorities;[47] shifting and reducing the federal role in public housing developments;[48] and creating two housing systems: a project-based subsidy applicable to an apartment building[49] and a tenant-based voucher applicable to a family.[50] The latter, referred to as Section 8, dramatically transformed the way public housing was financed, and Nixon fulfilled his political promise by increasing the private building industry's role; by expanding the ability of private firms to construct and rehabilitate public housing through public-private partnerships, Nixon reinforced conservatives' belief that the "proper" and limited role of government was to reduce the cost of social welfare programs for poor people.[51]

During the 1980 presidential campaign, Reagan wrapped his political rhetoric in the "language of morality and racial fear" about poor black women who were undeserving of public assistance.[52] Reagan is often credited with creating the phrase "welfare queen," but it was originally printed in the *Chicago Tribune* in 1974.[53] Reagan's disparagement of the poor[54] and the negative racial, social, and public construction of poor people was integrated into the public domain. The political and media discourse made black women into depraved, illiterate, sexually promiscuous drug addicts, and poverty was deemed their moral failure,[55] which reinforced Reagan's unwavering campaign position about cutting social spending. By exploiting whites' fears about black Americans as "other," and by vilifying and demeaning black female welfare and public housing recipients, Reagan's political narrative during his campaign for the White House converged into one message: "The welfare state is broken, and I'm the man to fix it."[56]

Once he was in office, President Reagan's rhetoric became a political catapult to push through policy changes; under the guise of balancing the budget, Reagan cut funding and directed his aim at low-income families and single mothers by declaring that modifications in social policies were in their best interest. Reagan pushed to stop or reduce the building of new public housing developments; decrease the federal government's expenditures and its financial role in housing the poor; limit the total number of families residing in public housing; increase the percentage of income families paid towards rent; and incorporate a tenant-based voucher system to be used on the private market.[57] Reagan called it a fiscally cost-effective approach[58] and made the tenant-based voucher program under Section 8 permanent.

During President Reagan's first term in office, the media's focus on the crime wave and drugs became persistent, and Reagan used the politics of crime to make an immediate and long-lasting impact on social policies. Reagan pushed through the Omnibus Crime Bill of 1984, making the pursuit of drug dealers and their assets paramount. Following on its heels, the Anti–Drug Abuse Act of 1988 was the first "tough on crime" law to overtly connect the "War on Drugs" to specific communities. Together, the acts determined who could reside in public housing, changed the way public housing was managed, and extended federal funds to fight drug-related crime in public housing. The 1988 act reflected the power of political rhetoric about crime when used to meet electoral objectives.[59] Since 1988, policies have made poor people residing in public housing "criminal," but the connection among poverty, criminality, and living in public housing is tenuous, at best;[60] rather, the claim has been used to deny government-funded housing and other public benefits to convicted felons. The political goals were to demonstrate to the voting public that elected officials were purifying the public square of criminal elements in order to protect the public's safety and calling for "improved" and tougher anticrime and antidrug policies. The political rhetoric permanently cast drugs, crime, poverty, racial minorities, and public housing as synonymous terms, and politicians designed laws to socially disable those who fell into each of these categories.[61]

The 1980s crime wave, though not statistically more violent than earlier ones,[62] became a symbol of social, political, and economic unrest in urban areas. When a less expensive "new" drug, crack cocaine, took hold, politicians relied on socially constructed ideas of who was criminal to support policy changes.[63] Instead of confronting poverty and racial discontent, politicians used crime as a tool to pass retributive policies targeting black residents for punishment by the criminal justice system.[64] As discussed previously, politicians criminalized behaviors related to crack cocaine while ignoring criminal behavior related to powder cocaine, resulting in black crack cocaine users and dealers and white powder cocaine users and dealers being punished in vastly different ways for identical criminal behavior related to the same drug; race is the only factor that explains the different punishments for similar criminal behavior involving cocaine.[65] A large factor in driving the policy decisions was the way the media shaped the discussion about black crack cocaine users while ignoring white cocaine users. Media coverage focused primarily on the violence associated with crack cocaine, its distribution, and open-air drug markets where it was consumed, principally in urban areas,[66] which led to the development of policies that vilified black users and dealers, made all urban crime a drug problem, and supported the argument that the underlying causes of criminal behavior were related to drugs and the intractable problem of drug addiction, but ignored the economics of drug dealing and disregarded communities experiencing institutional abandonment.[67]

Studies demonstrate that different racial groups' drug use is historically consistent, and despite what the media says, whites use drugs at a higher rate than blacks, who use drugs at a rate proportional to their share of the general population, 12 to 13 percent, which is a usage rate lower than that of whites;[68] the Sentencing Project demonstrates that whites are more likely than blacks to sell or use drugs.[69] Yet, due to criminal policies, black Americans are punished more harshly than whites, especially when it comes to drugs.[70] I argue that this is due to racial prejudice, political rhetoric, and biased media coverage, which sends a message that black drug use is fundamentally out of proportion to white drug use. This argument, despite the lack of evidence, is used to justify punishing black crack cocaine users and dealers disproportionately to white powder cocaine users and dealers. To date, there has *not* been an objective national study suggesting that black rates of drug use or drug selling are higher than white rates; unfortunately, such facts are ignored in political and policy debates surrounding drugs, crime, and race.

Fighting drugs and crime became a problem with only one solution: a penal solution arrived at by merciless legislative "fixes" that became the dominant response to urban problems[71] and diverted precious resources designed to address poverty.[72] The rise of crack cocaine and the punitive policy response supported a racialized political agenda that remodeled the criminal justice system and public housing policies. The official response to the crack cocaine epidemic included increased arrest rates, prosecutions, convictions, and incarceration rates, as well as longer prison sentences for all black drug offenders, but the policies largely disregarded white drug offenders.[73] With the surge in black drug felony convictions, the number of black Americans serving long prison sentences for nonviolent drug crimes escalated in the 1980s and 1990s.[74] Quantitative and qualitative data demonstrate that the dramatic increase in drug arrests stems directly from racialized policies.[75]

The 1992 National Commission on Severely Distressed Housing

"Congress created the National Commission on Severely Distressed Public Housing and charged it with the legislative mandate to define and identify public housing developments that are severely distressed."[76] The percentage of public housing communities considered severely distressed consists of 6 percent of the national public housing stock; therefore, 94 percent of public housing is fundamentally decent. The reality, however, is that the 6 percent of distressed housing drove 100 percent of the policy recommendations and their subsequent development by the Clinton administration.[77] This was the result of politicians and the media convincing the public that black men were violent, that poor black people living in public housing were criminal, and that young black people were super-predators,[78] which necessitated the government passing harsh policies punishing poor black people in order to keep the public safe.[79]

The commission debated how to address national public housing issues,[80] making clear that traditional approaches to revitalizing distressed public housing placed too much emphasis on the physical condition of buildings without addressing the human conditions of its residents. The commission proposed a National Action Plan to eradicate distressed public housing, improve the physical space and management of remaining housing developments, coordinate community services for residents,[81] and provide funds to PHAs to fill gaps between the needs of tenants and social services.[82] The commission recognized that public housing provides a valuable resource and safe living environment for low-income families, exists to serve people who are without other options for safe, adequate housing,[83] and offers limited-income and vulnerable members of society a place to live,[84] but the commission also verified that public housing residents are getting poorer, and are economically susceptible to displacement. These conflicting concerns, as well as the number of federal regulations, made the commission's challenge of addressing public housing infrastructure and its residents' economic and social positions more difficult.

One of the biggest challenges of managing local housing needs within national rules is the number of regulations.[85] One rule states that "PHAs are required to give preference to public housing applicants who have the greatest need for housing,"[86] but contradicts other federal policies designed to assist the poor. For instance, poor people who meet rent regulations and income restrictions for public housing are likely to also be eligible for federal and state child care subsidies, food stamps, and other forms of governmental assistance; however, a small increase in earned income, such as merely fifty dollars a month, while not enough to lift a family out of poverty, triggers the loss of most governmental benefits. Such restrictions create major disincentives for working families to move into public housing, and the rules discourage recipients of government benefits from looking for gainful employment with higher wages in order to save money and eventually move out.[87] However, instead of tackling these financial disincentives and other contradictory rules like them, HUD regulations, and the organizational structure of PHAs, the commission determined that the only way to "fix" distressed public housing was to decrease the number of funding streams to poor people to reduce the percentage of poor residents living in public housing.

Using the politics of poverty, race, and crime, the commission advocated for mixed-income developments by "finding" that public housing was never designed to house the poorest of the poor, which is simply *not* true. Yet, this misconception became the foundation for public housing policies in the 1990s as the commission argued that federal and state monies should no longer be aimed towards programs for poor people. Instead, money should be directed towards building mixed-income housing developments for middle-class families, and the number of poor residents and families living in mixed-income housing developments should be strictly limited.[88]

The reality is that public housing needed a huge investment of financial capital, which was unavailable. The commission came up with a nonmonetary alternative by disavowing the historical purpose of public housing, a politically feasible option because poor people are not valued in society.[89] The commission's recommendations were in line with political and financial realities but also gave political cover to the federal government to stop investing in housing for the poor,[90] which set in motion the government's reduction in funds for public housing developments, the demise of programs for public housing residents, and the stoppage of investments in properties suffering from institutional abandonment.[91] At the exact moment when public housing residents were becoming poorer, the federal government destabilized the fragile and limited housing safety net, and diverted the funds for social services to crime fighting.

"One Strike and You're Out"

Public housing developments tend to be built on inexpensive property in blighted areas surrounded by distressed neighborhoods, and the very geographic location of public housing creates segregated neighborhoods removed from quality school districts and disconnected from commercial businesses and public transportation. Removing residents from economic opportunities, grocery stores, banks, and social networks that wealthier communities take for granted breeds poverty, crime, and problems associated with crime.[92] There is a strong relationship among economic disadvantage, residence in public housing, and the level of rehabilitation needed for public housing;[93] most public housing was built in the post–World War II era and needs to be refurbished, but because those buildings were built in undesirable areas, public housing residents are isolated in undesirable areas of the city.[94]

Despite these facts, President Bill Clinton shifted the narrative about public housing, describing it as a benefit for hard-working, law-abiding residents so he could push for the implementation of new policies to rid public housing of criminal enterprises. The president's revisionist history justified conflating public housing, drugs, and crime fighting into one set of policies. Under Clinton, the small percentage of severely distressed public housing drove 100 percent of the political posturing to merge the Anti-Drug Abuse Act of 1988 with the 1992 commission's findings: The result, despite a lack of national studies supporting the connection between public housing residents and criminality,[95] was the implementation of strict screening enforcement and eviction procedures that reinforced the false notion that all public housing residents were criminal. The Housing Opportunity Program Extension Act of 1996,[96] generally referred to as "One Strike and You're Out," focused on clearing public housing of crime and anyone convicted of a felony.[97]

In effect, the Clinton administration opened a new front in the "War on Drugs," and when the law went virtually unchallenged, a permanent underclass was created through the political and media-driven association between public housing and criminality. Clinton's actions and political rhetoric also reinforced the media's perception that there was a symbiotic relationship between poverty and crime. President Bill Clinton repeated the fictional account that anyone living in public housing was probably connected to criminality and was inherently criminal; as a result, this image became fixed in the public's mind,[98] and issues related to institutional abandonment and poverty, and the connection to public housing, went unaddressed.

To comply with "One Strike and You're Out," HUD introduced guidelines for tenant selection that were designed to screen out and evict tenants involved in criminal activities. Under the "Public Housing and Tenant Criteria" section of the law,[99] PHAs were given broad discretion to set policies and a choice of screening tools, including accessing the National Crime Information Center (NCIC) and other law enforcement databases, to run criminal background checks to retrieve arrest and criminal record histories of tenants and applicants.[100] Having the ability to access universal criminal records databases to screen applicants and tenants, PHAs can reject applicants, evict tenants, and enforce lease compliance on the basis of an arrest or conviction on or near public housing premises.[101] The result created a stringent national policy for local implementation;[102] the rules made clear that an arrest, pending criminal charges or a conviction, would trigger the start of eviction proceedings of an entire family, even if one household member was arrested but not convicted. The constitutionality of evicting and screening out tenants on the basis of an arrest without conviction is highly questionable, and evicting tenants on the presumption of guilt is extremely controversial.[103]

"One Strike and You're Out" also allows for the establishment of preferred tenants, so PHAs adopted a system of preferences to create wait lists based on local priorities.[104] PHAs' preferences cannot be used to deny admission on the basis of race, color, ethnic origin, gender, religion, disability, or age of an applicants' family, but preferences can favor working families, persons with disabilities, victims of domestic abuse, and single people who are elderly, displaced, or homeless. Such preferred applicants can qualify for designated properties intended for specific populations (i.e., elderly, disabled, or mixed-income developments). The practice of creating preferred applicants reinforced President Bill Clinton's stated goal of making public housing an earned privilege rather than a needs-based program: To ensure that public housing was not for poor people, the criteria for applicants were made more stringent. PHAs considered individual attributes like financial obligations (e.g., child support, debt, alimony), work history, documentation of disturbing neighbors or destroying property, evidence of habits that adversely affect the health or safety of tenants, and arrest records or criminal history. PHAs use the law to extend their discretion in such a way as to deny applicants they deem unfit for public housing.[105]

Technically, federal housing policies incorporate the notion of rehabilitation to encourage the review of individual cases by PHAs, but they often disregard HUD rules, ignore preapproved state rehabilitation programs, neglect to perform individual threat assessments, and take no notice of laws stating that felons are eligible for public housing three years after the date of their conviction.[106] Janaye, the twenty-nine-year-old black, single mother who decided to live with her children's father despite the unstable nature of their relationship, applied for public housing. Even though she knew she might be denied because of her conviction, she had had no entanglements with the police, hadn't been arrested since her felony conviction ten years earlier, and hoped that would make a positive difference: "The rules say I'm rehabbed."[107]

Janaye was referring to a HUD rule that states that a drug conviction can be used to deny applicants up to three years after the date of their conviction, *but* if an applicant is within that three-year window, the PHA is to consider what the applicant has been doing; if the individual has completed a preapproved state drug, alcohol, or counseling program, the waiting period can be waived. Otherwise, the PHA is to evaluate the individual by weighing his or her work history, participation in NA or AA or counseling services, other evidence of rehabilitation (e.g., family reunification), and criminal activity.[108] After such a review, if there is no additional criminal activity and the applicant has successfully reentered, the three-year waiting period should be waived.[109] If three years or more have passed since the last conviction, then drug felonies are not supposed to be considered in the review. Yet, in-depth interviews suggest that Newark PHAs do not do this; instead, Newark PHAs get around federal law by placing individuals on waiting lists that are so long that they operate as an effective delay tactic that stretches endlessly into the future and becomes equivalent to being denied.[110] If rehabilitation were a legitimate goal, then PHAs would adhere to the federal three-year waiting period and conduct individual threat assessments for all applicants rather than use an old felony conviction as an overinclusive identity to exclude *all* felons from public housing. Instead, "rehabilitation" is a word that is not considered when public housing policies are implemented.

PHAs use the cover of federal law to exclude potential tenants with a criminal past, regardless of documented evidence of rehabilitation. Janaye's experience reflects PHAs denying an applicant on the basis of a felony without considering the applicant's crime, the time since conviction, or any documented rehabilitation efforts.[111] Janaye was either placed on a wait list or denied outright by all of the PHAs she applied to:

> Before the background check comes back, I get put on the [wait] list, but then I get denied. I mean they say come back, but, look, you know, they know, and I know that I can't get Section 8. I'm denied. I mean, everyone denied me. Eddison Housing Authority denied me. 550 Broad Street denied me. Somerset Livingston Housing. All of them, anything that was open, wherever it was, I'm denied because of this charge I've got. I've been denied Section 8 so many times now, but once when I asked [why], it was like they refused to give it to you straight, but I asked again, and they say, "oh, it's because you have this charge." Been going on nearly ten years [since her conviction], I've been good, no trouble, and yet I get rejected. Ten years of rejection.[112]

By ignoring the details of federal laws and HUD rules, PHAs deny housing to felons, making lifetime bans customary,[113] even though participants were otherwise rehabilitated and living crime-free lives.[114] Janaye's situation is particularly distressing because with limited access to money while caring for her minor children, she constantly struggles to reenter:

> I can't restart my life and reenter because I can't, because the conviction that I have, you know, it hinders me from housing, from anything that's available, you know, it's always that barrier if you've been convicted, you know. Before my charge, um, I use to get good jobs, you know, something that I was able to be there for me and my kids to live, nothing fancy, but I could provide my own housing, pay for my own school, pay for my own childcare, and everything else, but now. Well, now, I'm not really making it.[115]

Housing assistance is so limited for individuals convicted of a felony that it becomes a permanent social disability. Huxley, a male participant, was homeless upon release from prison, and it was only after family pressure came to bear that his sister took him in for a short period of time. When that did not work out, he moved in with his child's mother. In his own words, he is constantly searching for housing:

> Man, relationships are hard. So hard. I can't live with her and I can't live
> without her. [Huxley chuckles.] But I gotta live somewhere. Well, you know,
> because I am still homeless, not living on the street homeless like, but I have
> nowhere to live on a regular . . . and just because someone says come live with
> them doesn't make it a place to live. I'm still homeless. I bounce around from
> couch to couch, the shelter, holding on for something good to happen.[116]

Huxley looked for a different place to sleep every few days, and about a
year after he sat down for this interview, he was still looking for a permanent place to live and sleep.

"One Strike and You're Out" is so effective at denying felons an opportunity to access public housing that homelessness within the returning population is normal. As a result, individuals cannot plan for the
future or make positive forward movement to reenter, and when there
are no legal options for housing, hard decisions are made about where
one sleeps.[117] Gavin, a fifty-year-old college-educated man, was conscious of being socially disabled by his felony conviction, but his experience is unusual for many reasons. He earned a university degree in
African American studies; worked for many years; and was older than
most first-time felons. In his mid-thirties, he started dealing drugs as a
part-time job, but it escalated into a full-time job "because the money
was so good and came so fast." His life fell apart when he started using
his own product. Convicted of drug distribution and manufacturing, he
was incarcerated in 1995. Since then, he has been in and out of prison
and has tried to get clean but failed multiple times. Part of his failure to
stay clean was intimately tied to being homeless with few options.

> I grew up in public housing, so I knew the deal. I didn't even try for it
> because of the drug charge, didn't even try. You know how that feels?
> Knowing it wasn't a doable option, not for me? That hurt. I had to do
> what I had to do, look at my other options, a homeless shelter, the train
> station, the streets, and do what I do. I had a dual habit [drug and alcohol
> addictions] and was trying to make it clean each day, living with random
> people, being in places with people who sold drugs, and doing stuff, you
> know, to pay my own way. I was doing stuff, well, for my living expenses.
> I was in the illegal business, and I had to do what I had to do to stay out
> [of prison] because I didn't have a place to go to.[118]

Through a mix of philosophical musing and diatribe, using precise language, he explained the challenges of transitioning back to society without housing, and while he was talking about the reasons for his decisions, his nonverbal communication was measured. Gavin controlled his façade while talking to me, but it cracked as he became obviously frustrated when I asked clarifying questions. I wondered if his social veneer was his way of coping with the symptoms of prison-induced PTSD as Gavin exhibited irritability and hyper-awareness and continued to use drugs and alcohol, which I sensed he did to numb his pain. Gavin's life consisted of weighing his options and bartering illegal activities for a semi-safe place to sleep:

> I move around all the time, like six, seven times in the last year. Moving in with different people instead of sleeping on the street. I was having to do some things, like, not legal stuff, you know, like, like . . . [Silence falls as Gavin debates whether to tell me about what he did; he decides to disclose only some of his activities.] Okay, so, I had to watch the drug house, and do some similar kinda stuff, so I could have a place to sleep. It's a trade-off, not a good one, but it's too cold [winter in the Northeast] to be on the streets. . . . Getting locked up was very traumatic. I mean I wasn't use to the hopelessness, the craziness of it all, of being caged up; I wasn't that guy. There's a lot of us in prison like me, good guys that went wrong. We started going inside in our thirties. We the guys that aren't used to being locked up, so some of us went crazy and now have flashbacks about the violence we witnessed. It was out of my regular experience.

As a drug addict, Gavin sought treatment, but the system taught him that punitive practices are the norm, and there was no help for him in the system.

> Whenever you relapse, it is all punitive repercussions, even in drug court, and everything out here is punitive, if you slip up you go straight back [to prison] and then you come out, and you gotta keep turning it up [to make progress], but you further behind than you were before, older and tired. I'm real tired. I came in [to treatment] homeless, and I am still homeless. The housing situation is not there to help nobody, you know, that don't have an income or family, someone. Even though I'm in treatment,

they [the county] denied me [emergency housing] so I'm still out on the streets, homeless, because of the conviction, and if I fail drug court, I go back [to prison].[119]

Because Gavin is socially disabled by his felony conviction and ineligible for public housing, when he is not sleeping at the drug house, he is at a homeless shelter, both of which increase the likelihood that he will keep using and further limit his ability to access resources and programs that could help him get and stay clean.

In the shelter, all I want to do is leave, but you have to have money to get out of the shelter system. It takes a lot [of money] to get out. And with my sheet ["face sheet" or "jacket"] I am not eligible for programs that could help, but I can't do it on my own; I ain't got no family, and I need housing. I don't want to get locked back up, but without housing there is no hope. It's like you wonder when they [the police] going to catch up to me. Because, how is one supposed to get clean and get a job without housing? You stressed, especially living in a shelter, and you need housing to get a legal job. I said it was all a daunting task, but housing is the most of all.[120]

Other participants shared similar experiences of reentering and struggling to get on their feet when stable long-term housing was unavailable:

When you ain't got a place to sleep, you ain't thinking about nothing else, you only can think about a place to sleep. You sure ain't thinking about voting and stuff like that. Maybe you think about a job to get a place to sleep, maybe, but really nothing else matters except where you goin' sleep tonight. You know where you sleeping tonight? I don't.[121]

Exclusionary housing laws have a socially and psychologically disabling effect on those who cannot access public housing,[122] and when Maurice, the forty-three-year-old black man with multiple aliases, was released from DOC, he knew his effort to get public housing was going to be obstructed because of his drug distribution conviction in 1989. Maurice initially slept at the home of the mother of his children; it was a rocky relationship due to his past drug use and the time he spent "away" in prison, but Maurice struggled to keep the relationship he had with the mother of his children for a simple reason, a place to live.

I was trying to keep that relationship together to keep a roof over my head. So, when I was going through some problems with my girl, and I was going to get put out, and I *so* didn't want to go, I was like, man. Man! I thought about it, and I'm like, I was just living with a bunch of men, living in the shelter. Wow, I thought, that's going to be real tough [to go back to the shelter]. So, you know I swallowed my pride and I tried to make things work with her; well, it didn't work. After a while she was like "you gotta go, to a shelter or somewhere." She gave me a list [of shelters] and everything about what shelters that, you know, I could stay in and where I could still attend [AA and NA] meetings. So, I had to leave. Now, I'm homeless, for real homeless, with no place to stay.[123]

Maurice knew exactly what his options were for securing a place to sleep.

A homeless shelter, and I guess I could sleep in the park or the train station, but homeless all the same. And I'm clean [drug free] now, so getting a place to stay clean is real, real, real important. When I first got out, I knew it was going to be a rough road, but when my girl put me out, well, I was determined and went to see them [public housing officials for Section 8], and I slept where I could while I waited, and applied for city welfare, too, and had to wait for their decision, so when I was going through some stuff, I had to stay in the shelter for thirty-day stretches and then they [the city] might give you TRA [temporary rental assistance],[124] being that you just got out [of prison]. I was denied [housing], though, can you believe it, and even [denied] TRA, and every time I applied, when they saw I have a conviction for selling drugs, they was like "well, we're sorry sir, but we can't have you in here." I mean they didn't say it like that, all polite and stuff, they were mean-like, but that's the point they were trying to make: "Go away." So, I went away and slept wherever.[125]

Since leaving prison, Maurice has bounced from a homeless shelter to a family member to the streets, back to a family member, to a homeless shelter, and then back to sleeping on the streets. At the time of the interview, he said, "I got no clue where I'll sleep tonight, but it's getting warmer."[126] Maurice was attempting to downplay the reality that April in the Northeast is chilly and wet, and sleeping outside is unsafe and distressing.

Tony's arson conviction severed the fragile ties he had with his family, but it also prevented him from securing public housing and legal employment, and he lacked the ability to secure private housing because he had no income. Quickly approaching his fiftieth birthday, Tony knew that his current arrangement of taking on another season of construction work could not last much longer because his body was breaking down and in particular his knees couldn't take any more stress, but without access to regular health care and with no income, he was holding on as best as he could until something came up. He never was clear what that "something" could be.

> I lived in my car but I had to turn my car in because I wasn't making the payments so I lived at the truck stop, just hanging out, doing odd jobs, whatever I had to do, then I'd wash up at the truck stop, and do, you know, side jobs, and every week or so I'd get a hotel room, depending on what kinda money I had [and] what I needed to do, and then [at the hotel I could] do a full shower, laundry, you know, get some sleep, and I did that when I could.[127]

When Tony sat down for his interview, he knew that this was the best he could do, but like most participants he was realistic about what was possible and what he could afford.

Craig, a fifty-five-year-old widower, said his goal was to get a room to call his own, with his own bathroom, kitchen, and bedroom. "Not much, you know, something small and clean." He had no idea how he was going to accomplish this; family was not an option, as they didn't want him anywhere near them, let alone living with them. So, he was making it one day at a time.[128]

Lamar, a forty-year-old black man with an eleventh grade education and a GED he earned while incarcerated, had spent almost fifteen years in state prison, and transitioned into a halfway house upon returning home. When he sat down to talk with me, he was counting the days until he maxed out and could move in with his girlfriend, the mother of his children. Lamar was enrolled in a step-down program designed to help him transition back; as he met each program goal, restrictions were lifted. Lamar benefited from the program's short-term goals, but unfortunately the program did not incorporate long-term planning beyond the end of the program. Lamar knew that his time was running short, but he did not have a plan beyond moving in with his girlfriend when he maxed out. "They make me focus, stay straight, got some rules to follow, but not many, and I'm going to be with my girl, she'll help me get on my feet, so I'll be good."[129]

Lamar's felony prevented him from accessing public housing, so he did not even apply for it; Clifford was in a similar situation. Clifford knew he would be denied Section 8, so his plan meant relying on "his girl," which was risky, but not unusual. His relationship developed while he was incarcerated, and relying on a significant other, regardless of whether the relationship was established prior to or during incarceration, meant that while he was incarcerated he could plan his reentry and know where he was going to stay upon release. After being released and during the reentry process, however, some participants found that a "real" relationship was far more difficult and complicated than writing letters and enjoying random phone calls from inside prison.

A face-to-face intimate relationship required "communication and patience, and shit like that," and required difficult "mental and emotional stuff, adjusting to another person and how they do stuff."[130] Trying to make a relationship work requires at times difficult modifications, and sometimes the most problematic issue revolves around money; being 100 percent financially dependent on another person means that relationships take on a different level of significance when they are tied to housing and food.[131] Lamar explained:

> I'm with my mom. I have to live there [parole mandate]. Well, more like she let me live with her; I had no other options. I can't live with my girl, the mother of my two kids, we trying to work things out, and I see my kids and we do stuff on weekends. We mostly get along, but I have to live with my mom, so not sure what will happen after that. It's a place, and I got a part-time job, well, it ain't legal you know, because I can't report it [the job or the income to parole]. Just something I be doing, you know. I know a guy who does construction and I work on site, make sure it's clean, you know, keeps some money in my pocket. I can't afford to live [on my own].[132]

When Lamar started to talk about his financial situation, he contradicted himself; at the beginning he was upbeat and confident that he'd be moving in with his girlfriend when he completed his step-down program, but as the interview went on, he dropped his guard and shared a more authentic account of his life. After being in the field, I discovered that participants were more likely to start by telling me about their lives from a positive angle, and that the less savory details emerged in the latter part of our discussion. Lamar's interview followed this path, and the more we talked, the more facts he shared, but without the same optimism, divulging that he wasn't sure where he would be living if not for his mother; the notion that he'd move in with his girlfriend was highly unlikely, and he knew it, and he was not in the position to support himself.

The inability to access legal financial resources to "afford to live" is one of the biggest challenges for most of the participants reentering. "First housing" is a common mantra of reentry staff and counselors alike because housing provides stability with which to tackle a long list of critical needs, build social capital, and maintain relationships that are needed to ensure that one does *not* go back to prison. At twenty-two years of age, Jesus knew that housing was critical for him to reenter successfully: "I'm currently homeless, so I'm looking for housing. Housing is important, more [important] than anything else. No housing, you can't do nothing."[133]

"One Strike and You're Out" put public housing out of reach for participants, and as a result, participants like Gavin feel that they are victims of the public's hostility and lack of empathy, a sentiment that he sums up by saying, "They just want us to be homeless."[134] Without housing, felons live an "abnormal" existence as their felony maintains its power as a petite penal institution through socially disabling and exclusionary policies that deny *all* felons access to public housing[135] but that also include civil death,[136] internal exile,[137] and banishment from the public square to become twenty-first-century outlaws[138] who are more likely to reoffend and recidivate.[139]

Political rhetoric and the media have created a "felon monster" lurking in the shadows,[140] making it easy to consign convicted felons to permanent homelessness.[141] The act of making felons into contemporary outlaws exasperated Janaye, who asked some pertinent questions without answers:

This one conviction, the only one I have, in twenty-nine years of my life, you know, one mistake, and all opportunities are closed down for me. My housing opportunities are closed down. I can get no Section 8. I get no help. I can get no housing. How do they expect us not to repeat, you know, not do our dirt, and not to offend again if we can't come out and get housing, you know? If we can't get child care, and we get nothing, what then? If we can't get past the past, even if our past is in the past, you know, because my charge ain't going nowhere, it's back there, so what do they expect our future to look like?[142]

4

Education's Failed Promise

I got to be greedy, that fast money, it just all went off track
real quick. So, I know I need to start somewhere, to get back
on my feet, you know, and even though I got my licenses, I
now got a [felony] charge, so everything changes, so I need
more schooling or something to get ahead, but what? I need
to get back to working, but with a [felony] charge, that's going to be real hard, so maybe school.
—Curtis, February 13, 2012

A hush falls over the small room as Curtis's truth ricochets against the
hard silence while his simple words capture the entirety of his situation;
by acknowledging his reality as a felon, he demonstrates his awareness
of how his criminal actions have utterly *and* negatively changed his life.
Although Curtis would like to return to his "fast-money life," he knows
that he has to go back to school or get additional vocational training to
counter the adverse effects of his felony conviction.[1] Yet, he also recognizes that, first, he is not sure what will counter the negative impact of a
felony conviction, and, second, once he figures out what to do, he is not
sure his efforts will be adequate. As a result, Curtis did not know how to
start the process of figuring out what to do.

Many of those returning home with a felony on their public record
find themselves facing a similar conundrum: Educational attainment
combined with vocational training generally improves one's employment opportunities and increases economic and social stability;[2] however, this is not necessarily true for felons. Education is often insufficient
to offset a felony conviction. For instance, some reentry organizations
offer specific education and work-based programs, and individuals may
successfully complete the program but be unable to secure a job, producing disappointing outcomes for participants, who lose faith in themselves and reentry programs.[3]

Participants knew that stable employment would provide a strong incentive to desist from crime, but that finding and securing gainful legal employment would not be possible without their going to school, and that school would not guarantee them the opportunity to work. In order to understand participants' perspectives about education, this chapter explores their lived experiences with educational programs inside prison and their sense of how education could alter their lives but probably won't on the outside. Participants' narratives reveal how they view education in relation to equally important and related issues, like securing legal employment. In addition to describing participants' perspectives, this chapter analyzes federal education policies—one of the many obstacles that make attending school financially unattainable—in order to provide a wide-ranging picture of how educational policies, as currently structured, are not rehabilitating the vast majority of the returning prison population.

Education is critical to successful reentry because of its connection to employment; however, individuals with a criminal history are characterized as a hard-to-employ population,[4] and the challenges revolve around the fact that someone reentering society as a convicted felon is more likely to be unskilled and/or poorly educated. In spite of having little previous legal work experience, the vast majority of participants wanted an opportunity to interview for a legal job, explain their situation, and then be hired. Participants understood the important interaction between education and employment for improving their individual reentry success,[5] so they knew they would have to go back to school. Yet, attending school as a felon is complicated because the decision is not straightforward. Once home, participants have to figure out whether school is the right choice for them, and because a felony changes one's legal status, choices must be made in this altered legal context. Moreover, participants have to decide the best path to follow to satisfy conflicting expectations for themselves, the hopes of their family, and the unbending requirements of parole. The most important question participants had to answer was whether or not they thought they could attend school while traversing all of the hurdles and constraints that are unique to being a contemporary outlaw.

Despite the fact that participants had a history of dubious decision-making skills, an interesting detail about managing life's choices emerged during my time in the field and was affirmed by the interview data: When given time and several options to consider, participants' assessment skills proved to be sufficient, as they demonstrated the ability to weigh options, estimate the pros and cons of each, and then choose the best course of action. Participants proved they could be rational actors capable of conducting a cost-benefit analysis that showed that they understood that going to school is difficult due to daily struggles that can only be "fixed" with a job and legal income. Darren shared his thought process and how it related to his reentry decisions: "I will be honest with you, my problem is clothes, and other stuff, like taking care of my kids, you know, like eating, everyday stuff; all that costs money."[6] When one is hungry and trying to build a wardrobe from nothing, going to school is *not* a priority. One male participant explained his poor decision making in the past and his present need for money from a legal job in order to successfully to reenter society:

> It's just sometimes, you know, we don't think, and we do stupid stuff. It's like . . . it's like this, we messed up in the head and are smart but stupid, you know? I need a job. That's it. But [we come home, and] things be changing so quickly [like with technology], we have to catch up and make no wrong decisions when we back home. That can be stressful 'cuz we mess up, we go back [to prison]; no one wants that, not me, 'specially not me.[7]

In essence, participants knew they had made poor decisions, and while attempting to put their past permanently in the past, they had to navigate reentry under a high level of stress because they could not take a wrong step or make a bad choice. In practice, any decisions that did not have an immediate and positive effect on their lives were to be questioned, including going to school, because "it's hard reentering and stuff."[8]

Participants explained why education was not a priority as it related to the challenges of reentering, and their personal narratives offer a frank assessment of what they want, are able to do, and are willing to do, and why educational pursuits are not an integral part of their reentry plans. First-hand narratives provide context, explaining how their previous experiences shape their decisions not to go to school; from their position, going to school will not contribute to their immediate well-being or satisfy financial obligations because school is *not* an activity that pays legal costs, court fines, halfway house fees, or child support,[9] nor does school buy groceries or bus passes, pay rent, or cover a host of other financial obligations. Plus, studies show, and participants knew, that they would be socially disabled from Pell grants and face discrimination in the job market due to a felony conviction,[10] even with a university degree. Under these circumstances, school becomes a nonstarter.

Participants recognized that every educational program requires a long-term commitment that does not guarantee a convicted felon a fail-safe, full-time legal job at its conclusion—a reality often ignored in top-down analyses of reentry.[11] Participants knew the challenges of reentry better than any expert, so their underlying sense of why education is impractical, and why it is rarely considered a good investment of time and limited resources, is included in this assessment about the role of education. More importantly, participants articulated their beliefs about the role of educational attainment and asked hard questions that often go unanswered: Will the investment in an academic degree or vocational program remove the employment background check? Guarantee a job? Will completing a training program remove the stigma of a felony conviction? Will going to school change anything? These are legitimate questions related to the time and financial investment required to complete a degree program, and there is no guarantee that an educational program, certificate, or degree will lead to a legal job. Participants weighed this reality against their financial circumstances and then dismissed going to school because it was an unrealistic option. Huxley captured this sentiment when he stated, "If school will guarantee me a job, remove that damn background check, and let me work, I'll go get what you got [a PhD]."[12]

The Role of Education

After family and housing, education is one of the most influential institutions in providing a context within which to interact in society; education teaches social norms, rules of acceptable behavior, and societal expectations while also offering a resource bundle that can be accessed and used during social interactions throughout one's life.[13] For most people, education provides the mechanism for status attainment,[14] and when community-based schools are successful, communities prosper, and individuals are better able to navigate societal expectations, including securing employment to achieve a reasonable standard of living. Educational achievement reduces unemployment rates and social and income inequality, while increasing socioeconomic status and earning potential.[15] Education reduces criminal propensity and lessens future criminal activity of individuals who have already been convicted of a felony.[16] This is mainly true for participants reentering society with a solid family foundation, their high school diploma, and access to social capital.[17] This finding reaffirms studies demonstrating that formal schooling and educational attainment increase the chance that an individual will secure legal employment, reduce individual recidivism rates, and decrease the spiraling costs of the criminal justice system.[18] The reality, however, is that the majority of participants did not have family support, a high school diploma, or the needed social capital to move forward.

The "ecologically and economically different" communities to which a large percentage of former prisoners return are socially dislocated and suffer from institutional abandonment.[19] The concentrated number of former prisoners in some neighborhoods dilutes community resources, and the diffusion of social capital declines further as thousands of individuals return to similar neighborhoods that suffer from the concentrated effects of poverty, the dissolution of churches, a lack of grocery stores, and low-performing public schools. These negative effects are magnified in high-poverty areas.[20] Social institutions, like schools, hold communities together, but without the ecological niches that develop around shared public institutions, the organization of a neighborhood declines, and the distance between formal schooling and antisocial behavior deepens; the schism operates like an abyss into which many participants had fallen years before,[21] and the nature of prison makes it worse.[22] Neighborhood conditions make it difficult for those returning home after serving time to improve their social status; positive gains are possible, but there are exceedingly complex and intractable issues that must be addressed to wipe off the "social dirt" of a felony conviction[23] and reduce the social distance with the community.

The inability to access financial and social capital leads to food insecurity and material deprivation, placing individuals at risk of recidivating; even though prisoner reentry can be mediated by formal schooling, the urban environment is not necessarily conducive to going to school.

Attending classes towards a certificate or degree is highly dependent on acquiring hard resources, and such assets must be continuously available to pay for educational costs, as well as for living expenses. Although school has positive outcomes on social adjustment, when there are few resources in the home and in the community, there is an increased likelihood that obtaining an education, while not impossible, is unlikely. "Education is important, sure, but everything is important right now. Everything. And everything is hard. I don't have the money to be paying for something that don't offer me no job at the end."[24] Despite the grim outlook for participants, each of them understood the importance of going to school, especially parents, who believed it was too late for them but wanted their kids to graduate from university because they knew it would help them "do better in life."[25]

From participants' perspective, any educational pursuits and long-term planning without income from a legal job becomes folly when the social stigma of a felony is constant. Long-term planning is difficult when everything is hard, especially when several interconnected issues must be addressed before school can be integrated into a comprehensive reentry plan.[26] The intersecting challenges include low literacy rates, which play a central role in causing many participants to think in stark terms about their educational options. Many participants were lacking formal education, were undereducated or illiterate, and did not have a GED, which would require taking remedial adult education classes, if available, before starting an official program. If such classes are offered, there are often long waiting lists; and if the financial costs can be covered (or are free), a certain level of interest and commitment is required to complete any program. Then, financial resources must be available to pay for accredited exams related to the coursework, including the GED exam. Federal aid to pay for formal educational programs, including GED programs, qualifying exams, and postsecondary courses, were eliminated for prisoners and felons in the 1990s.

Education Policies and Prisoners

The Higher Education Act of 1965 (HEA) was the first major federal legislation authorizing financial aid to students in postsecondary programs, which strengthened the resources of colleges and universities.[27] The

HEA contains seven components addressing various higher educational pursuits,[28] establishing a prominent role for the federal government in higher education, and ensuring that more people can access higher education. Since 1965, the HEA has undergone several amendments and reauthorizations, but despite the changing nature of the political agenda, the political salience of financial aid for students endures, and the law continues to focus on its original commitment to increasing educational opportunities for low- and middle-income students.[29] The importance of the HEA cannot be overstated, as it fulfills a critical financial need in the form of Basic Education Opportunity Grants, commonly known as Pell grants. Established in 1972 through an amendment to the HEA,[30] the Pell grant system is the vehicle by which financial aid is delivered to students; originally, it included financial support for educational programs inside prison, but that program was abolished.[31]

Inside-Outside Programs

College-credit courses offered to prisoners have been in existence since the 1970s; known as the "Golden Age" of correctional education, that was when education was viewed as an important component of rehabilitation inside prison.[32] A variety of prisons partnered with accredited universities and colleges across the country to offer prisoners assorted courses leading to GEDs and associate's and bachelor's degrees.[33] Pell grants paid for prisoners' academic curricula and supporting material. In what are called "Inside-Out" programs, there are two main models. In one model, the prison partners with an accredited university and prisoners take classes "inside"; such programs are funded through private donations and courses are taught by volunteer teachers. In the other model, a prison partners with a university, and prisoners who pass initial screening evaluations are granted permission by prison administrators to become "inside" students who take university-level courses with "outside" students enrolled at a university, who travel to the prison throughout the semester. Both sets of students take classes together, read the same material, and engage in intellectual discussion; all of the students and faculty demonstrate a remarkable amount of educational and personal growth in the shared classroom.[34] In both models, taking classes is looked upon as a privilege for "inside" students.

Research shows that college-in-prison has a positive effect on the prison community, state budgets, the individual, and the individual's children.[35] Today, hundreds of university credits are offered in a number of medium- and maximum-level prisons,[36] and these courses tend to be offered by entrepreneurial professors who believe in making education accessible to everyone, including prisoners incarcerated across the country.[37] Further, such programs support the findings in *Changing Minds*: Education provides prisoners with the knowledge and skills needed to transition successfully out of prison, reinforcing the belief that education has a positive impact on the reentry process.[38] The vast majority of prisons in New Jersey do not offer Inside-Out programs, with the exception of East Jersey State Prison. Historically referred to as Rahway State Prison, after the city where the prison is located, it partners with Union County College to offer numerous college courses through "Project Inside." Despite quantified data demonstrating that education is effective at reducing recidivism,[39] the "tough on crime" political rhetoric and the "War on Drugs" took hold in the 1990s and led to major changes in eligibility for Pell grants and educational programs inside prison.

Pell Grants and the Violent Crime Control and Law Enforcement Act of 1994

Pell grants are the foundation of federal student aid, and became *the* primary source of financial support for postsecondary correctional education. Originally, qualified prisoners applied for a Pell grant and took approved educational curricula through correspondence or Inside-Out programs. However, the political and media attention focusing on the crime wave of the 1980s and the escalating "War on Drugs" dramatically increased the public's anxiety and fear of crime, and politicians felt pressured to respond. So, in a bipartisan effort closely aligned with the Anti–Drug Abuse Act of 1988 and the 1992 Commission on Public Housing, politicians responded by eliminating prisoner eligibility for Pell grants.

Using political rhetoric laced with dishonest claims, "tough on crime" politicians argued that prisoners were taking money away from good, worthy students. Leading the charge in 1993, U.S. Senator Kaye Bailey Hutchison (R-Texas) offered Amendment No. 1158[40] to the Violent Crime Control and Law Enforcement Act of 1994 to direct Pell grants away from prisoners and towards "deserving students." Senator Hutchison implored her colleagues to support her twenty-three-word amendment to protect "good" American taxpayers and the young people worthy of financial aid while undoing the ability of "bad" citizens to access the same funding. On the Senate floor, she argued,

> Last year Congress prohibited the distribution of Pell grant funds to prison inmates who are under death sentences or serving sentences of life without parole. This was a step in the right direction, Mr. President, but during the past year those who are serving lesser sentences—for offenses like carjacking, armed robbery, rape, and arson—received as much as $200 million in Pell funds, courtesy of the American taxpayer. This is not right. This is not fair to the more than 1 million eligible students who were denied Pell grants last year because there was not enough money in the program. It is not fair to the millions of parents who work and pay taxes, and then must scrape and save and often borrow to finance their children's educations. My amendment is aimed at stretching every possible dollar for those young people who stay out of trouble, study hard, and deserve a chance to further their education, [which is only] fair to working Americans who pay their taxes and do without in order that their children will have advantages they never had: a better education, more opportunities, a better future. The American people are frustrated by a Federal Government and a Congress that cannot seem to get priorities straight. They are frustrated and angry by a Federal Government that sets rules that put convicts at the head of the line for college financial aid, crowding out law abiding citizens.[41]

Senator Hutchison's argument was based on half-truths and a false dichotomy; to say that money was being taken from "good students" and given to "bad students" is incorrect. In reality, Pell grants are "noncompetitive needs-based federal college funds available to *all* [emphasis mine] qualifying low-income students."[42] Because Pell grants are allocated on the basis of financial need, applicants do not compete against each other; whoever is eligible and applies for funding gets funding. Pell grants are not a competition for a limited number of federal dollars allocated to the Pell grant fund; rather, if one person is eligible for a Pell grant, his or her funding does not eliminate or reduce the likelihood of another eligible person getting a grant. Further, once a student (or future student) qualifies on the basis of federal requirements, the grant is approved up to a lifetime maximum.[43] Despite these facts, Hutchison's political and bombastic assertions won bipartisan congressional support, and President Bill Clinton signed the bill into law. The punitive rhetoric upended the previous twenty-two years of correctional educational policy by making prisoners ineligible for Pell grants and removing federal funding for educational programs inside prison that have been proved to be effective. Senator Hutchison's amendment ensured that prisoners did not derive any educational benefit while incarcerated, and the amendment effectively turned prisons into warehouses for people.

The immediate impact of Hutchison's twenty-three-word amendment was direct and swift as prisoners were forced to stop taking university courses and states did not replace the federal funds.[44] This forced the cancellation of the majority of educational programs inside prison, but the "tough on crime" rhetoric and antifunding climate of the 1990s instigated other significant changes in correctional education; federal and state politicians, with voters' approval, eliminated or significantly decreased funding streams for other prison educational programs and put even modest programs under threat of being cut. In this political environment, politicians passed additional "tough on crime" measures that increased the size of the prison population, added to the total number of adults serving time, and decreased the number of GEDs earned inside.[45] One of those policy changes extended a blanket felony conviction clause to ensure that felons living in the community were ineligible to access Pell grants upon the completion of their criminal sentence.[46] The impact of this policy change means that current "Inside-Outside" programs in existence are supported by universities, private donations, foundations, and professors who purchase books and material on their own or through educational grants.

Prior to the elimination of Pell grants for prison educational programs, including college courses, they were available in more than forty states,[47] but a 2002 survey showed that only twenty-two states had instituted mandatory education for prisoners.[48] Recent data indicates that approximately 25 to 32 percent of federal and state prisoners participate in educational programming that leads to a GED,[49] and prisoners who do not participate are less successful at reentering society after release from prison.[50] Although most state prisons offer correctional programming in line with their institutional mission, these programs are not universally offered at every prison, and many of the programs do not lead to an accredited degree or certificate.[51] "Tough on crime" policies based on political untruths led to the abolition of valid education programs inside and the decline of prison-based programs despite four facts: completing and earning a high school diploma reduces criminal proclivities upon reentry into society;[52] education is proven to reduce recidivism;[53] prior to 1994, less than 1 percent of the Pell grant annual budget was used by prisoners;[54] and each of the fifty states' Departments of Corrections makes claims to have a mission related to education. The elimination of Pell grants and educational programs inside prison, changes in sentencing laws, and increased violence and overcrowding in prison led to a permanent change in the way prisoners are controlled.

Not Educated while Incarcerated

The New Jersey Office of Educational Services' (OES) mission is to ensure that prisoners are provided academic, vocational, and life skills courses that meet demonstrated prisoner needs within a framework that is congruent with the department's goals and aligned with state laws and correctional regulations.[55] OES educational programs are based on an "open-entry, open-exit" policy so that upon entry into a prison or a transfer between prisons, prisoners are able to enter or exit classes according to their educational level. In New Jersey, prisoners under the age of twenty-one are mandated to go to school. For those over the age of twenty-one, programs are available on a voluntary basis, but accredited educational classes that are valued on the outside are only available if prisoners' families can afford to pay for correspondence courses. OES policies claim that correctional education is "a critical element in [our] effort to develop constructive lives upon reentry,"[56] but when told of this policy, participants laughed bitterly. In their collective experience, OES policies fell remarkably short of supporting prisoners' educational pursuits.

The two most common programs offered in New Jersey state prisons are the Adult Basic Education (ABE) and the General Educational

Development (GED) program. Although correctional and educational classes are offered on a daily basis and in some prisons for several hours a day,[57] many individuals returning to Essex County, New Jersey, between 2011 and 2013 had not completed high school or its equivalent.[58] Many participants serving time in New Jersey prisons communicated that if the ABE or GED was offered, it was hard to get into the class because demand outstripped resources. The New Jersey DOC claims that it offers GED study materials to any prisoner who requests them, but when participants spoke about the study materials, they described the situation this way: When GED study books and practice tests *were* available, the test preparatory material was inadequate, dated, out of step with the latest test-taking requirements, and so heavily used that it was impossible to do the exercises without knowing the answers in advance. In addition to the inadequate preparatory material, participants spoke at length about waiting. Jermaine shared what it meant to "wait" while wanting to get his GED:

> Education inside, you was put on a waiting list, so I did some certificates, just waiting for my name to be called, but there is a very long waiting list to get through before your name get called. Plus, you don't just get signed up, it is not an automatic thing, you know, because you [have to] ask to do a class, then you gotta wait to get permission to get on a list [to be approved to take that class] and then you gotta wait to see if they going to say yes, and [if they say yes] then you get put on another list, wait some more [for a seat to open up], and then, like me, if you get transferred [to another prison] you start all over again.[59]

Other participants reiterated Jermaine's experience of waiting for permission to get on a waiting list. Huxley told me that he wanted to get his GED but when he had a chance inside, he could not go to the classes because the prison system forced him to wait.

> Look, I went in when I was like twenty-three or twenty-four, and all I wanted to do was get my GED so I wouldn't have to do it when I got out. I knew I needed to do some of the stuff that I could do, that I needed to do, do my time, you know, get the time [inside prison] to pass. I had years, so when it was my time, when I was allowed to finally do it [GED], I'm like

"let's go, I'm ready." Everybody, when they are like nine or twelve months short [of their release date], but not less, are allowed to go to school, when you could obtain all types of degrees and certificates, machine op [operations], all types of stuff. But it didn't happen for me.

After he waited years for an open seat in an appropriate class, when his name finally came up, prison administrators passed over him because his time was "way too short," meaning he had less than three months to go before his release date. Huxley said, "After all that time [waiting], I couldn't take the class when my name got to the top of the list."[60]

Submitting a request and then waiting for an administrative response takes time, and participants believed the long wait to get into an accredited class was a result of there not being enough GED materials or open seats in GED classes, and there were few proficient instructors who came into the prison to teach the material. In effect, former prisoners described how prison forces them to be inactive. "Waiting" was the result of the social control mechanisms inside prison, overcrowding, and violence or the threat of violence, forcing prisoners to serve more time locked down.

Ain't no one going to school when you on lock-down. Some guys who can't follow the rules end up making it [the rules] for everyone. That's the way it goes. One guy messes up, acts up, wildin' out, or somethin', and he gets everyone locked down and [then] new rules get made up. They kept us locked up [in our cells] for longer and longer [periods of time]. That's their way to control us, but people start popping off when they on lock-down, just because they bored, but popping off, that get us locked down more. Being locked down for twenty-three hours, allowed a shower two days a week, don't even come out for meals, that ain't no way to live, but that's what we had to do. Wait 'till they opened the [cell] doors.[61]

While participants waited to receive an administrative response, sometimes waiting months and in rare instances years before they got the required permission to take a class, participants described the waiting as pure frustration; however, asking permission to do anything and then being forced to wait for a response was normal in prison. That is the nature of living in a total institution: Taking the initiative is not an integral part of serving time; instead, waiting becomes a common pursuit that occupies large amounts of time because being resourceful or showing ingenuity can get a prisoner in trouble with guards, prison administrators, or other prisoners. Independent actions and free thinking are not encouraged.[62] Therefore, waiting becomes an enforced way of doing a bid as prisoners adhere to a schedule approved by unseen administrators,[63] and then wait for their cell door to open, enforcing an unnatural acceptance of waiting and being "held up" (i.e., caged).[64]

Waiting becomes a passive way to do prison time, but is also about control and is symptomatic of "tough on crime" policies and the lack of support from the state and federal government for substantive programs; the tendency to cut programs reinforces politicians' myopic focus on retribution rather than rehabilitation, and magnifies their failure to consider that 95 percent of incarcerated prisoners are released.[65] This political short-sightedness is common due to the pressure to trim state budgets even as the overall cost of incarceration escalates.[66] Prisons cannot reduce guards and staff that support front-line guards, and reducing the size of the prison population is a complex undertaking, so educational programs are cut; a vicious cycle of recidivism results as the programs inside prison that might improve reentry outcomes are eliminated. The result, Akeem explained, is that going to school in prison consists of

> [w]aiting. It's a joke, all the waiting, and after waiting, when you got to take a class [inside] it was all problems. I mean it, all problems. They don't have a lot of programs [and] all the school counselors are gone, well, all the good ones that teach you something. Cut. All of 'em, just gone, so we get no teaching.[67]

The need for GED courses, in addition to computer literacy courses, is great: The National Assessment of Adult Literacy (NAAL) indicates that individuals who are incarcerated are less likely to ever have used a computer (22 percent) while two-thirds (64 percent) of the general population has, which will increase the difficulty of taking the new GED computer exam.[68] Many participants sentenced in the 1980s and 1990s are coming home with a deep deficit in formal educational credentials and technological knowledge due to the advances in technology; as a result, most of the participants expressed a strong interest in learning how to use a computer and set up email and Facebook to reconnect with family. The fast pace of technological changes, including the use of smart phones, Twitter, Skype, texts, and apps, baffles many, and leaves those returning home socially disabled by their unfamiliarity with today's common forms of communication. Further, those who have served long prison sentences are reentering at an advanced age; more men and women are returning home in their forties, fifties, and sixties, and after serving decades in prison, they have aged at an advanced pace due to living an unnaturally confined life and eating an unhealthy diet, and therefore must contend with chronic and disabling illnesses, diminished cognitive capacities, and vision impairments.[69] The combination of time served and aging goes hand in hand with technological deficits, limited formal education, and inadequate labor market skills.

In addition to the physical and mental deficiencies, the lack of present-day job skills, forced waiting, the requirement to comply, and inactivity extend into the reentry process and accumulate into a tactic some former prisoners use to reenter the world. For instance, inside everything slows down and time lags, so when one is forced to wait, the challenge of reentering is adjusting to the speed of things on the outside and learning how to take the initiative for one's own success. This was especially true for participants who were on parole: Parole officers dropped by the nonprofit organization at random times, and an integral part of their job was to keep in regular contact with their assigned parolees. Every time parole officers visited the nonprofit organization, they displayed the extent to which the formal extension of the DOC's power stretched into the community.

As a result, it was imperative that while participants were at the nonprofit organization parolees' whereabouts were known, so parolees checked in with a counselor and obtained permission to step outside for a smoke or go down the block to get lunch;[70] such behavior was expected for those on parole.[71] However, even those who had maxed out and were not on parole asked permission and displayed "waiting tendencies." I witnessed adults hesitate before asking permission to go to the bathroom, to speak, and to step out to have a cigarette. Participants would ask for permission, and then wait for a response; taking the initiative was antithetical to the way they learned to survive prison. It was painful to witness, but easy to identify; prison takes away an individual's ability to make decisions and deprives men and women of their identity as adults with agency. Prison forces adults to ask permission to go pee[72] and imposes a warped sense of patience; the "waiting" tendency was apparent in the way some participants reentered society, as if they were waiting for someone to tell them what to do or waiting for someone to open their "cell" door.

Punishment as the Educational Curriculum

The reality of reentry is captured in a simple yet powerful phrase: "It's hard out here, a lot harder than I expected."[73] This is true because under the dominant model of punishment and retribution, politicians eliminated the "real" educational curriculum, despite it being a proven tool that reduces recidivism.[74] The lack of educational programs inside prison contributes to making reentry more difficult, as is evidenced by the fact that the recidivism rate, at approximately 67 percent, has remained steady while the range of GEDs earned (25–32 percent) inside prison is similar to the percentage of former prisoners who reenter successfully.[75] The available data strongly suggests that former prisoners who have their GED are more successful at reentering society.[76] However, the prison programs in New Jersey that I surveyed failed to meet the educational needs of prisoners; upon release, former prisoners tend to be uneducated and functionally illiterate.[77]

Participants who were incarcerated in the 1980s shared that while they were inside it was simple to get their GED because prison administrators made classes mandatory. "We were still locked down on a regular [basis], but it was still easier to get your GED in the '80s before all the crazy."[78] "All the crazy" refers to the prison environment becoming more dangerous for both prisoners and guards. Since "gangs running things now we just sit around [waiting for our release date], hang out, play cards, watch TV, when we ain't fighting or locked down. That's about it."[79] As prisons increasingly became hazardous environments, the improvement programs were removed as a punitive measure directed against defiant prisoners voicing their disgust at being locked down, and for safety reasons to protect guards and reduce prisoner-on-prisoner violence.

Crime is crime; we locked up for doing something that someone said was a crime, so they [public officials] have the power to make something a crime and take stuff away from us. I can't judge you, but I get judged, by the judge and everyone else, we all judged. Okay. And more people are judged to do life without parole, thirty to life, forty to life; that's your natural life. New Jersey doesn't have the death penalty anymore, so judges sending people away to die. That's really what gettin' thirty, forty, fifty years means, you be lucky to do fifty, and come out [alive]. That's a long time, and we use to have all kinds of educational stuff, now it's mostly gone. Time is all we get, ain't no programming, so it's all time and punishment and bullshit.[80]

Life sentences used to be reserved for the most dangerous criminals committing heinous, violent criminal acts and deemed beyond rehabilitation; however, the historic rise in long mandatory prison sentences reduced opportunities for parole and increased the total number of prisoners serving life sentences. The criminal justice system now hands out "life sentences" with an astonishing frequency for a wide variety of violent and nonviolent crimes:[81] Ten percent of state prisoners are lifers, and a similar proportion of federal prisoners are serving thirty years to life. The increased number of prisoners sentenced to life without parole or sentenced to the equivalent of a "life sentence," such as thirty or forty years, is the result of "tough on crime" policies[82] mandating that individuals serve decades in prison as if "life" inside prison is not really their *life*.[83] Participants inherently understood the predisposition towards long prison sentences, and many had served "long bids" for a variety of crimes that violated the social order, for acts of moral turpitude, for conduct not reflecting good moral character but in which no one got hurt or that involved drugs, for counterfeiting, or for guns. Participants differentiated between violent crimes and nonviolent crimes this way: "Ain't no one ended up dead or in the hospital, but we in as long or longer than those that killed or sent someone to the ER [hospital emergency room]."[84]

Tyrone, who served twenty-two years and seven months of a fifty-year sentence, said he sat around or got into fights because he didn't think a GED was necessary: "I could have had my GED, I guess, but when it was there, I didn't want to [go to class]. I thought I'd be in [prison] forever. No reason to study, I mean, study for what? I had fifty with twenty."[85] If Tyrone had served his entire sentence, he would have been in his seventies when released; technically, his was not a life sentence, but it was equivalent to one, which instilled a sense of hopelessness, a natural response to a sentence that is the equivalent to one's life. However, at some point Tyrone's mindset changed; he stopped fighting and began to tackle his anger about everything, including living in a cage. He was aware that his behavior was not the best, but in comparison to other prisoners,

> I'm pretty good. And I calmed down and started to go to groups and get my certificates. That was when I started to think that maybe I could get out. Maybe, but maybe was far off, maybe could be never, but I knew I had to show them [parole] I was ready to be released [prior to serving his maximum sentence].[86]

While explaining what it was like inside, he described why most of the educational programs are gone from inside:

> Politicians and then prisoners messed that up. Gangs got crazy, and then overcrowding. DOC took stuff away. New Jersey is a police state; prison is all about punishment. If they wanted to, they [politicians] could keep the numbers [of prisoners] flat and stop expanding the number [of prisoners], but they don't. It is overcrowded and dangerous, and it'll just keep on getting worse because there is nothing to do inside, we always locked down. People bored, so they fight.[87]

Socrates elaborated, detailing how and why inmates were on lock-down so often:

> We use to have vocational programs [in the 1980s], right, and then there was a couple of stabbings about something, so they took them [vocational programs] away. We use to do welding, too, but that became like a weapons class, inmates figuring out how to weld [unauthorized] stuff together into shanks.[88] So they shut that down. And, then one by one, they [prison administrators] take all the other programs away, they all gone [the classes], when they shoulda got rid of gangs.[89]

Participants believed that the disappearing educational and vocational programs inside, combined with "life sentences," are strongly correlated with the "War on Drugs"; political rhetoric calling for long punitive sentences for "average" criminals; politicians criminalizing more activities; elimination of "good time credits" and mandates that prisoners serve 85 percent of their sentence;[90] and the increased number of different gangs' members incarcerated in the same limited space. "There is more shit inside, you know, like all that anger [and distrust] must be worked out inside, somewhere, when people trying to protect themselves against all the crazy stuff and violence and the shit with the gangs protecting their turf."[91]

Policies have consequences, and when more people serve longer sentences, prisons become overcrowded, leading to increased violence. Violence begets more violence among *all* prisoners, who must protect themselves against the threat of violence,[92] and amid the "regular" violence, gangs serve as extralegal governance within the prison's social world; when norms fail within the community of prisoners, gangs exert violence to deter predators and to prey on weaker prisoners, and with more gang members serving time, the community rules are decided by gangs.[93] Aggression becomes the norm when prisoners are living on top of each other, literally, in assigned three-bunk bunk beds in open spaces (e.g., former gyms transformed into dorm-style sleeping quarters) or with two prisoners in a cell designed for one.[94] The limited carceral space becomes more constrained, the viciousness makes guards anxious, and the proliferation of gang violence escalates as they protect their prison turf, which all leads to more surveillance, lock-downs, the reduction of prisoner interactions, and the removal of programs, which is an effort to control prisoners but results in them having no outlet for their boredom, so fighting results.

All the Certificates in the World

Huxley explained the types of programming available when prisoners were allowed out of their cells to attend classes:

> The only place I've been [with education programs and support] was when I went to school with the feds [federal prison], and the teachers

came in from outside to teach the GED stuff. It was mostly calm [meaning there was not the random violence of state prisons] so classes were regular. But other than that, mostly inside [state prisons], they were taught by guys like me. The programs, the certificates, like the life skills and shit, they had all that [educational classes and counseling programs] but it was all run by inmates. I got those certificates.[95]

The types of certificate programs in most New Jersey prisons include addiction recovery, anger management, identifying criminal behavior and developing strategies to change it, increasing empathy for victims, humanity and kindness, character building and self-esteem, journal writing, finding one's purpose, goal setting, budgeting, resume and job interview strategies, how to be a good parent, and reuniting with family. In a few instances, participants described earning a certificate for successfully completing a trade skill like printing, silk screening, art, painting, interior decorating, auto mechanics, culinary arts, food safety, and landscaping. After completing each class, prisoners earned a certificate that served as proof attesting to their successful completion of a course. Much like appreciation awards granted for perfect attendance, certificates are printed on heavy golden ivory paper with elegant black text describing the topic and dignitary signatures confirming its importance, all framed in a decorative swirly black ink border with an ornate gold sticker attached. Those golden ivory certificates held a certain degree of influence as prisoners were told that they would assure a favorable response from parole and future employers.

Naturally, as a result of the power certificates held inside prison, former prisoners were proud of them; as a participant-observer, I recognized who was newly home from prison: The glaring "tell" was when someone came to the nonprofit organization to get assistance, to secure a copy of their Social Security card or photo identification, and pulled their stack of certificates out of a dog-eared manila envelope to show them off like a badge of honor. Participants would begin to speak about the certificate programs they had completed and what they had learned, telling counselors and staff, and anybody else who would listen, about their "work" inside. The certificates, they believed, were a sign of their willingness and ability to modify their behavior, verification of their personal growth, indication of a changed mindset, and evidence of their readiness to reenter society as a better person. But, eventually their bubble of hopefulness was burst when someone who had been home for a while would tell them that the certificates "ain't worth shit out here."[96] Bailey shared,

> When I was inside, I got all these certificates, got certificates in critical thinking, behavior modification, focusing on the victim, forgiveness, you know, all this emotional work. They were good, I guess, helped me to keep busy, do my time. But those pieces of paper aren't anything; they ain't good for nothing.[97]

Ryan was clear on the disconnect that existed between the certificates on the inside and working on the outside:

> I already have skills in math [and] language skills. Took all the certificate classes. All of them, but certificates are nothing. You need a license. I need real job training; stuff inside don't count out here. More schooling, you know, is what I gotta do; probably go to trade school, or something, vocational school maybe to learn computers, something that leads to something so I can get a job. I need to know computers. Ain't no damn certificate in that inside.[98]

The reality is that the certificates earned while incarcerated were not going to help anyone earn a GED, gain college credits, or secure legal employment. As Maurice stated,

> The whole idea was to get these certificates to be able to get a [legal] job. Well, that's what they told me, and you know, stupid me, I believed 'em. But they don't mean nothing out here. Guys walking around with files full of certificates but can't get no job. What does that tell you? They ain't worth shit. [And then, with a broad smile and a chuckle, Maurice said,] Nice paper, though.[99]

Maurice's sense of humor was his attempt at finding the positive in an otherwise grim situation, and as a convicted drug dealer and a self-proclaimed former drug addict, Maurice knew grim situations. But now that he had been drug free and clean for three years, he had an opportunity to connect with his kids and appreciated what he had versus being angry at what he did not have. He talked about how the certificate classes helped him to get clean and stay clean:

> I took a lot of them classes; every course they offered, I took it. They had Smart Recovery, Relapse Prevention, they had that, and I did that one like two or three times. There was a group called The Big Book,[100] and we'd meet every day for like two and a half hours and talk and talk and talk, and each month, they would give you a certificate if you completed it and went to all the meetings. You know, I was there every month, I was that serious. I had like fourteen of 'em [Big Book certificates] because I was dead serious about changing. I got the certificates to prove it, that I'm changed. Now, now I need a job.[101]

Some participants had completed the entire set of certificates offered inside prison, did many of the same courses several times, and were universally tired of the certificates and the associated classes. During one Group, some participants were at their wits' end, and talked at length—seethed, really—about how useless their certificates were. It was as if they finally recognized that they had been lied to, and realized that the promised job based on their certificates was not going to materialize. It was a demoralizing moment. Paula shared a common thought voiced by several participants: "I did the courses. I got my certificates, I've done them all. And I ain't got no job, no degree. Nothing."[102]

Xavier affirmed Paula's comment and said that it was no different for the men: "I did the certificates. All of them, and now what? Ain't gonna help me get a job, go to school, or nothing."[103]

Another participant remarked, "Yeah, you can say all you want about that [those certificates], they ain't no transferable skills in these certificates because ain't no one going to hire no felon." There was a wall of silence as everyone gazed at the floor, at the ceiling, out the window, or around the room as they looked for an answer. There was not one forthcoming.[104]

One participant summed up the reality of everyone's situation, "All the certificates in the world, and for what?"[105]

While addressing the uselessness of their certificates, participants discussed the craziness embedded in the certificate programs regularly taught by other prisoners who are estimated by prison administrators to be "good prisoners." Good prisoners are labeled as such because they have adjusted to living inside a total institution and avoided trouble. Tyrone described the obvious shortcoming in the certificate programs:

You can go to all the programs, get certified, and all that, and become the facilitator. But what's that about? They inside with me, sometimes [sentenced] for a longer time than I got. How someone inside with me going to teach me? What they know about character building and being out, about the noncriminal mind? They a criminal, just like I'm a criminal, what they know about changing their [criminal] mindset? It's crazy. Some guys, they do like five hundred hours [of programs], and then can be a facilitator. What is that about? [Tyrone answered his own questions:] All false hope, that's what. It's about nothing. Nothing for getting us ready to be out here.[106]

Other participants reported a similar belief about the practice of having "good inmates" teaching certificate classes. Osborn talked about the certificate facilitators:

Those guys, they get institutionalized to the ways of the prison and act as mentors and coaches and counselors and big brothers, and whatever, but they know nothing about the outside. These men, they been in there longer than me, and teaching me a class. Just dumb.

Osborn served twenty-five years in state prison for armed bank robbery, and was referring to the men he served time with, who were sentenced to life. Clifford picked up on the same theme:

That's the problem. They ain't never been successful on the outside and they the ones trying to give guys advice. Telling me stuff? Stupid, if you ask me. They don't know, and ain't been out for years so the information they do give is all wrong. I'm doing this [reentering] on my own. What they told me is all lies.[107]

While in the field, I learned that inmate-facilitators showed interest in the position for six reasons. First, serving as a facilitator helped make time pass by, as there was material to read and prepare on a regular basis, and offered a space where the facilitator had some control (i.e., the classroom). Second, facilitators are granted a small amount of power: "Being a facilitator or counselor, or whatever, that gives them power and some hope. Those guys are reformed lifers. They got life; they know they ain't leaving, so they like having the power, even if they institutionalized."[108] Third, becoming a facilitator provided purpose in a total institution where the only other objective was to "do time." How one serves one's prison bid is an important part of maintaining one's sanity, so having a purpose, even if it means managing time by becoming a facilitator, keeps the "crazy" at bay. Those who knew some of the facilitators reasoned that the facilitators did the classes "'cuz it helps from going cray-cray with boredom, gave the guys some freedom from the boredom, and those classes stopped 'em from getting in trouble doing stuff we ain't suppose to be doing."[109] Fourth, many educated inmates viewed being a facilitator as an opportunity to keep their mind sharp and get out of doing manual labor.[110] Fifth, those who were serving long sentences, but not a life sentence, were thinking about their future after they left prison, and believed that the experience of being a facilitator would help with future employers, despite their having been locked up. The sixth reason certain inmates became facilitators was related to a complex assessment of earning an early release date.[111]

Prior to 1997, becoming a facilitator offered a tangible way for prisoners to earn an early release date with "good time credits."[112] But New Jersey lawmakers, caught up in the "tough on crime" politics of the 1990s, terminated "good time credits" with the passage of the No Early Release Act of 1997, which mandated that prisoners serve a minimum of 85 percent of their sentence.[113] The No Early Release Act decreased the number of early-release parole-eligible prisoners, but with the elimination of "good time credits," lifers were the only ones who wanted to become facilitators; other prisoners had few reasons to be facilitators because they could not earn "good time credits." Participants explained that when prisoners found out that they could not reduce their time, and knew they had to serve 85 percent of their sentence, known as "ineligibility time," the incentive "to be good" was removed, and they responded accordingly. Participants spoke about "being good when that 85 percent was coming up, but not before. Why? Why be good? We was in there until they decide we can leave, and no sooner."[114] The No Early Release Act forced prisoners to serve longer mandatory minimum prison sentences; however, because of overcrowding and the lack of funding to build new prisons, "good time credits" in New Jersey are used unofficially to free up bed space. Participants thought that after serving over twenty years of a long sentence or at least 50 percent of a short sentence, depending on the crime, they had an increased chance of being paroled, which bears out in the time sentenced and time served of the participants,[115] and at that point they started to be "good."

Participants, upon returning home, were angry about being gullible and believing the certificates would help them on the outside, but they were also mad at the system for misleading them about the importance of certificates. Yet, participants also understood that they had to take the classes because they didn't have a choice, and were disgruntled about the contradictory nature of prison policies, including who taught the certificate classes, how the certificate programs operate as a form of "busy time" rather than offering substantive assistance that could be applied to the world outside or to "real school," and how the information was *not* applicable to reentry.[116] However, once participants started processing what was required to make good choices on the outside, and realized that while they might be struggling, the facilitators were still inside, participants shook their heads at the irony of themselves being outside and the "good inmates" being inside. Despite the ineffectiveness of their certificates, once they got their minds around their reality, they decided that being lied to was not so bad: "It ain't so bad when you think about it like that, we [out] here and they [in] there."[117] And, then there was general laughter as it was conceded that the certificates were not even worth the "nice paper" they were printed on.

Uneducated or Educated, Does It Matter?

Tony, a forty-nine-year-old black man who has remained out of trouble since his arson conviction in 1998, presented an honest assessment of his own life. Tony's earliest years with the education system vacillated between disappointing and bad. When I asked him about the highest level of education he had completed, he answered slowly, "Well, ah, um, well," and his voice trailed off. He looked at the back of his hands, flexed his fingers, and then turned his hands over and looked at his palms, rubbed them together as if his hands were cold, squeezed his palms together, tented his fingers, and then exhaled slowly. I could see he was struggling with something, so I patiently waited for his response. On another long, slow exhale, he said softly, "My education is very bad. Ah, I went to school but ah, didn't get an education, ever, it's bad." More silence; I gently probed for information, and Tony slowly opened up. Over our eighty-five-minute conversation, he shared his story, his struggles, and his experience of being passed from one grade to the next.

Although Tony had officially graduated from high school and had the paperwork to prove it, he was illiterate. This was what Tony was most ashamed of—his lack of literacy. Tony spoke openly about his arson conviction, how sorry he was, and how thankful he was for only damaging property, by setting a car on fire, and not hurting anyone. But while sharing his past and his troubled relationship with his ex-girlfriend, his voice inevitably trailed off when he talked about his schooling. Tony was bothered by his inability to become a "learned man" and told me how he'd developed coping skills to hide his illiteracy. "It's like I'm lying or something, but I can't read, and it's not something you want to tell people. I mean, who can't read?"

As the interview progressed, his deep shame became a significant part of our discussion. Tony's conviction and subsequent incarceration was not the fault of the criminal justice system, but at forty-nine years of age, he did not know how he was going to learn how to read: "I wish I had that chance inside [prison], ah, but my papers said I had my GED so you can't take the classes [inside]. Stupid, I think, right, because no one asked me, ah, and no one tested me." Tony knew that his lack of education was problematic, and fraudulent in a way.

> I can't do it, letters, I mean. It's like, it's like paper and words don't go [to-gether] in my head. My spelling, my spelling is awful. I can't spell. I went to elementary school then to high school, ah, but I stopped going and then, um, went back and then worked and then tried to go back to twelfth grade, but I, ah, then I enlisted in the military. I knew I couldn't read in 1981, so, um, going to the military, that was good, because it paid for my GED because I wasn't able to pass to get a diploma on my own, um, but

they still gave it to me. I mean I could read a little because I'm just reading like, ah, faking it, but not understanding; when they gave me that paper [diploma] in 1981, I couldn't read it for anything. Ah, I just couldn't read it. I knew it was wrong, to get the GED, you know. How were they [his GED teachers] going to pass me? For them to give it to me, that wasn't right. I couldn't fill out the [forms], you know, I couldn't even go and, ah, fill that stuff out [for public assistance], so I knew it was a lie, me getting it [his GED].

Tony's disgrace added to his feelings of humiliation.

Without the education, the ability to search out people that can help you, um, because it gets even more difficult because [the conviction] stays on your record so, ah, you know, whenever you go for a job, you know, it all comes up. Without the education, ah, um, well . . .

Tony's voice trailed off again; it was one of several instances when his voice became a whisper and then stopped as he searched for the words to capture his feelings, to explain or convey what he wanted to say. Each time he couldn't find the words he wanted to use, he tried again. Tony would exhale and look at his hands for the words he wanted, and taking a deep breath, he would slowly do his best to articulate his thoughts and feelings:

That's the hardest part, without the education and [not] being able to complete applications for stuff, and, um, it's getting the words together, you know, ah, it's real hard, and not being literate, and, um, and well, not knowing computers, it is all hard, to say, ah, what you want to say and not knowing the words, [and] not know how to get the words. It can be hard; it's always hard.[118]

Tony represents what Harlow and her colleagues found when examining educational attainment differences between the general public and the incarcerated population: Those who are incarcerated tend to have completed fewer years of formal education and have higher levels of learning disabilities and illiteracy rates, which is associated with low educational attainment.[119] "Many people go through the world and get through but cannot read or write but learn how to mask it."[120] Tony masked his illiteracy, and his shame prevented him from asking for help.

Low literacy rates and illiteracy tend to lead to poor labor outcomes, but having a felony guarantees an even tougher labor market experience regardless of one's education level.[121] Participants knew that education, employment, and a felony are intimately related: A felony conviction prevents them from getting a job, so why should they go to school when their conviction will always be on their record? Maurice explained his situation: "I'm not a dumb person, I just made dumb decisions. I got caught up, then got caught. School ain't going to fix that."[122] Darius understood the ramifications of having little education:

> Yeah, people look at that, you not having a high school diploma, but that felony is why they don't want to hire you, right there is the answer, and the thing with my background [his charge]. I went through a course to get my GED. I went to take the basic courses to try to and get my stuff up [studying in preparation] for the test, whatever, and I was going to have to take the test, it's just a step I haven't been able to accomplish. I was going to school, and they gave me a date to go [take the exam], and whatever, it was right there, for me to take the GED, but I didn't get there [to the test site]. Walking to the place, and I just turned around. So, I was just like this is a waste of my time. I can be working, trying to do other things and I thought I would just come back to that [to get his GED], but I never did. Wish I did. I didn't think it was going to be so hard with the charge, but with no high school [diploma], it's *really* hard [emphasis original].[123]

"Education is the only way I'm getting out," Duncan, a forty-four-year-old black college student, declared. He understood the importance of school and how it would differentiate him: "Going to school is the difference between them and me." Duncan's challenge is to get beyond his former world and become a "new man." At the time of his interview, he was wedged between two worlds: "I was a baller, you know, and my 'hood status matters to me. I'm just working on moving away from it. Had to change myself. But it's still hard to keep it [the change] going." As a former drug dealer who "moved weight," Duncan admits that the hardest part of reentering is "the people in my life." Many of his associates are still "working the block" and invested in his 'hood status; although Duncan said he was "out of the game," there were several people in his social network who wanted to know when he was coming back to the streets.[124]

"Change is a beautiful thing, right, but it's a struggle, challenging, keeping on track all the time is hard, but there is a pay-off at the end, right? Right, and it will be worth it, right? Beats the crazy days." The crazy days are when Duncan was running the streets and dealing drugs.

> The streets have changed so much, and when I go back, just hang out, you know, I know the "old folks" now and those who ain't dead, fucked up [on drugs], or locked up. I've been away for a bit, you know, serving short bids, they [the police] got me with a distribution charge, and then I was in and out, but in 2005, my activities caught up to me, and I was looking at federal time, long time, and I couldn't make the charges go away, and that's when I said, "I'm done." That last charge, wow, that last charge was not cool. My girlfriend at the time, she left, she was a casualty; there were lots of casualties along the way.

Throughout the interview, Duncan seemed to be saying all of the "right" things about having a change of heart, making amends to the "casualties" of his illegal activities, claiming he was no longer dealing drugs, and being responsible by going to all of his university classes. Duncan knows that earning his degree is the difference that will open up other options: "Being a college graduate, that will be worth it, right?"[125] Duncan knows that his drug charges will prevent him from many opportunities, but not all; his plan is to stay in school, and build a new life.

Employment Trumps Education

Some scholars estimate that educational and vocational programs create false and unrealistic expectations of reentry success; prisoners returning home are told that a diploma will get them a job and then everything will be alright.[126] The reality, however, is that going back to school after being imprisoned, for many adults who may be undereducated and may have suffered from negative previous school experiences, leads to high levels of frustration that expand the length of time they stay in the gray area.[127]

Many participants hit a variety of roadblocks when trying to earn educational credits in anticipation of securing legal employment because the constant message communicated and repeated by multiple actors in their social network is to get a job. Family members who took care of them while they were in prison are tired, significant others want them to contribute to the household, children require clothes and school supplies, and parole and probation officers, whom participants want off their back, all send the same message—"Get a job"—which trumps other pursuits, including taking classes. But for many participants, legal income represents more than just income: "When you have money, that you earned, you know, legally, you feel like a man and parole gives you a break."[128] Walter knew the importance of going to school, but because of the cost of paying for school, doing so was not in his best interests:

> [Parole] said I could take this class and go through with schooling, but it gets to the point that all parole does is give out mixed messages, "go to school to get a job, but you need to get a job." It's all a mess. So, that means all of those financial loans and grants and stuff that I have to take to go to school, I'm going to owe that back, but it's going to put more debt on me, so I just need to work and forget about school.[129]

Socrates captured the conflict among school, work, and parole:

> P.O. [Parole Officer] is focused on doing his job, and [we] need to recognize that he has a job to do. Their focus is on us getting employment, but to get a job you need a GED or high school diploma, something that you can show to get a job that's official [not a certificate]. That sets up conflict. A GED improves chances to work, and if I could work part-time and go to school part-time, that would be best. But my P.O. ain't going to allow that. I'm willing to do the work, do both, but my P.O. don't want me to do both. "Job. Get a job." That's all you hear [from parole]. You can get sent back [to prison] if you don't get a job. GED isn't important to them, so it's not [important] to me.[130]

Walter simplified the dilemma: "School is fantasyland. I ain't got no time to go to Disneyland. I got bills to pay, and my kids need uniforms for their own school. I don't have the luxury of sitting in a classroom when we gotta eat."[131]

In an ideal world, accredited educational programs taught by certified instructors would be effective and available *inside* every state prison. While incarcerated, prisoners could be required to attend classes, which would have positive rehabilitative outcomes and be a helpful tool for administrators to schedule time inside; instead, laws focus solely on punishment, and prisoners return home in the same educational position as when they went into prison, or worse. The lack of formal education keeps felons socially disabled, and the detrimental consequences extend into the area of employment. Sonja explained her specific challenge:

Look, I have college credit. I was good at school, but I was heartless, had sticky fingers. I had everything but I got agitated, never being able to pay for stuff, so I'd go for a semester and work a semester, on and off, and eventually I stopped going to make money, and well [Sonja's voice trails off]. Now what? Now I got a record, and it's terrible for people like me. It's so hard; my ex-husband, he was abusive and [it] took me a long time to get away; now my kids stuck with a no-good father, so I need to be there for them, but I'm homeless. So, I can't see my kids because I'm [considered] a bad influence on them. So, I'm a felon, and now even if I wanted to go to school, no one is going to hire me if I did finish.[132]

5

Not Working and Unable to Work

Since I've been out [of prison], well, I've only been working under the table and stuff like that and [there is] no need to go into it [the details about any of the off-the-books illegal jobs], but that's 'cuz of the [drug] conviction. No one will hire me; I didn't kill no one, I'm not violent, but no one wants someone like me at their place [of business] and I have to have [legal] employment to not get violated [and sent back to prison]. Hell, I have to have a job for everything.
—Gavin, April 11, 2012

Gavin hung his head, defeated by his past criminal behavior and felony, and he was not alone. Upon first returning to the community, participants' preferred way to meet their financial needs was with legal employment because the difference between succeeding and failing at reentry is directly related to working in the mainstream economy. Yet, many participants are unable to find stable and legal employment to take care of themselves as they face a number of critical financial responsibilities while attempting to rebuild their lives and support their families, including, in many instances, minor children. Darren put it this way:

> My problem is not about housing. I know you need it, I got it and am very glad for that. But you know there is other stuff, like "daddy, let's go to the Smurf movie" and they be growing and always need new clothes, 'specially shoes. You want to take them to do stuff, like the zoo, make sure they have stuff they need, but you don't have no money. And it hurts you, right, you know what I mean? It gets to you, not having no money. That's what makes all of this [reentry] so hard. No money.[1]

For participants, legal work serves as a place to go that occupies large blocks of time and provides a steady stream of legal income, but more importantly, a job decreases the lure of going back to hustling, banging, or looking for a "pay-off" in the streets.[2] Some, despite their felony conviction, reenter society, secure legal employment, and never commit another crime, as is evidenced by the 33 percent of individuals convicted of a felony who do not recidivate.[3] However, their success cannot be replicated due to divergent levels of formal education, know-how, skills, and varying access to social capital, housing, and familial support to meet basic needs, like acquiring clothes.[4] Additionally, because the vast majority of felons are disqualified from collecting public benefits, finding and securing legal work is the difference between overcoming the socially disabling effects of a felony and going back to prison.

To explain why securing a legal job is not routine for convicted felons,[5] this chapter explores a number of intersecting issues, including a survey of local, state, and federal policies that impose financial burdens on individuals while incarcerated and a description of how these fees continue upon reentry, creating crushing levels of debt; participants' experiences looking for legal work as felons; the way criminal background checks create government-approved unemployment; and what participants think and how they respond to the public's hostility, which keeps them socially disabled and unemployed. By analyzing these interrelated topics, I demonstrate how the petite penal institution of a felony conviction disables participants from entering the legal workforce.

Out of Work and in Debt

Reentry is different for each individual, so the time in which a former prisoner reenters society and remains unemployed varies, and can last a few weeks, several months, more than a year, or permanently; 60 to 75 percent of former inmates are unemployed up to a year after release.[6] The longer the time frame of unemployment, the greater the frustration and apprehension because of what a job signifies: A legal job increases the ability to earn money so one does not have to rely on family or intimate partner; boosts the possibility of being able to pay criminal justice fines, legal debts, parole, and halfway house fees; decreases the likelihood of committing a new crime, going "back to the streets to make bank,"[7] and being sent back to prison; and reduces the threat of violating parole due to inability to secure a legal job or pay on one's debt.[8]

Many local and state courts impose general fines while parole agencies charge supervision or administration fees, and both charge late fees for missed payments, with nonpayment resulting in a potential new jail or prison sentence.[9] Former prisoners must pay all their fines, as well as related fees for court-mandated drug tests, and if assigned to reside in a private halfway house for a portion of their parole, they must pay housing fees to the corporation that manages it.[10] These fees accrue, and if they are not paid back in whole or through an approved payment plan, devastating consequences can result.

> They get you for everything; I have to pay house fees [to the halfway house for room and board] but they [the corporately run halfway house] don't let you out to work a job, always locking us down for [any number of undisclosed] "security" reasons, and I pay to pee in a cup [for a drug test]. How crazy is that? They don't tell you straight out, but if I have to pay and then pee, what that tell you? And if I don't pay, they can say I'm dirty [meaning his urine is "dirty" due to drug use] and jack me up [send him back to prison].[11]

For parents reentering society, fees are added to any accrued unpaid child support that accumulated while they were incarcerated. This practice became customary when President Bill Clinton and the U.S. Congress reformed welfare in 1996, which included the Temporary Assistance to Needy Families (TANF) and the Personal Responsibility and Work Opportunity Reconciliation Act (PRWORA).[12] These two laws made child support enforcement a top priority, and the Clinton administration's efforts were effective at collecting billions of dollars in delinquent child support for minor children. The two interrelated policies aimed at reducing a single parent's reliance on welfare and access to other public benefits while sending a message to parents who owed child support about their responsibility in honoring their parenting obligations.[13] An unintended consequence of child support enforcement, however, was the way it targeted incarcerated parents with established child support orders.[14]

State courts vary in the way they treat child support obligations while a parent is incarcerated, but no state automatically modifies child support payments when a parent enters prison;[15] in twenty-one states, incarceration is not a sufficient reason to justify eliminating or reducing an existing child support obligation.[16] For instance, state supreme court justices in Montana argued, "[A] father should not be able to escape his financial obligation to his children simply because his misdeeds have placed him behind bars. The meter should continue to run."[17] In other cases, state supreme court justices argue that a prison sentence should be considered alongside standard measures in a modification request according to the answer to one basic question: Is the parent able to pay the child support order?[18] To reduce a child support order while incarcerated, a prisoner must submit a written request for modification, include a financial affidavit, and provide ancillary documentation to either the court of jurisdiction or child support agency. The process is cumbersome and lengthy, it requires legal representation, and responses are highly variable.[19]

The accumulated debt of past due child support payments, court and parole fees and fines, and related late fees and interest converts into an unrealistic monetary burden that becomes onerous to pay off due to the inability to find legal work.[20] For instance, PRWORA authorizes the suspension or restriction of licenses, including professional, occupational, and driver's licenses, due to child support arrears,[21] and the Child Support Recovery Act of 1992[22] allows state police and federal agents to arrest noncustodial parents for willful nonpayment of child support, which can lead to criminal charges, fines, and imprisonment. In New Jersey, once one is out of prison, nonpayment of child support and criminal justice fees can have the catastrophic effect of leading to arrest and reincarceration as warrants can be issued to arrest poor people who do not pay towards their criminal justice debt. In New Jersey, when individuals are charged and convicted of nonpayment of fees and fines, and they are unable to pay the amount owed, they can be reincarcerated and fined for nonpayment. New Jersey counties, twice a year, issue bench warrants to arrest people who are behind on their child support payments; some of the "deadbeat" parents also have fees and fines related to being incarcerated, and if they are unable to pay, it is a fourth-degree crime with a maximum eighteen-month prison sentence and up to a ten thousand dollar fine, on top of the accrued debt.[23]

A direct result of the accumulation of criminal justice debt and child support arrears for parents is that it discourages many from looking for work in the mainstream legal economy; this way, the state cannot find them through payroll records. When participants spoke about their debt, they spoke about making the conscious decision to take "off-the-books" work in the underground economy because they knew that states used automated payroll deductions to collect upwards of 25 percent of every paycheck to pay towards their criminal justice debt and unpaid child support, even if the collection amount or child support order did not reflect an individual's ability to pay. Participants shared that after the payroll deduction, they were left without enough money to buy food or pay rent, utilities, and transportation costs.[24] "The state can fuck you up; something gotta give, either I get a [legal] job and they take all my money [through income withholding] and I'm left with nothing, ain't got enough to live, or I work off the books to live, [but] they snatch you in Jersey for not paying [on your debt]. Fucked nine ways to Sunday."[25]

Technically, debtor's prisons are unconstitutional, but the 1983 U.S. Supreme Court decision in *Bearden v. Georgia*[26] made criminal fines constitutional, with the caveat that courts cannot imprison someone for failure to pay unless nonpayment is willful. Willfulness is not presumed by nonpayment alone, but in practice, local and state courts are incarcerating poor people for nonpayment alone, without proof of willfulness, leading to de facto debtor's prisons. Despite *Bearden's* stipulation, poor people unable to pay on their amassed debt are being locked up, and the supposedly archaic institution of debtor's prison is standard practice for jurisdictions that view criminal justice fees as a revenue source to defray the costs of the criminal justice system.[27] The onerous fees become unreasonable due to the sheer number of punitive fines imposed on defendants prior to conviction, including, in some jurisdictions, fees charged for each mile the police drive to serve an arrest warrant for failure to pay or, when an individual is arrested, for his or her failure to appear in court; if a person is unable to pay the fines, police in smaller jurisdictions where the court may only meet once a week will jail people for nonpayment, and charge them up to sixty dollars a night for "room and board" until their case is heard.[28] Impoverished defendants' lives are disrupted: as they wait in jail for their hearing, they are fired from jobs and lose their housing. In the case of child support payments, nonpayment is considered a crime against the state, and "Criminal Nonsupport" statutes exist in some form in all fifty states.

In many jurisdictions, debts are transferred to private "probation collection companies" that impose additional fees, including having probationers pay for their own ankle monitoring,[29] which results in poor people being trapped in a continuous cycle of debt and makes felons more vulnerable to recidivating. The system fails to acknowledge the economic reality of those who experience deep poverty, who do not have access to the needed capital to pay the fees and fines, and who are often homeless and unemployed. Moreover, the system fails to recognize that trying to collect on criminal debt that quickly snowballs into a huge amount of money undermines reentry efforts as the oppressive debt operates as retribution; when this debt is combined with the socially disabling laws that restrict felons from securing a legal job, it all becomes hopeless.[30]

No One Wants to Employ a Convicted Felon

An integral part of a felon's job search is experiencing rejection, and learning how to deal with the frustration:

> I've been home, maxed out, and it's real hard; I'm fighting [struggling] to stay out [of prison]. It's hard out here. Ain't got the tools, you know, to make it. I want to work, and some people like me get jobs, but no one is hiring *me* [emphasis original].

Xavier blamed his unsuccessful job search on his felony. "There is nothing for people in Newark, at least for people like me."[31] His sense of defeat was common; participants spoke about rejection and about literally being told, "You're not wanted"[32] and that any contribution they could make is not valued.[33] Dejected by his job search, Xavier flatly joked, "Who wants to get rejected today?"[34] Uneasy laughter followed his attempt at humor. Xavier's challenges were many, including his age (he was nearing fifty), long jacket, and lack of legal work experience.

> I've been on the street, [and] I was like about twenty-one, or no, I was like twenty-two years old, and then inside [prison] for twenty-five years, so I only know the street, hustling, doing time; didn't have time to get a job, but now? Now, *right now* [original emphasis his], I need to get a job, and

I'm scared that I won't [find one]; if I don't find work, I will fall back to the street and what I know [which is a life of crime].[35]

The inability to secure legal work is not simply about income but also about avoiding the negative ramifications of not working, which were evident on any random day at the nonprofit organization. One participant, who attended Group on a regular basis, was picked up on a technical parole violation and mandated back to federal prison because of his inability "to find and maintain legal employment," a common condition of federal and state parole.[36] One day he was there, and the next he was gone. Parole was ubiquitous, and a constant reminder of a felon's socially disabled status. Participants shared how parole officers would badger them to get a job to pay their fees and in the next breath hang the threat of prison over their heads if they failed at both; parole officers have the authority to revoke somebody's parole and send him or her back to prison, and such bullying tactics became a normal part of the reentry narrative. Alyssa openly stated that getting a job was the only thing that mattered:

> Okay, so I have to get a job to keep parole off my back, and they just ride you. They don't give you anything but a hard time, even when you doing right, you know. It's still a hard time. I want to say this, I mean they are doing their job, but it's like, you know, give me an opportunity. Because they say, "well, you need to get a job." But when you get out there, look for work, not many people want to give you a job. And so they [parole] want to violate you [send you back to prison] if you don't have a job. Here you are doing everything you can to find a job, and you tell 'em that, you know, you show them, 'cuz I'm not trying to fool them, but they don't want to hear that and [they are] always throwing it in your face, "why don't you have a job?" Like it's all my fault, like I'm doing nothing, and it's like [Alyssa's voice trails off, and then she says quietly,] It's all just impossible.[37]

Silence filled the small office where we sat, and as the faint noise of traffic filtered through the dusty windows, she said, "It's like they want to put you back inside [prison] because you can't find a job, especially if they [parole officer] having a bad day, you are violated, and sent back."

More silence. We sit motionless in the sharp silent space, until she hisses in a hard, low voice: "They want for me to fail."[38]

Tyrone experienced similar pressure from parole:

> Parole want you to get a job, like that's all that matters to them. I think I could get a job if I had more schooling. We all know that schooling is going to help me get a job, and then I can get a better job, and move on up in time. But parole, they don't care about you learning anything. "Gotta get those fees paid" is all they tell me. It's all about work, so that's what I'm doing. A job matters to them, so that's what matters to me. You'd be doing that, too, if you were in my situation.[39]

Tyrone understood the importance of education and its connection to gainful employment, but for those who cannot find work, the financial pressures of reentering make education irrelevant;[40] education is not valued by participants in the same way as a legal job is because the failure to attain an education does not lead to a technical parole violation that sends one back to prison.

When legal employment is not available due to the constraining effects of a felony and socially disabling policies, most participants' goal is to

> [n]ot end up living on the streets [at which point crime becomes a rational option] because when you got nothing, you got nothing. I want to work, it comes first, you know, it's all about a paycheck. I've been looking, but got nothing but rejects.[41]

Even knowing with certainty they would be barred from most legal employment opportunities, most participants continued to look for a job: "The biggest fear, getting started, knowing you going to get put down, cursed at, looked down at."[42] Despite the constant risk of rejection and feelings of worthlessness, participants knew that work represented "freedom, and would do it [look for jobs] one thousand times to have a chance at one [employer saying] yes."[43]

Walter's contained fury was evident in his tense body as he lamented, "I just want to work." Walter's first conviction occurred when he was forty-eight years old, and three years later, at the age of fifty-one, he wanted his life to revert back to the way it used to be:

I always used to work while I was doing my dirt [dealing drugs]. Had lots of jobs, in restaurants, as a driver, doing my dirt was a way to make some extra money, like a second job. You can't make nothing working for someone else. I was always working, and then it was like I woke up and knew I'd never make it [have enough money to live on from a minimum wage job]. I knew some guys, one thing led to another, but where I went wrong is that I did some drugs, nothing heavy, but started using my own stash when my mom got sick. She died in 2009, and then my dad, he got sick and died, and well, by then I was a drug dealer and using. You ain't never supposed to use, and never your good stuff [hard drugs]. Never. Drug dealers have to be drug free, because you gotta keep your stuff clean, keep a low profile, drive low-key cars, dress plain, keep it all on the low so people don't be getting jealous. Keep your money stacked. Don't be flashy. I did all that, except I used [drugs], and messed everything up. Now, I just want to work again, like I use to.[44]

Walter referred to what several participants, as former drug dealers, did prior to being convicted. They shared how they tried to appear inconspicuous and normal by "going to a regular job so that they could blend in while stacking their cash."[45] Former drug-dealing participants aspired to be like the successful drug dealers they knew who had a legal job and saved their drug earnings to buy a house or invest in real estate or a legitimate business, like a deli or laundromat, with the intent to build their wealth slowly, the legitimate way. Participants, in effect, were talking about laundering their own money in such a way as not to draw the attention of the police or their neighbors. "It's like we the bankers over there [pointing out the window and across the Hudson River to Wall Street], they bankers corrupt as shit, make millions doing shady shit. But us, we deal drugs, so we the enemy."[46]

Now, "the enemy" needed a legal job to avoid going back to prison. Collectively, most participants had a strong desire to work because they wanted to turn their lives around, and by securing a legal job they would be able to get their own place, pay bills, feel connected to society, make a positive contribution to their family's and kids' well-being, stay out of trouble by avoiding criminal activity, and be an adult who takes care of things without being dependent, which was universally loathed. Yet, getting a legal job is one of the hardest things to do with a felony conviction because securing legal employment is dependent on convincing a potential employer to hire one, but employers "are wary of us, people like me, they don't like people like me," Clifford shared. "That's the hard part, they real suspicious of us [felons] and real careful; so they hire someone, anyone else, really, as long as they ain't got a charge."[47]

Ray Charles endorsed this viewpoint: "They [employers] have to be extra careful hiring a convicted felon, and most times won't. They just won't do it. They can hire someone without the record; [they] still might get ripped off, but they feel better."[48]

Tyrone affirmed Clifford's and Ray Charles's experiences: "It's all about the charge. That felony; it will get you rejected every time looking for a job. *Every time*" (emphasis original).[49]

Brandon explained his situation and how he felt while trying to re-enter society; his understanding of reentry echoed the comments and experiences of other participants:

> Work comes first, it's all about a paycheck, you know, and like [drug] treatment comes second when it should be first, so after all that comes the rest [such as housing, education, and vocational training], but how you suppose to get established right, when all you can think about is you hungry? Doors get shut in your face, you have challenges, all they [potential employers] see is that conviction. I did my time, got clean, and all you hear is "get clean" [off drugs] and you'll get a second chance. Maybe for them [white guys], but not me. I did what they tell me, got clean, but nothing; it's just crazy, all racial shit, really. White guys [who are convicted felons] do better.[50] Not us [black guys]; I go out and do the best I can, but I still got nothin'.[51]

The relentless challenges of reentering society make it difficult to remain unaffected, but the alternative, going back to prison, is even more depressing. Some participants, unable to find work, hit the proverbial wall and started a downward spiral as they thought about the magnitude of not getting a job; starting with an indiscernible shift in energy that could be easily missed if one was not paying attention, participants' deportment would subtly change, and then suddenly the angst was palpable and unmistakable. There were days at the nonprofit organization when a shadow of despondency fell like a veil across a participant's face, the smell of despair and homelessness perfumed the air, or the emptiness in the eyes of those seeking help was vast as some participants grappled with their inescapable reality. The *Diagnostic and Statistical Manual of Mental Disorders* connects indifference, dispassion, or a catatonic state with post-traumatic stress disorder (PTSD).[52] Gavin had reached this state, and he knew it, describing his feelings and circumstances this way:

> It's like I'm just waiting for it [something bad] to drop, I got nothing, so you kinda know what's going to happen next [like going back to crime to support himself], and I'm waiting until I do that because it just needs to happen, I got nothing, so gotta do something to live.[53]

Forced Unemployment: Government-Produced Joblessness

The most prevalent socially disabling effects of a felony conviction is in the area of employment, as most employers embrace the use of criminal background checks or require an occupational license. Such practices are utilized by government agencies at the local, state, and federal levels, have been quickly adopted by private companies and nonprofit organizations, and are maintained and promoted as a tool to screen out "bad" applicants.[54] The negative externalities of being denied a legal job because of a background check force participants to make decisions not conducive to successful reentry, and such ramifications are not calculated into the degree of punishment imposed by the original sentencing court.

Over and over again, participants shared their job search experiences, which can collectively be summarized as equal parts stigma, socially disabling policies, and rejection:

> No one will hire me, and I want to work. Tried to get a job, tried lots, but . . . [Jermaine's voice trails off as he collects his thoughts.] It's that background check, big fail, and there ain't no second chance, none, no other options. Your record comes up [on a background check], and that's it, ain't no one hiring you after that [felony] pops up. I can't find work, so what you want me to do, huh?[55]

Jermaine's question about what society wants him to do is never recognized by politicians who write socially disabling policies that deny public benefits and approve the use of background checks to deny felons legal work opportunities. Criminal background checks, in particular, are common in the job market, and used for a wide variety of other reasons.

Criminal History Background Checks

Initially, a criminal background check was not designed for every job applicant; rather, it was a tool intended as one way to assess the character of applicants for specific positions: in the legal profession; with law enforcement (e.g., state, county, and local police and sheriff's offices and agencies requiring security clearance, such as the Federal Bureau of Investigation and the Central Intelligence Agency); and the United States military. However, the use of a criminal background check expanded after the passage of the Brady Handgun Violence Prevention Act of 1993 (Brady Act)[56] requiring federal firearms licensees (FFLs) to run a criminal records check on an individual prior to selling him or her a firearm. The act's permanent provisions went into effect November 30, 1998, when the National Instant Criminal Background Check System (NICS) became operational.[57] With the creation of NICS, firearm dealers could run instant background checks with the goal of determining whether a potential gun buyer had been convicted of a federal felony, which would disqualify the buyer from completing a gun purchase.

Following the implementation of NICS, Congress created the National Criminal History Improvement Program (NCHIP). The original purpose of NCHIP was to maintain criminal arrest *and* conviction records for use by law enforcement for national security purposes. However, to ensure that data was regularly entered into NICS, Congress provided financial assistance to states to automate and upgrade their criminal records systems to enable them to connect to NICS;[58] a result of NCHIP is that the annual number of arrests and felony convictions entered into NICS has skyrocketed. As policies shifted to address longstanding and new and emerging political concerns,[59] the proliferation of surveillance techniques post-9/11, the enhanced scrutiny of minority religious communities, and the increased political pressure to "do something" about crime led to additional information about more suspects being entered into NICS and FFLs and local and state agencies running more criminal records searches.[60] Alongside the shift in policies and increased number of entries, law enforcement agencies across the country saw their respective budgets increase in an effort to militarize police units under the auspices of being "tough on crime." Combined with advances in technology and database management, the integration of government efforts means that NICS is a national criminal records database capable of responding to interstate records requests using common variables such as name, date of birth, race, and sex to identify individuals.

With the increased number of laws mandating a background check,[61] the national database is accessible via the internet; agencies, institutions, and every jurisdiction of the United States has the ability to run a nationwide state and federal criminal history records check. With advances in database administration, criminal background checks are an inexpensive tool used by a variety of public and private organizations. Although non–law enforcement agencies cannot access the entire database, NCHIP allows federal, state, and local agencies, as well as private companies,[62] to use the data for a variety of aims, such as denying social benefits and employment opportunities by identifying individuals and barring them from purchasing a firearm; owning a gun if they are the subject of a protective order, outstanding warrant, stalking conviction, or domestic violence conviction, or if they have been deemed a threat to public safety; working in positions concerning children, the elderly, or the disabled; and holding employment licenses for specific positions, as mandated by state and federal laws.[63] Criminal background checks are used by Departments of Motor Vehicles; landlords to review tenants for public, affordable, and private housing; higher education institutions to determine eligibility for federal funding, work-study, and faculty and staff hiring decisions; foster care and adoption agencies; the U.S. State Department and agencies that issue passports and international travel documents (e.g., visas); county election offices in states that deny felons the right to vote;[64] government agencies that approve public benefits; and government and private agencies that grant commercial driver's licenses (CDL) and commercial motor vehicle (CMV) licenses.[65]

Employers' Use of Criminal History Background Checks

Prospective employers across industries utilize a criminal background check for hiring decisions and tend to exclude *all* felons from employment. Blanket policies excluding applicants on the basis of a felony are common and do not include a threat assessment to evaluate the actual or perceived risk posed by an individual; to weigh the nature and gravity of the crime alongside the responsibilities of the job;[66] or to consider evidence of rehabilitation, behavioral changes, or the amount of time that has passed since the date of conviction.[67] Some felony crimes face more scrutiny, such as violent crimes, crimes that threaten the public's safety, or crimes that suggest an employer's bottom line will be negatively affected.[68] Paula, charged and convicted of fraud and cashing bad checks, considered deceitful and deceptive practices used for financial gain, cannot get a job:

> Yeah, your charge comes up, always, can't hide from it but you can't get a job because of it, when all you want to do is hide it. It's the specific charge that should matter. I don't have no drug charges, ain't messed with kids, sure as hell didn't kill nobody, but I still can't get a job because of the felony. They probably scared I'm going to steal they money. [Paula moaned.][69]

As for participants with a history of violent crime, it is ironic that what works to their advantage inside prison works in reverse on the outside: "It's the violence that scares people out here, but gets you mad respect inside, but if you ain't messing with kids or raping women, you should be okay with most people."[70] This is not how the outside world works. Employers are reluctant to hire a person with a record of violent crime.

The Society for Human Resource Management (SHRM), the largest and oldest international human resource organization, shares best practices with HR professionals, including the use of criminal background checks. SHRM data indicates that approximately 69 percent of reporting organizations conduct criminal background checks on *all* job applicants; 52 percent conduct background checks to reduce legal liability for negligent hiring; and 49 percent do so to create a safe work environment.[71]

SHRM data also shows that background checks are regularly conducted by potential employers for employment reasons and for occupations that require a security clearance or to safeguard protected populations, such as children, the elderly, or the disabled.

Max hoped he could get an interview because then, he believed, he could explain his situation and decrease the impact of his criminal record:

> Once you get a chance, you can talk about how you did your time. I was good in prison [meaning he was not written up for fighting or violating the rules]. I made a mistake and served my time, paid my debt to society. I worked while I was in prison; I took the opportunities when they were presented, like doing certificates and carpentry, welding courses, food services, so I made good choices while I was doing time. That should count for something.[72]

Max was optimistic, but SHRM data shows that 96 percent of reporting organizations do *not* extend a job offer to someone with a violent felony and 74 percent of the time job offers are *not* extended to nonviolent felons. Three-fifths (58 percent) of the companies offer some job candidates the opportunity to explain their conviction before a final decision is made to offer a job.[73]

Private entities and public institutions are reluctant to hire felons, claiming that professional practices necessitate not hiring anyone convicted of a felony to protect their image, assets, property, and reputation, and their clients, employees, and customers.[74] The reluctance to hire felons is associated with stigma and fear, and when employers go looking for what they fear, they are more likely to *not* hire an individual when his or her criminal record becomes known.[75] As a result, entire groups targeted and arrested by the police but never charged or convicted of a crime are unduly screened out of the candidate pool, harming racial minorities, who are more likely to have an arrest record than whites.[76] Employers can use an arrest record as a proxy to discriminate against all black applicants, and employers' prejudicial views of who might have an arrest or criminal record and conviction then become reason enough to never interview or hire from this group of applicants.[77] An expanding number of private companies mimic the government's use of criminal background checks to exclude individuals with an arrest or conviction record. Participants were cognizant of how race and a felony merge to leave them in a socially disabled position.

> It [reentry] should be all about second chances, because shit I don't want to go back [to prison]. It's only guys like me in there [black men], but that doesn't mean we can't do good. Black success is never highlighted.[78]

Despite the long odds, many participants demonstrated a willingness to try to overcome the challenges by submitting a resume to jobs that seemed to match their skill set, but receiving a call-back for a job interview and offer was difficult. Paula knew what she had to do, but doing it was difficult:

> Gotta stay out [of prison] somehow and hold on. That's the only choice that makes sense. Because, the longer you stay out but sit still, doing nothing, the harder it gets to stay out. You gotta do something to stay out, gotta have something to hold onto, gotta have some money. So, you gotta hold on until something comes up whenever it comes, if it comes, and keep on trying to find something to do. Big thing to try and change, but that's what it takes.[79]

Occupational Licenses

An occupational license is a grant of permission or special privilege entitling the licensee to work in a particular field for which he or she would otherwise be ineligible.[80] Employment licensing restrictions based on statutory provisions extend to a diverse set of professional and occupational categories, and each license acts as a barrier to accessing a profession. Jurisdictions across the country have their own rules pertaining to acquiring a license and which professions require employees to be licensed. Regardless of the jurisdiction, licenses are mandated for two main reasons: regulatory provisions and revenue raising. Regulatory licenses for occupations serve as one of the greatest restrictions to employment and require special training, education, completion of an apprenticeship, or some combination of all three requirements.[81] A revenue-raising license is similar to an employment tax imposed on individuals prior to their entering a profession, and is used to control access to certain vocations;[82] applicants pay a fee, submit to a background check, pass an occupational competency test or supply proof of proficiency through educational credentials, and provide to the jurisdiction proof of business eligibility or incorporation papers. In return, the applicant is granted a license to work in that profession.[83]

Under both Republican and Democratic presidents, federal rules restricted felons from professions by denying them occupational licenses. Legislators argue that by requiring a license as a prerequisite to work at an occupation, including unskilled and semiskilled positions, they are protecting the public's interests, health, morals, and welfare by connecting competency tests and good moral character tests to an occupational license.[84] The national government took the lead in establishing standards for occupational license requirements and exclusions, and while no one has an affirmative right to a particular job or profession, the increased number of statutes excluding felons from being able to gain an occupational license means that the government's active role restricts felons from accessing vocational jobs and leads to unemployment while socially disabling a particular subgroup.[85] One example is the Sentencing Reform Act of 1984,[86] which accelerated the use of civil disabilities and employment restrictions in numerous occupations.[87]

States followed the federal government's lead, and the combination of "tough on crime" politics and the "War on Drugs" led to the passage of a long list of legislated types of professions requiring an occupational license.[88] Ostensibly, a license is needed to protect the public's safety, and increasing the number of professions requiring licenses restricts individuals convicted of a felony from accessing a range of jobs. As states and the federal government passed more laws restricting individuals with a felony from legally accessing an occupational license through statutory time limits or lifetime restrictions, a permanent state of government-enforced unemployment was formed.[89] The power to deny or revoke a license is at the discretion of the state licensing agency, and most states deny or revoke an occupational license if someone is convicted of a felony while licensed.[90]

Obtaining an occupational license is crucial to legally entering a number of regulated trades. Eligibility requirements for various occupations depend on the state, the type of license, and the industry, creating a hodgepodge of inconsistent, illogical, and piecemeal restrictions based on a broad set of characterizations and assumptions.[91] The state of Ohio, for instance, has 291 record-based employment restrictions barring individuals with a felony from a host of employment options,[92] and the same is true for licensed professions in all fifty states. For example, New Jersey requires a license for grounds maintenance workers (e.g., tree trimmers, pesticide applicators); social workers and rehabilitation, substance abuse, and behavioral counselors; construction workers (e.g., earth drillers and construction equipment operators, plumbers and steamfitters, and sewer pipe cleaners); health care assistants (e.g., dental and home health aides, orderlies); automotive technicians and heating and air conditioning mechanics; hairdressers, stylists, cosmetologists, manicurists/pedicurists, and makeup artists; and non–farm animal caretakers (e.g., dog walkers).

To date, the number of restrictions has been documented,[93] but there have been no studies on the cumulative effectiveness of licensing laws in protecting the public's safety or community morality. What is known is that felons are excluded from industries requiring an occupational license;[94] in particular, policies introduced following 9/11 became more restrictive,[95] and the licensing requirements have grown more numerous as additional occupations are targeted by politicians.[96] Most of the post-9/11 statutes impose lifetime restrictions on felons, even nonviolent individuals, preventing them from acquiring a number of jobs.[97]

> I worked before [my conviction], you know, and I want to work now 'cuz when you work, you don't have to struggle. When you have to struggle [financially], you lose focus about what you are suppose to be doing and end up in the streets. You just fall back to the old ways and doing whatever. There is some work, but without a license, I ain't going to get that work.[98]

Even if an individual has an occupational license, a felony conviction can be used to revoke it: "I have my [occupational] licenses, and all that. I've been working a long time, work has always been part of my life, but it all went off track for a little while, you know, [and now I'm a felon]."[99]

The courts have ruled that occupational licensing regulations are civil in nature, and consequently are not considered punishment,[100] thereby creating a "mythical divide" between punishment imposed by criminal courts and penalties levied by civil institutions.[101] Yet, employment restrictions are based on the criminal justice system's determination of guilt of a felony crime, and the employment ban is a result of criminal proceedings, which I argue operates as retributive punishment; the only practical difference between "punishment" and "penalties" is the agency imposing the hostile policies. The employment penalties connected to a felony are based on political calculations related to moral and public safety concerns that are justified by politicians who believe that offenders will always be unfit to work[102] because they are permanently flawed and unchanging.[103] As a result of this thinking, politicians pass restrictions that operate as a blanket exclusion that presumes every felon poses an equal threat to public safety and shares the same likelihood of engaging in future criminal behavior, resulting in the vast majority of felons being restricted from acquiring an occupational license.[104] Such record-based laws make every individual who bears the label "felon" identical under the law,[105] and legislators have created an environment in which socially disabling laws crisscross a variety of jurisdictional and institutional boundaries, and are found in a diverse body of laws.[106] Restrictions become cumulative in nature,[107] as politicians integrate additional stipulations that applicants must meet in order to obtain an occupational license, such as the inclusion of good moral character tests.[108]

Good Moral Character Tests

When applying for an occupational license, applicants have to "pass" a state's morality test to secure a license to work in a trade, but what is good moral character? Is a good morals test related to the occupational skills of the license?[109] The courts have struggled to define good moral character. The U.S. Supreme Court declared, "It can be defined in an almost unlimited number of ways for any definition will reflect the attitudes, experiences and prejudices of the definer."[110] The Court declares that employment license prerequisites must have a rational relationship to the public's interest; be conceived to achieve a legitimate purpose connected to the employment or work tasks; be connected to the requirements of the occupation; be reasonable; be linked to the hiring decisions involved in a job; and be related to the conviction.[111]

For instance, in *Schware v. Board of Bar Examiners of New Mexico*,[112] the Court declared that when granting a license, states can establish qualifications for entry into a profession but the qualification(s) "must have a rational connection with the applicant's fitness or capacity to practice [the occupation]."[113] In *DeVeau v. Braisted*,[114] the Court stated that employment restrictions barring individuals with a felony were "a familiar legislative device to insure against corruption."[115] Such reasoning indicates that restricting individuals with a felony from certain occupations is an acceptable legislative tactic to avoid fraud or deceit within a trade or profession as long as the reasons for the restriction conform to a legitimate state interest.[116] Some lower courts agree, and have upheld statutory codes that restrict access to occupational licenses using standards of moral turpitude or violation of community norms or values, but other lower courts have declared that "occupational barriers imposed on former offenders are irrational" because such restrictions are put in place by a legislature, are removed from the judiciary and the criminal courts, take effect without consideration of the appropriateness of the restriction, and do not take into account evidence of rehabilitation.[117] Due to the variable definition of "good character" and the subjective nature of what is judged as "worthiness," the application of such tests varies,[118] but "good character" tests categorically exclude felons from obtaining an occupational license. Although such tests differ across jurisdictions and occupations,[119] the use of good moral character tests implies that it is impossible to secure a license if convicted of a felony. However, there is some variation if a person was licensed prior to his or her conviction.

> The big thing is licenses. It is hard to get one if you haven't had one because you can get the training, and do all the schooling and still be denied. It's easier if you had a license and just have to get the money together to pay up any late fees and re-register, if they let you.[120]

Legislators argue that occupational licenses and "good moral character" tests protect the public's safety. In reality, the nature of exclusionary statutes locks felons out of work and keeps them unemployed.[121] Participants argued that licenses do not protect the community from potential criminal behavior; rather, "all they do is jack us up."[122] Finding a job is the difference between reentering *or* being sent back to prison, which makes occupational licenses and good moral character tests counter-productive;[123] they increase the likelihood that an individual will remain unemployed and commit a new crime,[124] helping to explain high recidivism rates.[125]

Struggle, Lie, or Commit a New Crime

Max knew exactly what he had to do to successfully reenter: "Get a job."[126] Mahoney felt the same: "Getting a job, it's all that matters. It's really hard, and I ain't got no real [work] experience, but that's what I have to do, find a job."[127] Shortly after returning home, many participants learned that occupational licenses and good moral character tests restricted them and prevented them from accessing many legal trades. In response, some participants altered their strategy and purposely looked for "hiring" signs in the windows of potential employers seeking to hire someone for a low-skilled, entry-level position that did not require a license, such as a dishwasher, line cook, mailroom clerk, or loader/unloader of tractor-trailer trucks.

The general thought was that notwithstanding their lack of legal work experience, if participants had an opportunity to talk to a hiring manager about a job, they could reduce the harm of their felony conviction appearing on a background check by talking about how they can carry out the related job's responsibilities on the basis of the work they did while incarcerated. Everyone who is physically able to do so works while incarcerated: Prisoners work in the kitchen preparing meals and baking bread; in the laundry; as barbers in the prison's barbershop (only for well-behaved prisoners due to the need to use sharp instruments); as part of the prison's operations and maintenance "labor force" as plumbers and electricians who repair and maintain the air conditioning, heating system, and ventilation units and as landscapers, painters, and general workers who clean and maintain buildings and grounds; and in the commissary (i.e., the prison store). Yet, even for entry-level jobs that do not require an employee to interact with customers or handle cash, a background check is inevitably run, and participants are rejected. Therefore, the vast majority of participants remained unemployed and cut off from the tangible benefits of employment despite their best efforts to find a job.

When a criminal background check denied a participant a job opportunity, many became frustrated because they knew they were running out of options: "It's sad, really, I'm not eating, can't get hired, got fines, and I gotta eat, so I'm going to do what I gotta do."[128] When participants reached this point, it was as if they disclosed an unspoken truth that all of them could, and if necessary would, go back to doing their thing in the streets. Many participants were honest about the fact that it would be easy to return to their old ways, but they would not make that decision lightly because it would probably lead back to prison. Gavin stated, "Don't want to, sure don't want to go back [to prison], but what else is there out here when there ain't no kinda help and no one hiring when you got a charge."[129]

Bailey made implicit what he would do if he could not secure legal work; he'd go back to the streets. "I had like one interview, but they checked me. And that was that. Done."[130] Others echoed Bailey's attitude and outlook on life as a felon:

> I want to do the right thing, I want to be a good story, a lot of guys do, but I need a chance. We all need a chance. I know I need a job; without one, well, you know, I'll do my thing.[131]

While a former prisoner is looking for work, the continual rejection leads to increased frustration and thoughts of going back to the streets or going back to prison arise, as Gavin asked, "Really, what else is there?"[132] A few participants, like Tyrone, remained philosophical. He recognized that his felony status was a problem when it came to a criminal history background check:

> The background check is going to happen, whatever they check they going to check, so you have to be upfront and change the terms of the conversation. Be honest. They don't need to know everything. The hard part is explaining the time I've been away. That is hard, but if you are honest, I hope, it'll work out. I mean, if it doesn't, and I don't get a job, I'm going back [to prison].[133]

Xavier knew this challenge first-hand: "Man that hurts, trying to explain stuff. Saying it was a long time ago doesn't work. People get scared, especially if they find out you violent."[134] The need to overcome the social and legal stigma of a felony without legal work experience may depend on the type of charge, and Tony knew his arson conviction would always be his problem:

> My charge, it will stay with me. It is very hard, it's a problem. No one wants an arsonist, even if it was just a tragic situation and a one-time thing; I have to live with that for the rest of my life. I didn't hurt nobody, just burned a car. It happened to be my girlfriend's car, but no one got hurt. I think for me, to be honest, at forty-nine years old, for me, first and foremost is to be able to live, not to have an expensive place, but live. Like I need five hundred dollars a month, but I haven't had a job, and it's going on six weeks and my rent is going to be due on the first and you know the landlord knows my situation but still the pressure of not being able to pay and meet expectations, that [pressure] builds until you ready to explode.[135]

Tony is struggling, and the lack of work is taking a toll on his health:

> My health issues, you know, get to me. High blood pressure, high sugar [diabetes], which I went to the hospital for, and when I was in the hospital, and I couldn't get the, I didn't get the charity care because I hadn't filled out the paperwork for that [because he cannot read], and the bills are coming in now, so I'm calling the people and making arrangements, paying like five, ten, twenty-five dollars when I can. Not much, but it's all I can do.[136]

Other participants spoke about their expectations of finding a job and what needs to happen for them to work. One said,

> I will work. I don't expect nothing, I want to work, will start at the bottom, and I want to show you [future employer] what I am worth, and then move up. I just need a chance, then I can be alright.[137]

The combination of getting a chance to work and "be alright" was a common mantra; participants explained that "being alright" meant gaining back their self-respect and making their family proud; carrying their own weight by paying their own bills; becoming independent by living in their own place; having a legal job to get parole off their back; and doing whatever else was necessary to not go back to prison.[138] Securing a legal job was so important that when a job search failed, it was an emotionally draining setback. Randall captures this sense of struggle: "You get tired always grinding, always working hard for nothing, and then something is taken away [such as being laid off when a construction job comes to an end or finding a temporary job with no potential of becoming a permanent one,] and just when you ready to get situated, it's snatched. It's a constant struggle, lots of downs and little up."[139] Randall expressed hope that his efforts would land him a legal long-term job; he was able to secure short-term temporary jobs, but then his hopes would be dashed when he would be laid off because of a background check, and he would have to start his job search all over again, going to job interviews and leaving dejected, understanding that he would not get a call-back because of his felony. "All of this is hard. There aren't too many [employers] hiring people like me."[140]

The inability to secure legal employment results in a type of pressure that some find unbearable; with no job, the likelihood of being sent back to prison increases exponentially as parole hangs getting a job over one's head like a guillotine. Before breaking under the pressure, most participants kept their negative thoughts to themselves, but eventually someone would ask in Group, "How we suppose to make it?"[141] There is not a satisfactory answer to this question; instead, participants came face to face with their reality and the consequences of committing future crimes.

Some participants, frustrated by their inability to find a job, tired of the rejection, hungry, homeless, denied public benefits, and socially disabled by their felony conviction, would step up to the precipice and then back off while praying for what seemed like a miracle. Other participants talked of the pressure being applied by parole to get a job or family members voicing their own frustration about carrying them financially; this combination merged to form a critical juncture when a decision had to be made: Stay struggling or find another way.

Xavier expressed his sense of inadequacy:

> People go back to what they do because they can't get no job but need to eat and got bills to pay. End up back and forth, in and out [of prison], it's

hard. Reality faces you, you get over the wall [prison], put it in your rear view [mirror], leave it all behind but it's hard out here.[142]

Xavier had struggled since returning home, and continues to face challenges, so the longer his struggle extended into the future, the more likely it was that going back to crime, and then prison, would become his reality. He was not alone.

The consequences of returning to the streets were easy to calculate: more prison time and disappointing people whom they loved and who loved them. During my time in the field, I was introduced to family members who stopped by the nonprofit and would stay for fifteen or twenty minutes, sometimes longer. Family members brought food, shared family stories, and introduced kids born while the participant was incarcerated. These types of exchanges provided a good reason for participants to avoid hustling or banging, and getting sent back to prison. Experiencing family love made the struggle to stay out of prison worth it, but love does not pay the bills or vanquish a felony conviction.

Not a single participant wanted to go back to prison, but under some circumstances illegal activities may be the only viable way to put cash in one's pocket to pay rent and buy food. Many participants were at their wit's end, feeling the pressure of parole closing in as they were repeatedly rejected for jobs, while the streets were beckoning them back to the "easy money." Paula explained how easy it would be: "To do wrong, it's one phone call away. I can call somebody right now and be back doing the do [selling drugs]." Paula knew that if she did not find legal employment sooner rather than later, selling drugs was a viable option to secure an income to take care of her kids, buy food, and keep a roof over their heads.[143]

Selling drugs or going back to a life of crime was not each participant's first choice; most wanted to successfully reenter. Many did not want to go back to hustling for a distinct reason: "It's dangerous getting shot at, and shooting at randoms [random people] will get you more time."[144] Instead of going back to the streets, participants thought of how to get around the socially disabling effects of a felony conviction as it related to a criminal history background check and good character test. So, prior to making *that* phone call to go back to a life of crime, participants discussed the "best" crimes to commit for quick cash and which crimes they could commit without being caught and sent back to prison. One option discussed was to lie on job applications, a calculated risk but also a coping mechanism to secure a legal job. Walter explained his thought process:

> I just want to work. I've always had a job. I'm a good worker, so I'll be able to find a job. Keeping it, well, maybe that's something else, but not 'cuz something I do, it's 'cuz everyone be checking [conducting a background check]. It's all that I'm doing now [is looking for work]. I can't go back [to prison]. I ain't got another bid in me. That would take too much out of me. [Being inside] made me appreciate stuff [on the outside]. I got like eight grandkids and I pick some of them up from school now and we hang out. That's what I do now, but I need to work, too. Work will make things better. Look, I've always worked. But having that record, they don't want to hire someone like me, and I got work experience, and they still don't want to hire me. They want to hire someone without a charge. What does that tell me? That I'm not checking that box no more. Ain't worked since October [2012; Walter sat down for an interview in February 2013]. I'm not checking the box no more and I got some interviews coming up. I'm lying. Straight out. If they don't run a [criminal history background] check, that's on them. I'm not telling them nothing. They can find out on their own, but I'm not telling 'em.[145]

Walter knew the importance of finding legal work, and the best way to overcome the socially disabling effects of a felony:

> So, when I am doing applications it will ask you on there, "Have you been convicted of a felony and is it alright for a background check?" And, well, before I never said yes, always no, and I would work, but that was before the computers got so good and so advanced as they are right now, catching up to you; now, you can't get away with those little lies.[146]

Many job applications contain a question to screen out felons: "Have you ever been arrested or convicted of a crime?" This question about a conviction is found on application forms for everything from entry-level jobs to management and other professional positions across industries and is used by a wide assortment of public and private organizations and companies. Criminal screening laws allow employers to ask applicants about their criminal history at the time of application, meaning that felons are weeded out prior to the job interview. Recent campaign efforts "to ban the box"—that is, to ban the problematic question about past convictions from all job applications—have been effective in forty-five cities and seven states, and the Equal Employment Opportunity Commission (EEOC) is prosecuting employers who use a felony conviction as a blanket denial when making hiring decisions.[147] Changing past employment practices is a slow process, however, and some cities and companies continue to use discriminatory practices to deny job applicants on the basis of a past felony conviction.[148] Participants knew that the criminal background check was going to be a problem, so they talked about ways to get around the initial screening process. Participants decided that when the question about a past felony was on a job application, they would lie: "Lying works [to get a job], and it's a chance you have to take. You getting sent back [to prison by parole] for not having a job, so lying is a small thing to prevent that from happening."[149]

The decision to check the box "no" during the application process had the desired outcome; participants got hired:

> Saying no, I'm not a felon, and doing that so you know, you can start working, and you work for a little while, a few weeks maybe, until the system catches up to you, and maybe the system doesn't ever catch you, so you just keep on working. Maybe that's possible, but now that's less possible. I mean, I went to apply for a job and tell 'em [that I have a felony], which I know that with my background I wasn't ever going to get the job, so I figure by the time I filled in the forms [the application], and handed it in, get hired, I could work some. Put some money in my pocket, you know.[150]

Many knew that lying on one's job application is not the best option, but "a man needs money to live, no one can live without money, and I ain't going back [to prison], so I'm doing what I need to do, skirt the law by not doing something worse."[151] Walter encapsulated participants' thinking on the "felony conviction box" on job applications:

> I got a felony, I got a record, been to prison. I don't tell them what I did. What matters, should matter, you know, is what I'm doing now. I check

the [yes] box, and no calls. Nothing. And then I started putting "no" on the applications, not checking that box, and everything changes. I get calls for food service jobs I applied for. I get to the interview and I'm honest. I did time. I give no details on what I did. It's what I'm doing now that matters. I volunteer at a church. I don't really volunteer, though, but I don't have a choice, I gotta lie, make myself look good, so I tell them what they want to hear, and I know how to talk about my reentry. I sometimes get hired, and they get me later [background check], sometimes not, and I work when they don't.[152]

In effect, participants would rather lie on a job application and skirt employment laws than revert back to their criminal ways because the latter would probably lead back to prison. Participants said they would revert to their former criminal behavior only after trying to get a job the legitimate way, like after the hundredth job application goes unanswered. As one participant put it, "Lying [on an application] seems like the best option out of a lot of bad ones."[153]

Randall was more practical about his approach to lying on job applications: "Switch Social Security numbers, get a new identity, you know, it's really all that would work. Because I need to be someone else. Being me, well . . ."[154] Randall's voice trailed off into silence.

Tyrone quickly pointed out the problem with the type of identity theft proposed by Randall: "Can't report that income to parole because it's not you. That will send you back [to prison]."

"Yeah, I know," Randall snapped.

D'Shawn responded, "Lying. That's it. Better than stealing someone's identity, and you never know who has a clean record. Wouldn't that be fucked up? You get a stolen identity and that name has a jacket." Laughter ensued over the comical set of errors that could unfold: "Could you imagine, maybe your jacket is better?" More laughter.[155]

When participants are socially disabled and unable to secure legal employment after making legitimate attempts, they feel as though they have a right to do what is necessary to secure legal employment. "They [the government] is keeping us down. We served our time, paid our debt, so, what am I going to do? Lie on my application, that's what."[156]

Participants knew that despite their past illegal behavior, they needed to work to earn a paycheck and to resist their former criminal ways in

order to avoid going back to prison, and since no one wanted that return, lying on an application seemed like the best option. Participants'
decisions to lie on a job application, I believe, is a logical response to
socially disabling laws that make it easy for employers to run a criminal
background check and not hire a convicted felon. Moreover, in the collective experience of participants, no one had been arrested for lying on
a job application. They were fired, but never sent back to prison.

Participants felt that the legal rules required calculated misbehavior
to increase their ability to remain legally in the community. The combination of a felony conviction, criminal background check, occupational
licensing restrictions, good character tests, and other disqualifying tools
that dissuade employers from hiring a felon signals to felons that they
are not able to legally work. This is the crux of the challenge for participants as it pertains to the socially disabling effects of a felony and
the difficulty in securing a legal job; legal employment decreases the
propensity to return to a life of crime, but politically created policies
increase the likelihood of former prisoners going back to crime because
there are few legal options to getting a job. The result is high rates of unemployment, persistent financial struggles, food insecurity, and homelessness, and in some instances, the inability to secure a legal job *will*
divert some desperate individuals back to a life of crime to resolve their
financial needs.[157] Some participants, after trying to get a legal job, reasoned that crime pays more and pays faster than any legal job available
to an unskilled and uneducated worker.[158]

Scholars and practitioners argue that employment is the *critical* component that leads to desistance from crime[159] and the *number one factor*
that reduces recidivism.[160] A wide variety of employment opportunities
would reduce the overall recidivism rate,[161] but exclusionary laws that
treat all felony convictions as a proxy for unworthiness to be employed
will keep recidivism rates high. This potential labor force is highly variable, but the pervasive legal restrictions preventing felons from securing employment reinforce their inferior status, and their felony becomes
the socially disabling restriction that far outweighs the original penal
punishment handed down by the courts. The collective process of un-
dermining the efforts of individuals convicted of a felony to work at a
legal job undermines successful reentry,[162] which begs the question, At
what point are felons allowed to work? When, if ever, is a second chance

granted to those who have been released from prison? Employment restrictions call into question the value society places on justice, punishment, and the opportunity to reenter. When social conditions are such that felons have to make terrible choices between what their conscience tells them they should do and the necessity to survive, what should they do? What would you do?

Conclusion

Public Hostility

It's like they want me to fail [at reentry]. If I fuck up in any
way, I go back [to prison] to rot. If I do wrong [and violate
parole], I go back. If I do what I need to, what I know, to get
myself reestablished, you know, to eat regular like and get a
place [to live], I get sent down state [and locked back up];
but if I do right [comply with the law] I ain't got shit. We
fucked if we good or bad, we fucked both ways.
—Field Notes, January 30, 2013

Once one is caught in the web of the criminal justice system, Socrates
explains, the biggest hurdle is the felony conviction itself: "It's all about
the charge; no one cares about anything else."[1] As convicted felons, when
participants were released from a local jail or state or federal prison,
the vast majority of them struggled to secure housing, and the lack of
available options meant they experienced varying degrees of homelessness. Without a place to call home, participants had to make decisions
based on what was realistically possible; many quickly grasped that
regardless of their level of interest in enrolling in an educational or
vocational program, going to school was impractical due to their being
denied Pell grants, not having the financial resources to pay for necessary expenses, and lacking the proficiency in writing and reading skills
required to be successful. Before being able to look for a job, participants
had four strikes against them: they were uneducated, homeless, poor,
and convicted felons. With this as a foundation upon which to reenter
society, all of the participants experienced varying degrees of unemployment because they could not pass a criminal history background check.
The inability to secure legal employment was the toughest obstacle to
overcome because without a continuous legal source of income, it is

impossible to find a place to live and pay rent and focus on overcoming the socially disabling effects of a felony conviction.

In the opening chapter, I posed several pertinent questions about the purpose of a felony conviction, and they all focused on one issue: Are felons ever allowed to serve their time, pay their debt, *and* reenter society without the public's hostility shadowing them? The answer to this question for most felons is no, which necessitates asking, What social good or public aim is served by the permanent stigma of a felony conviction? What is achieved by socially disabling felons after they have completed their court-mandated sentence? The answer to these questions is that a felony conviction has many "useful" political and social "benefits" for anyone not convicted of a felony.

Historically, punishment was intended to be degrading and humiliating so that the individual and the family were exposed to public derision.[2] Today, the same practice is continued by foisting the word "felon" permanently onto millions of bodies. A felony conviction maintains a division between "us" and "them," and the insidious discourse across different time periods has created two separate groups within society; one group is viewed as respected, contributing members of society, and the other group is regarded as having no value. The negative externalities of a felony conviction restrict felons from accessing critical public assistance and entering the legal work force. It is a powerful contemporary tool that fuses distinct social-economic institutions, such as housing, education, and employment, to the criminal justice system. A felony conviction is a simple short-cut that widens the net of policies, maintains the broader social system of white supremacy, supports "tough on crime" politicians, determines an individual's worth as he or she reenters society, operates as a long-term form of punishment, and engenders failure in the returning prison population. This research demonstrates the excessive character of a felony conviction, which validates the willingness of the legal and political systems to socially disable anyone convicted of a felony. In essence, a felony conviction ensures high recidivism rates so that there are bodies available to be incarcerated.

When one examines the lived experiences of men and women reentering society with a felony conviction, retribution seems to be the only justification for post-punishment penalties. Yet, retributive policies have created an illusionary sense of balance. Retributive theories presume that when a crime is committed, the social equilibrium is thrown out of balance, and punishment is designed to restore the balance by holding the criminal accountable by having them pay a debt to society.[3] A prison sentence has become the official governmental response to the lawless nature of offenders, and the current system is out of balance because its retributive focus extends punishment beyond the original sentence and the reach of the criminal justice system. Upon exiting prison, the burden to reenter is placed on the individual, who is unable to access public benefits; these policies are wrapped in the political language of being "tough on crime" and strongly suggest that politicians are more concerned with retribution than with other societal or community objectives. The larger significance of this study is that a felony conviction is an effective tool with which to prevent offenders from fully reentering and participating in society, and policies and administrative regulations that use a felony conviction to deny benefits are anti-felon and pro-punishment, which have made yesteryear's felons today's contemporary outlaws.

The process of releasing prisoners and blaming them for their inability to reenter is dishonest; the failure to reenter society reinforces cultural norms, bolsters politicians' call for more "tough on crime" legislation, and allows for excessive punishment to be inflicted upon "others" who have already been sentenced.[4] Politicians can rationalize and pass "tough on crime" policies because there is "no powerful constituency [that] will be affronted," so politicians compete on who can be the "toughest" to avoid the label of being "soft on crime."[5] Participants knew that people in power rarely, if ever, think about *after* prison: "I did my time for my wrong, but now what? That's all I think about, now what the fuck do I do? Ain't no one with any kinda power thinks about after they lock us up. No one."[6]

Politicians have the ability and power, if they wanted to, to reduce, or even eliminate, the most egregious social disabilities of a felony conviction. This would be possible with targeted policy changes that would require a fundamental modification in the politics of punishment, such as elected officials reforming sentencing laws *and* taking prisoner reentry seriously by investing in educational opportunities inside prison and employment prospects for felons living in the community. But, politicians fear being tagged as "soft on crime." Michael Dukakis's experience in the 1988 presidential election is *the* example of why politicians step lightly when thinking about changing "tough on crime" laws, for the "Willie Horton-izing" of crime politics has not diminished. Although there have been some recent preliminary bipartisan efforts to reform the criminal justice system at the state and federal levels, those efforts are fragile; despite consensus on the human and financial costs of locking up so many people without a measurable increase in public safety, the discussions are tenuous because the same dynamics of being "soft on crime" that were present in 1988 are still present today. So, politicians pass criminal justice policies that emphasize harsh penalties while arguing that such policies are needed to protect the public's safety. But do they protect society? There is no definitive study on whether the cumulative effect of long criminal sentences, exclusionary statutes, and socially disabling laws protect the public's safety; rather, what we do know from the reentry narratives of participants is that policies preventing convicted felons from accessing public housing and educational and employment opportunities lead to negative outcomes.

The Importance of Narratives

Using first-person accounts, this book sheds light on why men and women convicted of a felony struggle to reenter, how the public's hostility is embedded in laws, in what way a felony operates as a petite penal institution, and by what means a felony *changes* individuals and the law *transforms* them into contemporary outlaws. The discourse of illegality surrounding a felony conviction remains as a permanent characteristic affixed to a person's public record, and as a result individual men and women are stigmatized and set up to fail. Personal narratives, coupled with the policy analysis, fill in critical gaps about reentry, and expands our understanding of why reentering society is so challenging; moreover, the policy-focused inquiry reveals how the mark of criminality becomes an extra-legal designation that converts felons into a permanent inferior class and denies them a host of societal opportunities.

Framing participants' narratives within social disability theory provides an important framework within which to question public policies, draws attention to the political choices that impact individuals convicted of a felony, and develops new insights about prisoner reentry. A felon is "disabled" by his or her conviction, and socially constructed barriers ensure that they remain impaired. The application of social disability theory to prisoner reentry exposes some of the societal costs of socially disabling individuals convicted of a felony, and illustrates how the negative externalities connected to a felon's body are due to the historical constructions attached to blackness and centuries of political investment in punishing criminal bodies. My approach extends social disability theory to a felony conviction by confronting the types of oppression individuals convicted of a felony experience, and by showing how policies prevent felons from being able to improve the quality of their lives. Participants' narratives reinforce our understanding of how policies make the theoretical notion of social disability a tangible, felt experience, and reveal why it is so difficult to follow a linear reentry path: The real world of reentry is messy, consisting of stops, starts, and wrong turns, including returning to the scene of participants' crime, which can evoke memories of when the police shackled them and took them away, and of the prison door slamming shut behind them, which can cause PTSD-like symptoms. The application of social disability theory via a felony conviction also helps to expose how societal decisions, rooted in tradition and driven by racial bias, marginalize an identifiable group to create a socially constructed reality for individuals convicted of a felony.

The data I collected over the course of twenty-nine months in the field illustrates how reentry has changed over time and in what way it is an individual struggle. Convicted felons exist in a socially engineered environment where public attitudes support restricting the social rights of felons through isolation and exclusion. The extent of the exclusion varies, and while participants had diverse experiences returning home, and responded to hostile policies in different ways, the ethnographic data exposed behaviors that had a causal logic to them (e.g., lying in order to work); how some decisions were antithetical to what experts call for (e.g., not going to school); and how the act of being homeless was the norm (e.g., speculative thinking by a system that assumes family will provide housing is factually wrong in many instances). Narratives explain how and why individuals fail at reentry, and how socially disabling policies attached to a felony conviction punish individuals beyond their original criminal sentence. By integrating individual data with a historical, policy, and racial analysis, *Convicted and Condemned* expands our understanding of the complex human concerns that are central to what it means to be a convicted felon.

Personal narratives uncover how adverse outcomes are virtually guaranteed. By exposing the culture of reentry that encapsulates negative assumptions, instills the belief that a future arrest is inevitable, and presupposes failure, the narratives describe a cloud of doubt under which participants struggled to overcome the layers of administrative rules hidden in legislative language. By making a felony conviction its own petite penal institution, the vast set of contrary policies captures and treats murderers and drug addicts, arsonists and bank robbers, bad check writers and drug dealers, thieves and carjackers, and anyone convicted of conspiracy, robbery, or aggravated assault, alike. The label "felon" is an unchanging attribute that does not distinguish between different types of crimes or individual offenders, and does not take into consideration evidence of rehabilitation, despite the fact that all convicted felons are not the same and are convicted in individual trials. Instead, hostile policies treat all felons as one distinct subcategory deemed unfit to rejoin society.[7]

Felons' voices reinforce how policies' negative implications bound them to a set of spaces that delegitimize them from becoming legal actors in society, and make clear that the state's purpose is grounded in the politics of punishment. Participants were unable to get out from under the shadow of their felony to earn a lawful job, even after they had made legitimate and lasting changes in their lives. Many participants' lives became organized around their status as a felon, which shapes the way society responds to them and the way they respond to society, creating an all-consuming identity that is denied "everything that's good."[8] Participants felt society's hostility, and knew they were unwanted, so they engaged in illegal and legal options while hoping they didn't get sent back to prison as they waited for something good to happen.[9]

One underlying theme in the midst of the reentry narrative is that of survival. The survival narrative tells of how participants survived prison, are trying to survive reentry, and are looking for ways to survive the label "felon," exposing what it means to be thought of as a menace: "We the problem, and that's always going to be a problem 'cuz the system is designed to start chaos, and we the chaos they tryin' to put down and control."[10]

Failing at Reentry

"Tough on crime" political rhetoric operates as a social force to construct an "ideal criminal" and "felon monster," and that "understanding"
is translated into public policies. Such punitive policies teach prisoners
"how to jail" and "not go crazy,"[11] and communicate upon their return
to society that they are "nothing."[12] There is no expiration date on the
socially disabling laws imposed on a felon, and the current impact of
hostile policies is so acute that bad reentry outcomes are almost certain;
the recidivism rate has remained around 67 percent for four decades.[13]
If approximately 33 percent of released prisoners are not rearrested,
reconvicted, and reimprisoned, then the majority of former prisoners
recidivate, which means that a failure to reenter is "normal." Yet, the goal
of reentry should be to remove societal barriers and promote opportunities for individuals to build a crime-free life. Instead, one of the key
findings of this study is that policies use a felony conviction to undermine reentry via a felony conviction.

It is fundamentally challenging to reenter because the process is not
coordinated by any one agency or government department, and there
is no ritual of reintegration or formal procedure to help felons reengi-
neer themselves in such a way as to neutralize the debasing effects of a
felony conviction.[14] The lack of rehabilitation programs and integration
resources means that individuals reentering society are principally responsible for their own reentry. This is critical: as long as society looks
at felons as solely responsible for their reentry success, as being to blame
for failing to reenter, and as long as experts rely on an individual deficit
model to explain reentry,[15] society does not have to confront the hard
truth that reentry is basically a myth and a hoax.[16] When individual reliance is coupled with hostile policies, such policies contribute to the cycle
of recidivism; men and women are unable to reenter because the system
sets them up to fail.[17] Participants were unable to separate themselves
from their criminal status due to the insidious nature of a felony conviction outside of the criminal justice system.

The specific reasons why individuals fail at reentry are many, but one
participant described it this way: "Ain't no rehabilitation going on. [The
Department of] 'Corrections' ain't correcting nothing"[18]—because they
were sitting in prison doing nothing but "fighting and shit."[19] Partici-

pants knew that rehabilitation was not an integral part of their prison time, but the fact is that rehabilitation stopped being a basic part of the criminal justice system and prison programs a long time ago.[20] Once rehabilitation was deemed ineffective by experts, it was easy for politicians to cut programs inside prison and incarcerate more people under mandatory minimum sentences. The punitive rhetoric was then extended to reentry and reintegration programs. Reentry programs' budgets are slim, and the possibility of rehabilitation is rarely considered; instead, the politics of punishment and fear of blackness has created a "perfect storm."[21]

The perfect storm of hostile political rhetoric and related policies, a lack of funding, and the fear of blackness and all felons has created an environment that reinforces felons' social disadvantage, which is evident in high recidivism rates. Without access to public resources, participants are kept "down and out" and their identity as felons tends to overwhelm their efforts to become someone else.[22] The lived experience of participants demonstrates how they have to learn how to manage their "double direction"[23] of being nominally "free" but still ensnared by their past. They feel rejected by society, and are never given an opportunity to prove their worth after the completion of their sentence, which is a similar phenomenon to that of free blacks having to prove they were not slaves prior to the Civil War. Black exclusion has been a constant form of social control throughout American history,[24] and although not all felons are black, given that most prisoners in New Jersey and other states are black, the criminal justice system has reconstructed the color line.[25]

Reestablishing the Color Line

People of color are disproportionately affected by the criminal justice system, which has made a felony conviction a new form of racial discrimination.[26] The negative outcomes have created a color line that increasingly divides Americans who feel the weight of the criminal justice system from those who are insulated from its harsh penalties.[27] "Justice" is hard to achieve when racial bias exists at every stage of the criminal justice system, but most whites view the criminal justice system as fair, just, and impartial.

When hostile policies targeting felons are interpreted through a racial lens, the corollary contemporary effects of a felony cannot be disconnected from the vestiges of past practices, such as the shadow of the country's troubling historical and political discourse concerning slavery, race relations, racialized criminal laws, and policing. Today, instead of slave patrols and night watches, the police survey and attempt to control minority communities.[28] Historically, whites have maintained their status in society by utilizing the criminal justice system to impose punishment upon black bodies, and have ensured that justice and equality are *not* for all. Instead, racial animus is buttressed through "tough on crime" policies and politics,[29] and a felony conviction represents the structural investment that enforces a form of pervasive discrimination that maintains the color line.[30]

Racial animosity, an integral part of the criminal justice system, can only be tackled if it is addressed; hiding from it will accomplish nothing.[31] One specific example of the way the criminal justice system is racially discriminatory is the "War on Drugs," which has captured and incarcerated a disproportionate number of black men and women even though whites are the overall majority of the U.S. population at approximately 72 percent, and use drugs at the same rate.[32] The "War on Drugs" upholds racial disparities, as is evidenced by the fact that black males are imprisoned at higher rates across all age groups and races,[33] and this was evident every day in the field. The vast majority of participants and clients at the nonprofit organization were black.

The racial disparities with respect to who is incarcerated and who is released from prison mean that the negative effects of the system are felt predominantly in black communities; by social design, black communities are marginalized, and have been transformed into a venue for profit and punishment:[34] Millions of public dollars are used to militarize local police with weaponry more suitable to a war zone[35] to police black communities. Modern-day police tactics, like yesteryear's slave patrols, attempt to maintain the social order and protect property. Within this current environment of militarized policing, white fear of black men, criminal punishment, and public stigma are evident on the streets of most major U.S. cities.[36] The racial divide around crime and policing are explosive points of tension,[37] and recent police shootings and the acquittal of white officers indicted for killing black men and women have exposed the racial divide and fear of black skin in ugly ways.

As I write this conclusion, people are chanting #BlackLivesMatter, "Hands Up, Don't Shoot," and "I Can't Breathe" in civil protests across the country over the rapid escalation of situations in which police officers, within seconds of encountering unarmed black men and women, teenagers and children, employ lethal force. In effect, the police are operating as judge, jury, and executioner. Some examples in which protesters are calling attention to the killing of unarmed black men and women by the police include the following. In Tulsa, Oklahoma, Terence Crutcher, unarmed, was shot and killed by a white female officer, who was charged with manslaughter.[38] In Baton Rouge, Louisiana, Alton Sterling was killed by the police in the parking lot of a convenience store while he was selling CDs, and a few days later Philando Castile was shot to death in his car in Falcon Heights, Minnesota, a suburb of St. Paul. In Cleveland, Ohio, police shot 137 bullets into an occupied car, killing Timothy Russell and Malissa Williams, both unarmed.[39] In November 2014, there were two incidents within days of each other: an officer, seconds after exiting a police cruiser, shot and killed twelve-year-old Tamir Rice for playing with a toy gun at a park; and Tanisha Anderson died of positional asphyxiation while in police custody (her death was ruled a homicide).[40] In Baltimore, Maryland, Freddie Gray suffered a broken neck while in police custody, and died a week later.[41] In North Charleston, South Carolina, Walter Scott was shot by a white officer eight times in the back and died at the scene.[42] In Ferguson, Missouri, eighteen-year-old Michael Brown was killed by an officer and his body was left on display for several hours in the August sun. In New York City, Eric Garner was put in an illegal death chokehold by an officer for having sold loose cigarettes.[43] In Bastrop, Texas, Yvette Smith, unarmed, was shot by a county sheriff's deputy while following police orders to come out of her house. In Chicago, Rekia Boyd was shot in the back of the head by a white police detective.[44] In Dayton, Ohio, an open carry state, John Crawford III was shot and killed by white officers in a Wal-Mart while holding a gun Wal-Mart sold and talking on his cell phone.

This is just a fraction of known racially charged incidents, as there are many more cases in which unarmed black men and women are killed needlessly or for misdemeanor noncapital crimes, but these examples are evidence of racial animus, suspicion of blackness, and police practices targeting black bodies. I think that the overpolicing of black communities is intertwined with the racial effects of the criminal justice system, the "War on Drugs," the socially disabling effects of laws, and "tough on crime" police tactics and politics. In American cities across the country, the police operate as an occupying force pointing military-grade weapons at urban residents in a show of force that sends the message that the police are at war against economically and politically disenfranchised black residents.[45] In minority neighborhoods, the police incessantly pursue residents for petty infractions but do not do the same in white communities.[46] Such tactics and actions have a racial edge.

The shooting of unarmed black men, women, and children has increased black Americans' fear of the police, while the police's right to shoot and kill is reinforced, especially if they say, "I feared for my life." The language of fear is seen in Darren Wilson's grand jury testimony describing Michael Brown as having "the most intense aggressive face. The only way I can describe it, it looks like a demon." Calling Michael Brown an "it" and a "demon" is the language of fear, and became Wilson's justification for shooting Michael Brown. If trained police officers see a black body and shoot without consequence, that fear can be used as justification for others to shoot and kill black people. George Zimmerman fatally shot Trayvon Martin because Trayvon looked "suspicious."

The politics of fear and the language of black skin as suspicious have given the police, and others, a potent defense and "right" to be exempt from punishment for actions that take the lives of unarmed black men, women, and children. This mindset echoes historical policies focused on racial control. The language of fear is not new; in a dialogue about blackness and criminality, the language of fear makes felons easy political targets to dismiss as illegitimate actors and validates the political investment in passing "tough on crime" policies. Such laws include the Omnibus Crime Bill of 1984, the Anti–Drug Abuse Act of 1988, the Brady Handgun Violence Prevention Act of 1993, the Violent Crime Control and Law Enforcement Act of 1994, the Personal Responsibility and Work Opportunity Reconciliation Act (PRWORA), the Temporary Assistance to Needy Families (TANF) in 1996, the National Instant Criminal Background Check System (NICS) in 1998, and other federal and state laws. These net-widening policies target felons for exclusion.

What Can Be Done to Change Reentry?

Former prisoners who reenter society in cities like Newark, New Jersey, are greeted with the message that they are unwanted. Participants knew society was going to be unwelcoming, but societal disgust has the effect of defeating them before they even get started: "We nothing."[47] The political and social messages connected to a felony conviction mean that it functions as a form of "social dirt"[48] to fashion an unnatural legislated state of existence:[49] While in the field, I felt as though I was watching a displaced people acquaint themselves with a strange society.

If the existing socially disabling policies and the systems that enforce them are left unchanged, felons will continue to fail at reentry because socially disabling policies are not producing positive reentry outcomes; rather, the system maintains high recidivism rates. The adverse results when one is unable to reenter will continue to be felt chiefly in minority communities. Socially disabling laws do not boost public safety, improve societal well-being, decrease poverty, or improve communities experiencing institutional abandonment. The entrenched disablements undermine reentry, and the negative effects ripple across the community, but it does not have to be this way. Policies can be changed and structured to make successful reentry the objective rather than an exception.

Political efforts to change the system and decrease the lifetime consequences of a felony conviction are necessary, but to change negative reentry outcomes, there must be an accessible way to remove the label "felon" from one's public record. If that is not changed, then each law that prevents felons from accessing public benefits, including public housing and the legal job market, would need to be reformed. The current political and legislative climate makes this unrealistic: criminal justice policies—punishment and sentencing decisions that label individuals as felons—are principally a state issue, and asking each state legislature to conduct a holistic review of its policies with an eye towards transforming them to assist former prisoners reenter is naïve. However, politicians from both political parties across the country have recently called for criminal justice reform and seem to be coalescing around reforming sentencing for nonviolent drug offenders in an effort to reduce incarceration rates; codifying changes in the way the criminal justice system punishes crack versus powder cocaine;[50] and decreasing the use of long prison sentences for most offenders. The call for reform is *just* political talk to date, but if these changes become statutes and are fully funded and implemented, then the new laws would be a step in the right direction. Yet, sentencing reform efforts are the low-hanging fruit in any discussion about overall criminal justice reform.

Sentencing reform *only* addresses the front end of the system, such as the amount of time spent in prison. Shorter sentences would be beneficial for the mental and physical well-being of the hundreds of thousands of individuals who are incarcerated for felonious offenses, and reducing incarceration rates and changing the way society punishes criminals are important goals, but these changes leave in place a felony conviction. The policy chapters analyzed the back end of the criminal justice system and brought into focus the unsystematic mix of countless laws that target participants and those similarly situated. When the laws are examined inclusively, it becomes obvious that any serious reform efforts must *concurrently* address both the front end of the system—policing, arrest, conviction, and sentencing—and the socially disabling hostile policies at the back end of the system.[51] Changing back-end policies in tandem with reducing the prison population could be possible with a "one and done law" rather than political wrangling over separate bills that could be amended in nefarious ways, terminated in committee or voted down in a floor vote, or vetoed by a governor or president. The only effective way to topple current socially disabling laws is to create substantive policy changes that offer a realistic option for every person convicted of a felony to expunge and remove the felony label permanently from his or her public record.[52] If a felony label is removed, and former prisoners are able to exit the criminal justice system completely, then it would be possible to reduce the effect of hostile back-end policies that currently undermine reentry.

Any monies saved from reforming the criminal justice system, including reducing the incarceration rate, should be directed towards benefits that build social capital, including accredited educational programs inside prison, and toward linking those programs to vocational training and real jobs outside of prison. Such programs existed in the past, and study after study demonstrates the need for employment in order for a former prisoner to succeed at reentry; to secure employment, education is required, and therefore, these two areas should be the main focuses of any new program initiatives inside prison. If jobs and education were combined with stable housing, reentry outcomes would probably improve beyond 33 percent. But, without a concerted effort to remove the "felon" label, job training and educational programs will be for naught, as punishment would continue to be endless. The political challenge is how to reform a system so as to allow felons to exit it and become emancipated from their conviction.

One possibility for reform was introduced by Senator Rand Paul on July 8, 2014, and was reintroduced by Senators Rand Paul and Corey Booker on March 9, 2015. The Record Expungement Designed to Enhance Employment Act, or the REDEEM Act, aims to amend the federal criminal code to give nonviolent and juvenile offenders the opportunity to seal or expunge their criminal records.[53] The REDEEM Act also proposed amending the Personal Responsibility and Work Opportunity Reconciliation Act of 1996 (PRWORA) to allow individuals charged with nonviolent crimes, such as drug possession, use of a controlled substance, or distribution in part due to drug addiction, to be eligible for public assistance, including lifting of the lifetime ban of many drug offenders from receiving benefits under the Supplemental Nutrition Assistance Program (SNAP, food stamps) and Temporary Assistance For Needy Families (TANF, welfare). The REDEEM Act is a politically safe start; unfortunately, it does not address state-level convictions, which are the most numerous, and only applies to covered federal nonviolent offenses, which means the list of exceptions on who is *ineligible* for benefits is long—violent and/or repeat offenders, members of organized crime syndicates, and terrorists. Thus, the eligible pool of former offenders is negligible.

The terrorism category is particularly problematic. The legal definition of "terrorism" in New Jersey constitutes someone making a threat during a domestic dispute, threatening violence that causes public inconvenience, posing a threat that the victim believes is immediate (e.g., bullying and cyberbullying), having an argument with an angry spouse while going through a bitter custody dispute, or making speech-based threats that include the intent to terrorize, harm, or intimidate.[54] Similar terrorist-threat laws were passed in most states post-9/11, and have expanded so much that they capture almost anyone who gets into an angry argument. Several participants served time in state prison for being found guilty of making a threat deemed terroristic in nature; otherwise, they have nonviolent drug convictions, but due to the terroristic threat conviction, they would be ineligible for benefits under the REDEEM Act. However, politicians making any start to reform the system have to be encouraged, especially if the ultimate goal is to reduce the negative effects of incarceration and a felony conviction.

In another effort to reduce new crimes *and* recidivism rates, the Obama administration's Department of Education (DOE) was pursuing efforts to undo the 1994 amendments to the crime bill that eliminated Pell grant eligibility for state and federal prisoners. In what is called the Second Chance Pell Pilot Program, DOE is testing new models to allow incarcerated students to receive Pell grants and pursue post-secondary education programs and vocational certificates. A 2013 RAND Corporation study demonstrated that individuals who participated in correctional educational programs were 43 percent less likely to recidivate within three years after release than prisoners who did not participate.[55] Under the Pell Pilot Program, prisoners who meet the eligibility requirements and are eligible for release will be able to access Pell grants; approximately twelve thousand prisoners began receiving them during the 2016–2017 academic year. DOE argues that it has the authority to promote education and job training programs for those who are incarcerated in an effort to reduce recidivism rates, and is using a portion of the HEA that allows DOE to conduct pilot programs, but the program has met resistance from Republicans in Congress.[56] Republicans argue that the administration does not have the authority to make prisoners eligible for Pell grants because the HEA, as amended, prohibits prisoners from receiving Pell grants. In an effort to bar the pilot program, Republican representative Chris Collins of New York introduced a bill entitled the "Kids before Cons Act."[57] While the ban on prisoners remains in place until Congress acts, as part of its effort to assist prisoners and reintegrate convicted felons, the Obama administration was attempting to pressure Congress to amend the HEA. As U.S. Department of Labor Secretary Tom Perez has stated, "[Without legislative changes] we're squandering [an] opportunity by not giving people with a criminal record a second chance, [and] many of the people we're trying to help, frankly, didn't have a fair first chance."[58] This debate is fraught with political disputes based on "tough on crime" attitudes and divergent stances on prison programs and prisoner reentry, which means that the debate will continue long after President Obama leaves the White House. The Pell Pilot Program will be contingent upon future administrations supporting DOE's efforts to educate prisoners.

If punishment is intended to have an end date connected to completing one's sentence and if society wants recidivism rates to decline, then these reform efforts and others like them must continue, with or without voters' consent, and be made permanent in the form of statutory changes that allow felons to serve their criminal sentence and then fully exit the system.[59] As the system is currently configured, any reform efforts are important because participants' narratives exposed that they do not trust the system, and expect to get screwed even when "we doing what we suppose to do."[60] Narratives reveal how reentering society has no practical meaning within the criminal justice system because it only focuses on punishment; participants knew they would be incessantly referred to as felons and considered to be criminal. The consequence of increased punishment for all felons is not less recidivism; rather, the exacerbation of post-punishment restrictions ensures that a large number of individuals convicted of a felony end up back in prison because they are hungry, homeless, uneducated, and unable to secure a legal job.

Knowing that one could exit the system completely would change the mindset of participants, and reducing the use of a felony conviction outside of the criminal justice system would give those reentering the hope that they would be able to have a second chance at becoming part of society rather than remaining part of the problem. Second chances seem only to be granted to white, wealthy felons (e.g., Martha Stewart); for poor minority felons, hostile policies only create homelessness, undermine future employment opportunities, and push felons away from school, which makes new criminal activities more likely. The implications of this research demonstrate that current policies set participants up to fail and government agencies and agents cannot rely on former prisoners' families to take care of their loved ones. Although the notion is quaint, it is not practical. "You can't wait for help. I ain't got no family, so it's all me."[61] Participants lacking family support, and with no social capital or public benefits, found it difficult to become "free" to build a noncriminal life because of the institutional constraints embedded in a felony.[62] Society maintains its hostile glare long after the criminal justice system is done with prisoners by shifting power to institutions that implement socially disabling laws that create an inescapable Panopticon.[63] The pejorative nature of the word "felon" marks individuals for life, and so many fail to reenter before they even get started.

Another important implication of this research is that it reveals how and why negative sanctions attached to the denial of public housing, education, and employment are the *key* policy areas that undermine successful reentry. Failing to reenter is a politically spawned phenomenon,[64] and society cannot felonize its way out of hard social challenges. Socially disabling felons is built into public policies, and the surveillance tentacles of the criminal justice system produce inequality, discrimination, and more punishment. Structural inequality, in turn, breeds contempt for the law. The United States has tried to incarcerate its social problems of crime, poverty, and racial animus with punitive brute force, and yet the same problems remain.[65] The solution to fixing prisoner reentry is not more brute force; rather, it is a model that moves away from punishment as an only option and replaces it with a system that is willing to incorporate rehabilitation, reintegration, and second chances.

Like the outlaws of yesteryear, today's felons have acquired what Foucault calls a "history,"[66] and that history has a permanence that lasts long after someone has served his or her time and paid his or her debt to society. The intersection of hostile policies and a felony conviction functions to reproduce punishment and a social hierarchy with felons on the bottom. Hostile policies are not offering a remedy to create a more just society; rather, such policies exercise endless power over marginalized "others."[67] The divide is exacerbated for felons because the implicit and explicit meanings of a felony hold their strength in an uncomplicated dichotomy—felon and nonfelon. The deceptively simple language makes the desired default position, nonfelon, unobtainable, and participants knew that they would not be able to alter this reality.

It is time to deconstruct socially disabling policies and the dominance they hold in felons' lives with the goal of increasing former prisoners' ability to reenter society successfully. Such reform efforts would require breaking from the past and reimagining a future that values justice and fairness; if the system were changed, there would be less contempt for the law from participants, and others like them. There is no justice when laws and policies make a felon socially disabled; when there are few ways to escape the label and become a nonfelon, and it is impossible to prove one is rehabilitated, then contemporary outlaws will demonstrate contempt for the law, and "do what we do to survive."[68] This attitude pervaded the mindset of participants, and if policies do not change, the same attitude will probably cross the minds of the approximately 12,500 prisoners released from prison this week when they realize that reentry is harder than they imagined.

METHODOLOGICAL APPENDIX

TABLE A.1: SUMMARY OF PRISONER FILES

Table A.1 provides a list of the type of information that the DOC and each prison collects about each prisoner. A prisoner's general file is an integral part of the penal system as it relates to managing bodies in each prison and between prisons, but is also used to manage the prisoner's sentence and release date; therefore, it is imperative that the information in each file be correct. The information constitutes the Department of Corrections' perspective about a prisoner, so a prisoner's file forms the basis of how the criminal justice system treats that individual. The data in the file is supposed to ensure that the prisoner is not deprived of rights. Prisoners lose the right of liberty and freedom, but they do not give up all of their constitutional and civil rights when they are imprisoned. The file is one tool to protect individual prisoners' rights so they receive fair and timely access to appropriate legal and medical assistance. The file also ensures that the DOC upholds its legal responsibilities to the prisoner, including reconciling grievances and formal complaints.

In terms of this research, it was important to understand what was in a prisoner's file to show how that information could be used to assist DOC in matching prisoners to appropriate programs. However, as demonstrated by participant narratives, rehabilitation was not a focus of New Jersey's DOC. Instead, prisoner files were used to match each person to a bed at the correct security classification. Yet, the data could help prisoners reenter society. The general file contains information about family and the type of support the prisoner is likely to have upon reentering society. This supports my assertion that when someone is released from prison, the DOC knows whether that person will be homeless on the basis of the prisoner's visitor's log (Has family visited, written letters, put money on their commissary account?); whether that person has earned any educational credits; and whether that person has any work experience applicable to jobs on the outside. The information in a prisoner's general file could be used to improve reentry outcomes rather than just to control the movement of bodies between prisons, determine release date and the date of eligibility for parole, and allocate staff and the delivery of services inside prison. If DOC can use the information to calculate where prisoners are incarcerated, it could use the information to help prisoners reenter successfully.

TABLE A.1: Summary of Prisoner Files

Activity	Information Contained in Prisoner's File
Classification and Placement	· Sex and age of prisoner · Criminal record (arrests and convictions) · Detention · Order of commitment · Security classification · Length of incarceration · Transfers · Prisons · Codefendants
Personal & External Contacts	· Social background · Prisoner contact with family · Notify family members (e.g. death, serious illness, injury, transfer) · External contacts · Legal representative · Personal effects inventory · Religion
Health and Well-Being	· Psychological profile · Mental health · Medical records · Dental records · Medications (prescribed and received) · Dietary requirements
Discipline	· Nature of transgression · Sanction imposed · Complaints and grievances · Prisoner behavior
Gang Involvement	· Gang involvement · Social ties inside
Rehabilitation & Employment	· Needs assessment · Treatment program · Progress reports · Employment details · Earnings (spent and earned)

TABLE A.2: INTERVIEWED PARTICIPANTS AND THEIR
CRIMINAL CHARGES

Table A.2 is a list of the fifty-three participants who were interviewed; they were chosen from the larger client population utilizing the available services at the nonprofit organization, were identified as key participants from the ethnographic fieldwork, and demonstrated knowledge about reentry from different viewpoints.[1] They were selected on an ongoing basis with assistance from staff members. Prior to each in-depth interview, I introduced myself and conducted a brief face-to-face initial meeting that explained the purpose of the interview, laid out my expectations about their time commitment, stressed the voluntary nature of their participation, and emphasized the anonymity of the information they shared with me.[2] If they demonstrated a willingness to be interviewed, we sat in a private office where the interview was conducted. Interviews were semistructured and directed by an IRB-approved interview protocol; however, flexibility was built into the protocol during each interview, which produced dynamic exchanges and added value to understanding the project of a felony conviction.[3]

The age of participants ranged from eighteen to sixty-one at the time of the interview. The average age was forty-three and a half years. Most of the participants who interviewed, twenty, were in their forties (37.7 percent); fourteen participants who were interviewed were in their fifties (26.4 percent); four were in their sixties (7.6 percent); seven participants were in their twenties (13.2 percent); another seven were in their thirties (3.2 percent); and one participant was eighteen years old (1.9 percent).

TABLE A.2: Interviewed Participants and their Criminal Charges

Interviewee Pseudonym (alphabetized)	M/F	Age (at time of interview)	Race	Felony Conviction(s)	Maximum Term of Prison Sentence	Time Served Status at time of Interview	Length of Interview (Hours: Mins)
Alton	M	43	B	Robbery Receiving stolen property Aggravated assault Carjacking (2 counts) Theft, unlawful taking Escape Weapons, unlawful possession	10 Years 5 Years 9 Months 27/26 Years 5 Years 10 Years 5 Years	19 Years, 11 Months Released from South Woods	1:03
Alyssa	F	46	B	CDS—possession		** Out of State	0:29
Bailey	M	48	B	Receiving stolen property CDS manufacture, distribution, dispense Weapons, violation of regulatory provisions	6 Months 20 Years 1 Year, 6 Months	20 Years, 1 Month Released from Rahway	0:28
Bishop	M	41	B	Resisting arrest—eluding police officer CDS possession CDS manufacture, distribute, dispense Distribute drugs on school property	180 Days 1 Day 1 Day 8 Years	4 Years, 2 Months Parole	0:38
Brandon	M	48	B	Burglary	4 Years	2 Years, 3 Months Released from NJ DOC	0:42
Carolyn	F	34	W	Theft by unlawful taking CDS possession	12 Months 3 Years	1 Year Parole	1:08
Chase	M	61	W	Weapons—unlawful possession handgun	5 Years	3 Years, 4 Months Parole	0:25

192

Interviewee Pseudonym (alphabetized)	M/F	Age (at time of interview)	Race	Felony Conviction(s)	Maximum Term of Prison Sentence	Time Served Status at time of Interview	Length of Interview (Hours: Mins)
Craig	M	55	B	Burglary Theft—unlawful taking, disposal of moveable property	10 Years 5 Years	5 Years, 4 Months Parole	0:32
Curtis	M	50	B	Unlawful possession of weapons	12 Months	4 Months	0:38
Darius	M	26	B	Simple assault		*** NJ Charges	0:27
Darren	M	32	L	Threat to kill Weapons possession, defaced firearm Weapons, possession for unlawful purpose Criminal mischief Obstruct administration of law		*** NJ Charges	0:38
Decker	M	34	B	CDS distribute drugs on school property	4 Years	1 Year, 10 Months Parole	0:49
Duncan	M	44	B	CDS manufacture, distribution, dispense	4 Years	1 Year, 10 Months * Federal ** Out of State	0:58
Elton	M	47	L	CDS possession	3 Years	5 Months Parole	0:29
Emmanuel	M	41	B			* Federal	0:18
Gavin	M	50	B	CDS—distribute on school property CDS—manufacture, distribute, dispense	7 years 1 Year	4 Years Parole	0:46
George	M	48	L	Theft, unlawful taking, disposal Burglary	4 Years 3 Years	13 Months Parole	0:49

193

Interviewee Pseudonym (alphabetized)	M/F	Age (at time of interview)	Race	Felony Conviction(s)	Maximum Term of Prison Sentence	Time Served Status at time of Interview	Length of Interview (Hours: Mins)
Hunter	M	49	B	Robbery Resist arrest Weapons	15 Years 4 Years 9 Months	10 Years, 5 Months Parole	0:33
Huxley	M	33	B W NA	Driving while suspended in NJ Possession of a CDS Aggravated assault Weapons/unlawful possession/handgun Weapons/unlawful purpose—firearms		* Federal ** Out of State *** NJ Charges	1:08
Janaye	F	29	B	Aggravated assault Weapons/unlawful possession/handgun	1 Year 1 Year	1 Year Maxed Out	0:22
Jermaine	M	44	L	Aggravated assault CDS distribute on school property CDS distribute	5 Years 5 Years 5 Years	6 Months Released by South- ern State	1:05
Jesus	M	22	B L	Receiving stolen property Resist arrest—elude while operating vehicle Terroristic threats Burglary	4 Years 4 Years 4 Years 4 Years	2 Years, 2 Months Released by North- ern State Prison	0:22
Johnny	M	50	W	CDS possession heroin	5 Years	1 Year, 8 Months Parole	0:13
Jordan	M	29	L	Robbery Resist arrest—elude while operating a vehicle Conspiracy robbery or car jacking	5 Years 6 Years 1 Day	4 Years, 3 Months Released from Southern State	0:35

Interviewee Pseudonym (alphabetized)	M/F	Age (at time of interview)	Race	Felony Conviction(s)	Maximum Term of Prison Sentence	Time Served Status at time of Interview	Length of Interview (Hours: Mins)
Lamar	M	40	B	Weapons/defaced firearms Weapons/unlawful possession of handgun Murder Assault/aggravated	1 Year, 6 Months 5 Years 30 Years 10 Years	15 Years, 1 Month Parole	0:38
LaTonya	F	18	B	Burglary		*** NJ Charges	25
Leon	M	60	B	CDS possession heroin	10 Years	18 Months Parole	1:07
Mahoney	M	22	B	Conspiracy CDS—possession CDS—intent to distribute Possession/distribution within 500 feet of public housing		*** NJ Charges	0:30
Mason	M	58	B			* Federal	1:12
Maurice	M	43	B	CDS—1000 feet from school Wandering		*** NJ Charges	0:59
Max	M	51	B	Robbery	7 Years	4 Years, 3 Months Parole	0:15
Molson	M	35	B	Defiant trespasser Driving on a revoked license CDS possession		*** NJ Charges	0:20
Morgan	M	42	B	Theft by unlawful taking, disposition Robbery Weapons, unlawful possession of firearm	3 Years 6 Years 4 Years	5 Years, 4 Months Released from CURA	0:38

Interviewee Pseudonym (alphabetized)	M/F	Age (at time of interview)	Race	Felony Conviction(s)	Maximum Term of Prison Sentence	Time Served Status at time of Interview	Length of Interview (Hours: Mins)
Nicholas	M	49	W	Robbery	5 Years	4 Years, 11 Months Released from Southern State	0:21
Norton	M	45	B			*** NJ Charges	0:20
Ortiz	M	52	B	CDS distribute drugs on school property	3 Years	18 Months Parole	0:26
Osborn	M	55	B	1978 Atrocious assault/battery Armed robbery 1987 Receiving stolen property 1993 Weapons unlawful possession 1995 Terroristic threats Robbery Burglary—armed	5 Years 5 Years 5 Years 3 Years 10 Years 20 Years 10 Years	5 Years, Maxed out 5 Years 3 Years 3 Years Served: 26 Years, 1 Month Parole	0:45
Pablo	M	51	L	Theft by deception	3 Years	1 Year, 9 Months Parole	0:27
Paxon	M	55	B	Carjacking Weapons possession	15 Years 1 Day	10 Years, 9 Months Parole	0:46
Peace	M	59	B	Assault/aggravated Robbery Weapons/unlawful possession	10 Years LIFE 5 Years	29 Years, 7 Months Parole	0:27

Interviewee Pseudonym (alphabetized)	M/F	Age (at time of interview)	Race	Felony Conviction(s)	Maximum Term of Prison Sentence	Time Served Status at time of Interview	Length of Interview (Hours: Mins)
Rich	M	21	B	Aggravated assault Conspiracy Receiving stolen property Resisting arrest	3 Years 1 Day 4 Years 12 Months	1 Year, 7 Months Parole	0:43
Ryan	M	44	B	CDS distribution on school property	5 Years	2 Years, 2 Months Released from Mid-State Correctional Facility	0:42
Sampson	M	60	B	Robbery—threat of bodily injury CDS possession, use, or being under influence	12 Years 3 Years	9 Years, 4 Months Parole	0:17
Sandi	F	32	B	CDS possession, use, or being under the influence Distribute drugs on school property	1 Year, 6 Months 3 Years	1 Year, 8 Months Parole	0:20
Savannah	F	34	B W O	Robbery	7 Years	5 Years, 10 Months	1:25
Socrates	M	57	B	CDS possession, heroin	5 Years	2 Years, 10 Months	0:23
Stuart	M	44	B	Criminal trespass Unlicensed entry	18 Months 1 Year	11 Months Released from Kintock	0:20
Taye	M	60	B	Manslaughter—aggravated Weapons, possession of firearm	20 Years 7 Years	7 Years Parole	0:30
Tony	M	49	B	Arson, property	* Federal	1:22

197

Interviewee Pseudonym (alphabetized)	M/F	Age (at time of interview)	Race	Felony Conviction(s)	Maximum Term of Prison Sentence	Time Served Status at time of Interview	Length of Interview (Hours: Mins)
Tyrone	M	42	B	Aggravated assault Robbery Weapons, unlawful possession	9 Years, 6 Months, 1 Day 50 Years 4 Years	25 Years, 7 Months Parole	1:36
Van	M	27	B	Possession of a weapon Robbery Unlawful possession of handgun Unlawful purpose—firearms Conspiracy Eluding law enforcement officer—failure to stop		*** NJ Charges	0:53
Walter	M	51	B			*** NJ Charges	1:06
Xavier	M	54	B			*** NJ Charges	0:17

Race   B (Black); L (Latino); W (White); NA (Native American); O (Other), as defined by the Participant

Criminal Charges
(based on archival research)

* Federal Charges; federal face sheets are unavailable to non–law enforcement individuals.

** Out of State Charges; unable to locate records to verify time sentenced and served.

*** NJ Charges; participants' felony conviction was verified verbally by staff, and in these instances I was able to access charging sheets, but was unable to verify their conviction, time sentenced, and time served through archival research. This was probably due to the fact that these participants were charged with a felony but served time in county jail, which has different records access than the New Jersey Department of Corrections.

NOTES

PREFACE AND ACKNOWLEDGMENTS

1   Field Notes, March 28, 2012.

2   Interview with Max on May 30, 2012.

3   Atkinson, 2000, 215.

4   Field Notes, January 30, 2013.

INTRODUCTION

1   A "face sheet" contains an individual's criminal history and administrative infor-
    mation such as legal name, any aliases known to the authorities, birth date, and a
    picture often referred to as a "mug shot." For each conviction, the date, criminal
    code of the charge, and the term of sentence (minimum and maximum) are in-
    cluded. Face sheets vary because law enforcement agencies at the local, state, and
    federal levels compile different types of data.

2   Society for Disability Studies (retrieved from disstudies.org).

3   Field Notes, June 27, 2012.

4   Brantingham & Brantingham, 1981.

5   See Ostermann, 2011.

6   "With paper" or "on paper" refers to being on parole or probation (Glaze & Parks, 2012).

7   See Muhammad, 2009; Alexander, 2010.

8   See Alexander, 2010.

9   Wacquant, 2000, 2001, 2002a; Wilson, 1980, 1987.

10 Wacquant, 2001; Jordan, 2004; King, 2008; Mallach, 2010.

11 Lewis, 2013, 18814.

12 Armour, 1997; Finkelman, 1993; see Balko, 2013.

13 Quotation marks are used for the phrase "War on Drugs" due to its politically
    motivated nature and the way "war" is used as a metaphor that relies on milita-
    rized police surveilling minority communities (see Middlemass, 2014b).

14 Coyle, 2003; Middlemass, 2014b; Barak, 1994; Brownstein, 1996.

15 Miranda, n.d. Drugs are inanimate objects that cannot be compelled to behave;
    instead, they operate as a symbol with which to demonize people and target them
    for punishment.

16 Chin, 2002.

17 Bobo & Thompson, 2010; Chin, 2002; Cardoso, Gaviria & Zedillo, 2009; Cronkite,
    2006; King, 2008.

18 Estrada, 2004. The PATRIOT Act of 2001 changed the FBI's role in domestic investigations and operations, allowing ethnic and racial profiling (FBI Domestic Investigations and Operations Guide, 2013).
19 See Schneider & Ingram, 1993a, 1993b, 1997.
20 Exceptions: Pinard, 2004, 2006, 2007; Wacquant, 2010b.
21 Travis, Solomon & Waul, 2003.
22 My decreasing access required minor adjustments to the data collection, and reminded me to "check any proclivity I had toward egocentrism" (Sutton, 2011, 50). An important part of ethnography is to remember that participants' lives are the focus; any inconvenience to my research design was insignificant and peripheral.
23 Field Notes, May 16, 2012.
24 Whitehead, 2005.
25 Participants viewed the words "prisoner" and "inmate" differently, as referring to two different types of people who are incarcerated. The term "prisoner" is a legal term used to describe a person sentenced to serve time in prison for a felony conviction. The term "inmate" refers to prisoners who are institutionalized to the ways of prison, abide by all of the rules, and become part of the prison. For the purposes of this book, the term "prisoner" is most accurate, while the word "inmate" is used sparingly to denote a particular type of prisoner.
26 Bosk & DeVries, 2004, 5.
27 Pseudonyms are used throughout the text.
28 Middlemass, 2006, 2014b; Marable, Steinberg & Middlemass, 2007; Boxer, Middlemass & Delorenzo, 2009; Boxer et al., 2011.
29 Woods, 1994; Calavera, 2008; White, 1980.
30 Whitehead, 2005; Anderson, 2003; Gold, 1997.
31 Gurney, 1985; see Whitehead, 2005; Anderson, 2003; Gold, 1997.
32 Exceptions: Fenno, 1978, 1986; Scott, 1998.
33 Clear, 2009; Leverentz, 2014.
34 See Massey, 1998.
35 Schutt, 2012.
36 Gurney, 1985; see Massey, 1998; Whitehead, 2005; Richardson, 2000; Woods, 1994; Hammersley & Atkinson, 2007; Bogdan & Biklen, 1998.
37 See Srivastava & Hopwood, 2009.
38 Gurney, 1985.
39 Specifically, iterative analysis, content analysis of policies, and data triangulation across all types of data sources were used (see Olsen, 2004; Calavera, 2008; Hussein, 2009; Jick, 1979; Law, 2004; Thorpe, 2012; Srivastava & Hopwood, 2009).
40 Travis, 2005.
41 Cobbina, 2010, 211.
42 Ford, 2001; Thorpe, 2012.
43 Middlemass, 2007; Russell-Brown, 2004; Russell & Milovanovic, 2001.
44 Eagleton, 1979; Bal, 2004.

45 See DiCicco-Bloom & Crabtree, 2006.

46 Spradley, 1979; Hammersley & Atkinson, 2007.

47 Geertz, 1973; Sutton, 2011.

48 Whiting & Lee, 2003, 289; Fetterman, 1989; Massey & Walford, 1999; Schutt, 2012.

49 Whiting & Lee, 2003; Sutton, 2011; Fetterman, 1989; Massey & Walford, 1999; Calavera, 2008.

50 Sutton (2011) uses "key informants"; DiCicco-Bloom & Crabtree, 2006.

51 Petersilia, 2003; Travis, 2005.

52 Middlemass, 2007; Russell-Brown, 2004; Russell & Milovanovic, 2001.

53 Purely quantitative methods and data are unable to capture the sights and sounds of hopelessness and distress (see Pettit & Western, 2004; Uggen, 2000).

54 Other workshops included how to create a resume, interview practice, and job etiquette.

55 My field notes were handwritten and I typed my notes shortly after being in the field. They contain personal accounts describing participants' interactions and conversations at the reentry organization.

56 Goffman, 1957.

57 Ibid. Foucault (1979, 231–56) discusses the prison as a mechanism of coercion that has complete and "total" power over inmates.

58 Goffman, 1957, 1961.

59 Field Notes, March 27, 2013.

60 Field Notes, March 28, 2012.

61 Field Notes, July 25, 2012.

62 Field Notes, June 6, 2012.

63 Field notes, several days; see Wacquant, 2010b.

64 Field Notes, May 30, 2012.

65 Sutton, 2011; DiCicco-Bloom & Crabtree, 2006.

66 IRB Protocol #11–306M.

67 Schnitzer, 1993; see Methodological Appendix.

68 One challenge with interviews is participants' capability and willingness to express personal information; some were verbose and others were taciturn, hence the varying interview lengths.

69 DiCicco-Bloom & Crabtree, 2006.

70 Personal interviews and field notes, several days. In keeping with participants' voices, there are several instances in which they used the word "crazy" and communicated that it was the most accurate word to describe their situation.

71 Methodological Appendix, table A.2, "Interviewed Participants & Their Criminal Charges."

72 It was rare to see women of any racial or ethnic identity at the nonprofit organization; fortunately, women returning to Essex County are able to access services geared to their specific concerns, such as Women in Strength Empowered (WISE Women) at Essex County College and Integrity House. Six women sat down with me to be interviewed, and fifteen regularly participated in Group.

73 New Jersey is one of only a handful of states with a high black-to-white prison population ratio (12.4 to 1) and a high Latino-to-white ratio (3.3 to 1) while the incarceration rate of whites in the state is low (Mauer & King, 2007).

74 Marable, Steinberg & Middlemass, 2007; Boxer, Middlemass & Delorenzo, 2009; Boxer et al., 2011; Middlemass, 2006, 2007.

75 Clemens, 2013, 1; see Vrij, 2008; Bond & DePaulo, 2006.

76 Strömwall & Willén, 2011, 272.

77 See Volbert & Steller, 2014.

78 Garfinkel, 1956; see Hancock, 2004.

79 Phelps, 2013.

80 Stuntz, 2001.

81 Hylton, 1982.

82 Austin & Krisberg, 1981; Phelps, 2013; Leone, 2002.

83 Field Notes, June 27, 2012. "Jacket" and "overcoat" are slang for one's criminal record or face sheet. Some participants have "long jackets," referring to lots of criminal arrests and/or convictions, while others have "short jackets," referring to few arrests and/or convictions.

84 Grattet et al., 2009; Petersilia, 1999; see Phelps (2013) for arguments of net widening related to criminal justice reform and rehabilitation.

85 Middlemass, 2007; Russell-Brown, 2004; Russell & Milovanovic, 2001.

86 See Abberley, 1987.

87 Alexander, 2010.

88 Alexander, 2010; Marable, Steinberg & Middlemass 2007.

89 See Petersilia, 2003; Travis, 2005; Thompson, 2004, 2008.

90 See Middlemass, 2007; Russell-Brown, 2004; Russell & Milovanovic, 2001.

91 See Pinard, 2004, 2006, 2007.

92 Field Notes, February 15, 2012.

93 Field Notes, August 1, 2012.

94 Rodriguez & Emsellem, 2011.

95 Interview with Janaye on April 29, 2011.

96 Field Notes, May 30, 2012.

97 Field Notes, January 30, 2013.

CHAPTER 1. FELONY CONVICTION AS SOCIAL DISABILITY

1 Warren, 2008.

2 Travis, 2005.

3 U.S. Justice Department, 2013; Draine & Herman, 2007; West & Sabol, 2011; Rosenmerkel, Durose & Farole, 2009.

4 See West & Sabol, 2011; the number of 12,500 is based on the minimum number of 650,000 people released every year, divided by 52 weeks (650,000/52=12,500).

5 Davidson, 2008; see Burke & Tonry, 2006; Draine & Herman, 2007; Freeman, 2003; Immerwahr & Johnson, 2002; Boxer et al., 2011.

6 See Abberley, 1987.

7 Schneider & Ingram, 1993a, 1993b.

8 Edgell, Gerteis & Hartmann, 2006.

9 Chin, 2002.

10 Chin & Holmes, 2002.

11 Damaska, 1968, 347.

12 Chin & Holmes, 2002.

13 Travis, 2002.

14 American Bar Association, 2002, 2003, 2004.

15 Demleitner, 2000.

16 Cohen & Rivkin, 1971.

17 Love, 2011; Chin, 2002; Davidson, 2008; Demleitner, 1999; Mauer & Chesney-Lind, 2002; Pinard, 2004, 2006; Roberts, 2008; Tress, 2009.

18 Love, 2006, 2011.

19 Pinard, 2006.

20 Davidson, 2008.

21 Pinard, 2004, 2006, 2007; see Holl & Kolovich, 2007.

22 Pinard, 2006, 2007.

23 See Pinard, 2004, 2006, 2007; Holl & Kolovich, 2007; Davidson, 2008.

24 Chin & Holmes, 2002.

25 See Rodriguez & Emsellem, 2011; Kalt, 2003; Uggen, Manza & Thompson, 2006; Aukerman, 2005; Binnall, 2009. The Integrated Automated Fingerprint Identification System (IAFIS) is part of the Federal Bureau of Investigation (FBI), which collects fingerprints and criminal histories. A "Fact Sheet" from IAFIS indicates that there are over 67.2 million subjects' fingerprints in the National Criminal History Record File, the criminal master file of the federal government. The master file houses fingerprints and criminal histories of subjects, and includes a civil file with over 26.3 million subjects. This database increases by eight to ten thousand subjects each day (retrieved from http://www.fbi.gov). The National Employment Law Project estimates there are sixty-five million Americans with a felony record (Rodriguez & Emsellem, 2011).

26 National Employment Law Project, 2005.

27 Mukamal, 2001.

28 Sexual offenders are the exception, as they must contend with harsher socially disabling laws after completion of their sentence (Roberts, 2008; Vitiello, 2008).

29 Field Notes, May 16, 2012.

30 Foucault, 1979; Clear, 2009; see Gottschalk, 2006.

31 Thomson, 1997, 33; Murphy, 1990.

32 Garfinkel, 1956.

33 Russell & Milovanovic, 2001; see Russell-Brown, 2004; Middlemass, 2007.

34 Gerschick, 2000.

35 Devlin & Pothier, 2006; Gleeson, 1996; Golledge, 1993; Jenkins, 1991.

36 Koch, 2001.

37 Hu et al., 2001.

38 Koch, 2001.

39 Jenkins, 1991.

40 Siebers, 2011, 2001; Jenkins, 1991.

41 Stone & Priestley, 1996; Silverstein, 2000; Golledge, 1993; Oliver, 1990.

42 Levitas, 2000.

43 Jenkins, 1991; Devlin & Pothier, 2006.

44 Newell, 1999.

45 Golledge, 1993.

46 Stone & Priestley, 1996.

47 Gleeson, 1996.

48 Siebers, 2011, 2001.

49 Siebers, 2001.

50 Siebers, 2011; see Abberley, 1987; Barak, 1994; Baumeister et al., 2005; Hancock, 2004; Haney-Lopez, 1994, 1996; Massey & Denton, 1993.

51 Gerschick, 2000. Many individuals who are disabled live independently despite any challenges connected to their disability.

52 Gerschick, 2000.

53 Jenkins, 1991, 572.

54 Stone & Priestley, 1996.

55 Schur, 1984; Gusfield, 1996.

56 See Murphy, 1990.

57 Goffman, 1959, 1963; Jenkins, 1991.

58 Murphy, 1990.

59 See Siebers, 2011; Goff et al., 2008, 2014; Dolovich, 2012.

60 See Murphy, 1990.

61 See Gerschick, 2000; Jenkins, 1991; Martin, 2011; Parcel & Dufur, 2001.

62 American Bar Association, 2004; see Cohen & Rivkin, 1971.

63 The following groups are considered legally incapacitated: convicted felons, minors, and those deemed mentally incompetent by a court of law (American Bar Association, 2004).

64 Hill & Hill, 2002.

65 Pager, 2007; see Schneider & Ingram, 1993a; Bobo & Thompson, 2006; Hancock, 2004; Wilson, 1980, 1987; Marks, 1991; Phelps, 2013; Oreopoulos, 2003.

66 American Bar Association, 2004.

67 See Kalt (2003) and Binnall (2010) for a discussion about felon jury exclusion.

68 Hill & Hill, 2002.

69 American Bar Association, 2004; Chin, 2002; Davidson, 2008; Love, 2006, 2011; Mauer & Chesney-Lind, 2002; Steinacker, 2003; Thompson, 2002; Travis, 2002, 2005.

70 Thomson, 1997, 33.

71 Damaska, 1968.

72 Field Notes, April 19, 2011.

73 Middlemass, 2014a.

74 See Smiley & Middlemass, 2016.

75 Middlemass, 2014a.

76 Field Notes, June 6, 2012; see Middlemass, 2014a. When participants referred to illegality, they rarely named the specific activity; instead, they used a wide range of synonyms and alternative expressions.

77 Interview with Tyrone on February 27, 2012.

78 See Blumstein et al., 1986; Langan & Levin, 2002; Visher, LaVigne & Castro, 2003; Wolfgang, Thornberry & Figlio, 1987.

79 See Pager, 2007.

80 See Blumstein et al., 1986; Langan & Levin, 2002; Travis, 2005; Travis, Solomon, & Waul, 2001; Visher, LaVigne & Castro, 2003; Wolfgang, Thornberry & Figlio, 1987.

81 Smiley & Middlemass, 2016.

82 Field Notes, June 6, 2012.

83 Rich, 1971, 17.

84 Field Notes, June 12, 2013.

85 Interview with Janaye on April 19, 2011.

86 Field Notes, February 8, 2012.

87 Tuan, 1977, 23.

88 Luckermann, 1964, 70.

89 Foucault, 1980.

90 Tress, 2009.

91 Foucault, 1967, 1969, 1979, 1980, 2003.

92 Keyssar, 2000; Ewald, 2002; McWhirter, 2009.

93 Leviticus 24:17–21; Deuteronomy 19:21; Exodus 21:22–25; and Matthew 5:38.

94 Tress, 2009; Goebel, 1976.

95 Baker, 2002.

96 McWhirter, 2009.

97 Tress, 2009.

98 Olson, 2007; Itzkowitz & Oldak, 1973; Damaska, 1968.

99 See Greenridge, 1894; Steinacker, 2003.

100 Olson, 2007; see Kellaway, 2003.

101 See Olson, 2007.

102 Pillory: Used as a form of public scorn, punishment, ridicule, and humiliation, it was a wooden device with holes in which the head and hands of an offender could be locked for long periods of time. Ear cropping: criminals' ears would be completely cut off or nailed to a pillory with the intention of having them tear off; it was abolished in the United States in the 1820s and 1830s (Kellaway, 2003; see also Tress, 2009; Granucci, 1969; McWhirter, 2009).

103 Tress, 2009; Goebel, 1976; Stuntz, 2001.

104 Damaska, 1968.

105 Lippman, 2006.

106 McWhirter, 2009; Baker, 2002; Tress, 2009.

107 Tress, 2009.

108 Ibid.

109 Ibid.

110 Stuntz, 2001; Carpenter, 2010. Criminal laws reflect the times in which they are created. "New" crimes are not substantially broader today than they were centuries ago (Stuntz, 2001). The addition of laws criminalizing witchcraft (Tress, 2009), conspiracy, blasphemy, forgery, and solicitation (Lippman, 2006) were added after Blackstone's time.

111 Tress, 2009.

112 Blackstone defined the relationship among people and between the people and government, arguing that a felony should result in forfeiture (Maxeiner, 1977). Livingston argued for a written criminal code that incorporated defined sections: (1) crimes and punishments; (2) legal procedure; (3) evidentiary rules; and (4) prison reform (Tress, 2009).

113 Tress, 2009.

114 Ibid.

115 Tress, 2009.

116 Ibid., 465.

117 Ibid.

118 Goebel, 1976.

119 In *Ex Parte Wilson*, 114 U.S. 417 at 429 (1885), the court stated that "a crime punishable by imprisonment for a term of years at hard labor is an infamous crime." See *Mackin v. United States*, 117 U.S. 348 at 350–52 (1886) (a crime punishable by imprisonment in a state prison or penitentiary is an infamous crime within the provision of the Fifth Amendment of the Constitution); *Catlette v. United States*, 132 F.2d 902 (4th Cir. 1943); *Green v. United States*, 356 U.S. 165, 183 (1958); and *United States v. Russell*, 585 F.2d 368, 370 (8th Cir. 1978).

120 Lippman, 2006; Stuntz, 2001; Carpenter, 2010.

121 Stuntz, 2001; Carpenter, 2010.

122 The unlawful killing of a person is legally defined according to the circumstances and jurisdiction, including homicide (unlawful killing of a person with malice and premeditation); felony murder (killing a person during the commission of a felony crime); manslaughter (unjustified and inexcusable killing of a person without malice); vehicular homicide; crime of passion or sudden rage resulting in death; infanticide (killing of an infant); misdemeanor murder (New Orleans, LA); depraved-heart murder (callous disregard for human life); honor killing; consensual homicide (euthanasia); assassination; lynching; and contract killing.

123 Mayhew, 1974.

124 Stuntz, 2001; Chambliss, 2001; Simon, 2007.

125 Stuntz, 2001; Chambliss, 2001; Ross & Staines, 1973; Simon, 2007; Carpenter, 2010.

126 Stuntz, 2001; Carpenter, 2010. The courts rarely find criminal policies unconstitutional or unlawful, so the creation and expansion of criminal laws resides in the hands of state and federal legislators.

127 Hagan, Hewitt & Alwin, 1979.

128 Olson, 2007.

129 Yankah, 2004.

130 Doris, 2002.

131 Ibid., 123.

132 Reitz, 1996; see D. Roberts, 2004.

133 See Chambliss, 2001.

134 See Gilliam & Iyengar, 2000; Barnett, 2003; J. Roberts, 1992; Greer, 2007; Barak, 1994.

135 Sacco, 1995.

136 Cohen, 1972; Carpenter, 2010.

137 Stuntz, 2001; Carpenter, 2010; Dowler, 2003; Cohen, 1972.

138 Carpenter, 2010; Stuntz, 2001; Simon, 2007; Anderson, 1995; Barak, 1994; Cohen, 1972; Hurwitz & Peffley, 1997; Brownstein, 1996.

139 See Gilliam & Iyengar, 2000; Barak, 1994; Austin & Krisberg, 1981.

140 See Gilliam & Iyengar, 2000.

141 The phrase "missing white woman syndrome" was first invoked by Professor Sheri Parks, a professor of American Studies at the University of Maryland, College Park, during a March 14, 2006, interview on CNN. See Christie (1986) about "ideal victims."

142 See Black & Missing Foundation (http://www.blackandmissinginc.com). FBI statistics paint a grim picture about the intersection of blackness and disappearance in the United States: The media exposure rate and coverage of black female disappearances is particularly glaring in comparison to the attention given to white women who disappear. See also "The Faces of the Forgotten: Heartbreaking Plight of 64,000 Black Women Missing across America . . . as the Country Turns a Blind Eye" (January 18, 2012) retrieved from www.dailymail.co.uk.

143 Greer, 2007; Christie, 1986. Domestic violence made national headlines during the 2014–2015 NFL season, and continues to make national headlines, but has not resulted in a moral panic of new legislation.

144 Christie, 1986; Truman, Langton & Planty, 2013. The Bureau of Justice Statistics defines violent crime as murder, rape, sexual assault, robbery, and aggravated and simple assault. In 2012, the violent crime rate was 26.1 per 1,000 people (Truman, Langton & Planty, 2013). In 2012, rates of violence against residents in different geographical areas were as follows: 32.4 per 1,000 people in urban areas; 23.8 per 1,000 in suburban areas, and 20.9 per 1,000 in rural areas. Urban residents tend to be victims of violent and serious crimes at higher rates than residents in rural and suburban areas. Blacks experience violent crime at higher rates than whites and Latinos (Truman, Langton & Planty, 2013).

145 Gilliam & Iyengar, 2000.

146 Schneider, 2006; J. Roberts, 1992.

147 Greer, 2007; Goff et al., 2008, 2014. For example, see pictures of Brock Turner, who was convicted of three sexually based felonies, and yet his mug shot was not initially shown.

148 Christie, 1986; see "When the Media Treats White Suspects and Killers Better Than Black Victims," *Huffington Post*, August 14, 2014, retrieved from www.huffingtonpost.com, for an example of media headlines depicting black victims in a harsher way than the ones describing whites convicted of murder.

149 Ingebretsen, 1998.

150 Ibid., 99; see Goff et al., 2008, 2014.

151 Recent examples include "Charleston Shooting," *CBS News*, June 17, 2015, describing Dylann Roof, who killed nine people at the historic African American church, Emanuel African Methodist Episcopal Church (retrieved from www.cbsnews.com); Adam Lanza's shooting rampage at Sandy Hook Elementary School (December 14, 2012); James Eagan Holmes's shooting rampage at the *Batman* movie (July 20, 2012); and Wade Michael Page's neocon-fueled Islamophobia shooting attack on the Sikh Temple (August 5, 2012); see "Angry, Armed, and White," *Salon*, February 14, 2015. Retrieved from www.salon.com.

152 Example: the killing of John Crawford III in a Beaverton, Ohio, Wal-Mart after Ronald Ritchie, a white man, lied to a 911 dispatcher claiming Crawford was an active shooter and pointing a gun at white shoppers (September 2014).

153 Anderson, 1995.

154 Edsall & Edsall, 1991.

155 Anderson, 1995.

156 Higginbotham, 1996, 180–81; see Julia Klein, "Helms Ad Galvanized White Vote," *Spokesman-Review*, November 11, 1990.

157 Anderson, 1995; Bell, 1988; Dominguez, 1986; Goldfield, 1991; Oliver & Shapiro, 1997; Simon, 2007.

158 Edsall & Edsall, 1991.

159 "Nikko" is an election ad that evokes the racist "law and order" politics by using an image of a "scary black man" to appeal directly to whites' fear of black men lurking in the shadows waiting to rape and murder white women.

160 D. Roberts, 2004; Grinstead, et al., 2001; Reitz, 1996.

161 Kyckelhahn, 2014.

162 The Sentencing Project (www.sentencingproject.org).

163 Tom Hester Sr., "Governor Christie Working to Abolish N.J. Early Release Parole Program," March 30, 2011. Retrieved from www.newjerseynewsroom.com.

164 Veto Message for Bill S-2308, Governor Christie of New Jersey.

165 Barnett, 2003.

166 Interview with Ryan on August 22, 2011.

167 Field Notes, March 27, 2013. I had the sense to know that what Emmanuel constituted as "nothing" was based on his experience living with the oppressive surveillance structure inside prison.

168 Luckermann, 1964, 70.

169 See Dowler, 2003.

170 Kennedy, 1997.

171 Haney-Lopez, 1994.

172 Williams, Lavizzo-Mourey & Warren, 1994; Haney-Lopez, 1994.

173 Muir, 1993; Ladson-Billings, 1999.

174 Omi & Winant, 1994.

175 Williams, Lavizzo-Mourey & Warren, 1994, 26.

176 Gates, 1997a, 1997b.

177 Muir, 1993.

178 Gould, 1994, 67.

179 Ibid.

180 Watts, 1981.

181 Watts, 1981; Montagu, 1974; Haney-Lopez, 1996.

182 Blumenbach, 2000.

183 Gould, 1994, 66.

184 Haney-Lopez, 1994, 1996.

185 Blumenbach, 2000.

186 Ibid., 28.

187 Blumenbach, 2000; see Barkan, 1992; Ladson-Billings, 1999; Haney-Lopez, 1996.

188 Gould, 1994, 67.

189 Haney-Lopez, 1994, 1996.

190 Gould, 1994; Cook, 1941; Behrens, Uggen & Manza, 2003.

191 Watts, 1981, 19.

192 Miles, 1988.

193 Williams, Lavizzo-Mourey & Warren, 1994; Matsuda, 1996; Haney-Lopez, 1994, 1996; Gotanda, 1991; Telles, 2004; Watts, 1981; Gossett, 1997; Lieberman, 2005; Lee, 1995; Omi & Winant, 1994; Ladson-Billings, 1999; Muir, 1993; Kornblum, 1988.

194 Williams, Lavizzo-Mourey & Warren, 1994, 27.

195 Haney-Lopez, 1994, 1996; D. Davis, 1966, 1984; J. Davis, 1991, 1978; Gates, 1997a, 1997b; Muir, 1993; Montagu, 1974; West, 1993; Williams, Lavizzo-Mourey & Warren, 1994; Goldfield, 1991.

196 See West, 1993; Omi & Winant, 1994; Bell, 1992, 1980; Kennedy, 1997.

197 Field Notes, June 13, 2012.

198 The origination of the term "the color line" is often credited to W. E. B. Du Bois, who drafted a speech for the First Pan-African Conference (London, England, July 1900) entitled "Address to the Nations of the World." In that speech, Du Bois said, "The problem of the Twentieth Century is the problem of the color line." However, Frederick Douglass was the original person who used the phrase in an article entitled, "The Color Line," which appeared in the *North American Review* in 1881.

199 Lieberman, 2005; Blumer, 1965.

200 Kushnick, 1998; Blumer, 1965.

201 Finkelman, 2000.

202 Burgess, 1965; Wacquant, 2000, 2001, 2002a; Muhammad, 2009.

203 Grossberg & Tomlins, 2008.

204 Banner, 2002.

205 Finkelman, 2000, 1993.

206 Finkelman, 1993.

207 Finkelman, 1993, 2082; Morris, 1988.

208 Hening, 1809.

209 Finkelman, 1993; Morris, 1988; Wiecek, 1977.

210 Harvard Law Review, 2000; Cardoso, Gaviria & Zedillo, 2009; Chin, 2002.

211 Finkelman, 1993; Butterfield, 1996; Haney-Lopez, 1996; Keyssar, 2000; Morgan, 1975.

212 Segal, 1991; see Kappeler, 2015.

213 D. Davis, 1984, 1966; Finkelman, 2000, 1993.

214 Jordan, 1968; Finkelman, 2000, 1993.

215 Muir, 1993.

216 Defining blackness included the "one-drop" rule, which was used widely through-out the South to regulate the offspring of slaves and slave masters, produced through the rape of black female slaves who were more than three generations removed from African parentage (McRoy & Freeman, 1986; Simpson & Yinger, 1972; McKinney & Thompson, 1965; Stephenson, 1910).

217 Watts, 1981.

218 J. Davis, 1978, 106.

219 See Keyssar, 2000.

220 Grossberg & Tomlins, 2008; Butterfield, 1996.

221 Butterfield, 1996.

222 Ibid.

223 Ibid.

224 Ibid.

225 Butterfield, 1996; Wood, 1974.

226 Finkelman, 1993.

227 See Banner, 2002.

228 Butterfield, 1996.

229 Ibid.

230 Keyssar, 2000; Bell, 1988.

231 Segal, 1991.

232 Ibid.; see Keyssar, 2000.

233 Bureau of Justice Statistics, 2008.

234 Harrison & Beck, 2003; see Jencks & Mayer, 1990; Jordan, 2004; King, 2008; Lamb, 2005; Landau, 2002; Mallach, 2010; Marks, 1991; Oreopoulos, 2003.

235 Alexander, 2010.

236 Kennedy, 1997.

237 See Alexander, 2010; A. Davis, 2002; Hetey & Eberhardt, 2014; Marable, Steinberg & Middlemass, 2007; Bobo & Thompson, 2010, 2006; Western, 2006; Rattan et al., 2012.

238 Ladson-Billings, 1999.

239 Blumer, 1965, 323.

240 Blumer, 1965; Alexander, 2010; Butterfield, 1996.

241 Higginbotham, 1996; Butterfield, 1996.

242 Higginbotham, 1996.

243 Du Bois, 1901; Higginbotham, 1996; Manza & Uggen, 2006.

244 Shapiro, 1993.

245 Shapiro, 1993; see Sider, 1993.

246 Shapiro, 1993; Keyssar, 2000; see Demleitner, 2000; Manza & Uggen, 2006; *Ratliffe v. Beale*, 20 So. 865, 868 (Mississippi, 1896).

247 Keyssar, 2000; Mauer, 2006.

248 Keyssar, 2000; Manza & Uggen, 2006; Shapiro, 1993.

249 Higginbotham, 1996; Butterfield, 1996.

250 Shapiro, 1993.

251 Butterfield, 1996.

252 Tolnay & Beck, 1992.

253 Wacquant, 2001, 103.

254 Wacquant, 2001; Wilson, 1980, 1987.

255 Wilson, 1980, 1987.

256 Wacquant, 2001; see Jencks & Mayer, 1990; Jordan, 2004; King, 2008; Lamb, 2005; Landau, 2002; Mallach, 2010; Marks, 1991; Oreopoulos, 2003.

257 See Langan, 1991.

258 The Bureau of Justice Statistics shows that black men and women serve nearly 20 percent longer sentences than whites convicted of similar crimes (U.S. Sentencing Commission, 2013).

259 Bias exists at every stage of the process (Bobo & Thompson, 2010, 2006; Western, 2006; Rattan et al., 2012).

260 Haney-Lopez, 1996; see the U.S. Department of Justice, Civil Rights Division, March 4, 2015, Investigation of the Ferguson Police Department. Retrieved from www.justice.gov.

261 Interview with Gavin on April 11, 2011.

262 Nordgren, Banas & MacDonald, 2011; Hetey & Eberhardt, 2014.

263 Bouie, 2014.

264 Rattan et al., 2012; Hetey & Eberhardt, 2014.

265 Ghandnoosh, 2014.

266 Goff et al., 2014; see Goff et al., 2008; Hetey & Eberhardt, 2014; Holzer, Raphael & Stoll, 2006.

267 Three recent examples include Michael Brown (Ferguson, MO), Tamir Rice (Cleveland, OH), and Terence Crutcher (Tulsa, Oklahoma).

268 Goff et al., 2008; Clear, 2009; Thompson, 2008.

269 Wacquant, 2001.

270 Institutional abandonment refers to property disinvestment, blighted land, and areas that lack public transportation, financial services, parks, and considered unattractive for economic development (Northam, 1971).

271 Wacquant, 2001, 105; Jencks & Mayer, 1990; Jordan, 2004; King, 2008; Lamb, 2005; Landau, 2002; Mallach, 2010; Marks, 1991; Western, 2009.

272 Schmidt, 1971; Middlemass, 2014b; see Cardoso, Gaviria & Zedillo, 2009; Estrada, 2004.

273 Estrada, 2004.

274 Gilens, 1999; Middlemass, 2014b.

275 Chin, 2002.

276 Jacobson, 2005; Scott & Gerbasi, 2005.

277 Hedges, 2013; Coyle, 2003; Seddon, 2006.

278 See Brownstein, 1996.

279 The U.S. Sentencing Commission reported racial differences in crack and cocaine sentencing to Congress (1995); in 1993, 88.3 percent of crack cocaine offenders were black and 10.3 percent white (see Angei, 1997), and racial disparities increased after *United States v. Booker*, 543 U.S. 220 (2005) (Fischman & Schanzenbach, (2012).

280 Hatsukami & Fischman, 1996; Brownstein, 1996.

281 Hatsukami & Fischman, 1996; major differences between crack and powder cocaine lie in the level of dependence determined by how cocaine is used. When cocaine is injected intravenously, sharing needles increases the likelihood of acquiring HIV/AIDS, and smoking crack cocaine is reported to cause a more intense, quicker high than snorting powder cocaine (Hatsukami & Fischman, 1996).

282 Coyle, 2003; Hagan, 1992; Seddon, 2006.

283 U.S. Sentencing Commission, February 1995, Special Report to Congress: Cocaine and Federal Sentencing Policy, chapter 7: Sentencing of Cocaine Offenders.

284 Coyle, 2003.

285 Auerhahn, 1999a, 1999b; Chin, 2002; Musto, 1999.

286 The U.S. Sentencing Commission (2010) concluded that the 100-to-1 ratio between sentences imposed on cocaine defendants and sentences imposed on crack defendants was generally unwarranted and promoted racial discrimination.

287 Coyle, 2003; June 22 and 29, 1995, Hearing in the U.S. House of Representatives, Judiciary Committee on Crime Subcommittee, examined the U.S. Sentencing Commission's 1995 recommendations. In July 2010, Congress cut the sentencing disparities from 1 to 100 to about 1 to 18, when it passed the Fair Sentencing Act of 2010 (Public Law 111-220).

288 Walmsley, 2009; see Cardoso, Gaviria & Zedillo, 2009.

289 Scott & Gerbasi, 2005; Simon, 2007; Middlemass & Smiley, 2016.

290 Demleitner, 2000; Wacquant, 2000; Alexander, 2010; Reiman, 1995.

CHAPTER 2. UNWELCOME HOMECOMING

1 In *Ocean's Eleven*, Danny Ocean, played by George Clooney, leaves prison in his tuxedo. Ocean was arrested in his tuxedo, and he came out wearing his tuxedo.

2 Field Notes, May 1, 2013; see Smiley & Middlemass, 2016.

3 Exception: Smiley & Middlemass, 2016.

4 Blumstein et al., 1986; Langan & Levin, 2002; Visher, LaVigne & Castro, 2003; Wolfgang, Thornberry & Figlio, 1987.

5 Middlemass, 2014a.

6 Behrens, Uggen & Manza, 2003.

7 Foucault, 1979; Hartnett, Wood & McCann, 2011; DeVeaux, 2013; see Weinberg, 1942.

8 Goffman, 1959, 1961, 1963; see DeVeaux, 2013.

9 DeVeaux, 2013.

10 Moran, 2013, 2012a; Goffman, 1961.

11 Field Notes, June 27, 2012.

12 Field Notes, March 21, 2012. To "wild out" refers to acting crazy or behaving in a way that threatens or bullies those who are weaker. Participants' references to "wildin' out" refer to the "craziness" in prison.

13 Michael Schwirtz, "Rikers Island Struggles with a Surge in Violence and Mental Illness," *New York Times*, March 18, 2014, demonstrates the challenge of imprisoning ever increasing numbers of mentally ill inmates in an environment where harsh zero-tolerance disciplinary measures are used to control defiant and erratic behavior, which is detrimental for the mentally ill.

14 Wachtler & Bagala, 2014.

15 Field Notes, several days; DeVeaux, 2013; see Hartnett, Wood & McCann, 2011.

16 Methodological Appendix, table A.1, "Summary of Prisoner File."

17 Field Notes, June 27, 2012.

18 Field Notes, June 27, 2012.

19 Local jails serve as "holding pens" for prisoners with misdemeanor convictions and under a year of time sentenced; defendants before and during trial if they cannot secure bail; prisoners after conviction but before being sent to a state assessment center prior to being incarcerated; and prisoners being transported between prisons. Evaluations are not a priority.

20 Field Notes, June 6, 2012.

21 Field Notes, June 20, 2012. The term "your papers" refers to someone's official arrest and conviction record, and "being off paper" indicates "maxing out."

22 Field Notes, June 20, 2012.

23 Field Notes, June 20, 2012.

24 Field Notes, June 6, 2012.

25 Field Notes, May 23, 2012.

26 Field Notes, June 6, 2012. "Wilding out" refers to acting crazy, bugging out, going ballistic, going insane, freaking out, or arguing for no apparent reason.

27 Field Notes, May 23, 2012.

28 The American Medical Association and American Public Health Association set the sixty-feet-square dimensions as standard for physical and mental health of prisoners, including reducing the spread of communicable disease, stress, mental disorders, aggression, and physical and sexual violence (James et al., 1997; Innes, 1986).

29 Participants never named names and did not speak about the violence that was inflicted on them or that they inflicted on others, or about gangs, and they

avoided talking about illegal activities inside prison (e.g., prison rape, sexual violence, homosexual relations, drug dealing, and drug use) and did not talk about any specific guard.

30 Interview with Tyrone on February 27, 2012.

31 Field Notes, March 28, 2012.

32 Interview with Janaye on April 19, 2011.

33 Interview with Darren on August 15, 2011.

34 Field Notes, July 25, 2012.

35 Field Notes, May 15 2013.

36 Field Notes, May 15 2013.

37 Eisen, 2014; Grinstead et al., 2001. Prison visit costs include travel/transportation, hotel (most visitors must arrive in the city the night before because they must be at the prison early in the morning to pass through the security process), food, and wages lost from missed work.

38 Ronay, 2011; Grinstead et al., 2001; Glaze & Maruschak, 2008.

39 Moran, 2013.

40 Moran, 2013; see Robinson, 2008.

41 Field Notes, May 1, 2013.

42 Du Bois, 1903; Myrdal, 1964.

43 Field Notes, May 30, 2012.

44 Field Notes, May 1, 2013.

45 National Institute of Mental Health (NIMH) describing Post-Traumatic Stress Disorder. Retrieved from www.nimh.nih.gov.

46 Cavanaugh, 2011; Corry, Klick & Fauerbach, 2010; Dekel, Peleg & Solomon, 2013; Janoff-Bulman, 1992; Shaley, 2009.

47 DeVeaux, 2013; Innes, 1986; James et al., 1997.

48 DeVeaux, 2013; Binnall, 2008.

49 See Shalev, 2009; Glassford, 2013; and Cavanaugh, 2011.

50 National Institute of Mental Health. Retrieved from www.nimh.nih.gov.

51 Middlemass & Smiley, 2016.

52 Risman, 2004; Martin, 2004; Lorber, 1994.

53 West & Zimmerman, 1987; Risman, 2004; Martin, 2004; Lorber, 1994.

54 West & Zimmerman, 1987.

55 Messerschmidt, 1993; Kupers, 2005.

56 Kupers, 2005, 714.

57 Interview with Mason on April 15, 2013.

58 Ibid.

59 Field Notes, July 25, 2012.

60 Robertson, 2012.

61 Field Notes, February 8, 2012.

62 Field Notes, February 8, 2012.

63 Lord, 1995.

64 Ibid.

65 Dr. Laura Bedard, a corrections warden and jail administrator, writes about the creation of pseudo-families in women's prisons in "The Pseudo-Family Phenomenon in Women's Prisons," Oct. 20, 2009. Retrieved from www.correctionsone.com.

66 Selling, 1931; Heffernan, 1972; Forsyth & Evans, 2003.

67 Beer, et al., 2007; Heffernan, 1972; Greer, 2000.

68 Ward & Kassebaum, 2007.

69 Greer, 2000; Heffernan, 1972.

70 Heffernan, 1972.

71 Heffernan, 1972.

72 Forsyth & Evans, 2003.

73 See Greer, 2000.

74 DeVeaux, 2013; Binnall, 2008.

75 See Dekel, Peleg & Solomon, 2013.

76 Boxer, Middlemass & Delorenzo, 2009; Boxer et al., 2011; Corry, Klick & Fauerbach, 2010; Lynch et al., 2012.

77 Interview with Gavin on April 11, 2011.

78 Field Notes, June 20, 2012.

79 Field Notes, May 9, 2012.

80 Field Notes, September 24, 2012.

81 Interview with Maurice on April 11, 2011.

82 Field Notes, May 8, 2013.

83 DeVeaux, 2013; see Janoff-Bulman, 1992.

84 Field Notes, June 6, 2012.

85 Field Notes, June 6, 2012.

86 See Moran, 2012a, 2012b.

87 Field Notes, May 8, 2013.

88 Field Notes, May 23, 2012. "Wildin'" or "wilding out" is slang; synonyms include "to act crazy," "to bug out," "to go ballistic," "to act insane," "to freak out," or "to argue for no apparent reason."

89 Field Notes, May 9, 2012.

90 Interview with Stuart on January 30, 2012.

91 Field Notes, February 8, 2012.

92 Field Notes, March 19, 2012.

93 Field Notes, several days; see Corry, Klick & Fauerbach, 2010; Dekel, Peleg & Solomon, 2013; Shalev, 2009.

94 Field Notes, July 11, 2012.

95 See Ostermann, 2011.

96 Interview with Savannah on March 5, 2012.

97 Field Notes, June 20, 2012.

98 Shalev, 2009; see DeVeaux, 2013; Binnall, 2008.

99 Interview with Bailey on August 15, 2011.

100 Bailey maxed out, so he did not have to report to parole or probation, and has no restrictions on his movements (see Pew Charitable Trusts, 2014; Ostermann, 2011).

101 Field Notes, June 27, 2012; an integral part of prison security is surveillance. Knowing where every prisoner is at any time means that prison head counts are a vital component of the prison environment, and guards are required to count prisoners at least four times a day.

102 Field Notes, February 8, 2012.

103 Interview with Alton on August 22, 2011.

104 Ibid.

105 Field Notes, September 24, 2012.

106 Prisoners eat using a plastic spork, which is a hybrid eating utensil that is a spoon-fork combination; however, it is too shallow to eat soup and the prongs are too small to "fork" meat. Plastic sporks are used in prisons because the plastic is too flimsy to use as a weapon; regular forks, knives, and spoons are considered too dangerous for their potential of being fashioned into a weapon. Sporks are also a common utensil in the fast-food industry and primary schools, and often used by toddlers.

107 Field Notes, July 11, 2012. Emphasis is based on tone of voice of participant.

108 Field Notes, September 24, 2012.

109 *12 Years a Slave* (2013), movie adapted from the 1853 antebellum slave narrative memoir by Solomon Northup, a free black man from Saratoga, New York, who was abducted and sold into slavery.

110 See Wood, 1974; Butterfield, 1996.

111 Keyssar, 2000; see Alexander, 2010.

112 Interview with Huxley on April 18, 2011.

113 Interview with Maurice on April 11, 2011.

114 Ibid. Maurice had a great sense of who he was and his mistakes, and tried to find humor in everything.

115 Grinstead et al., 2001; Ronay, 2011; Glaze & Maruschak, 2008.

116 Smiley & Middlemass, 2016.

117 Field Notes, June 20, 2012; see Sabol & Lynch, 2003; Glaze & Maruschak, 2008.

118 Field Notes, February 29, 2012.

119 Field Notes, February 8, 2012.

120 Field Notes, several days.

121 Field Notes, several days.

122 Field Notes, several days.

123 Field Notes, May 20, 2012.

124 Field Notes, several days.

125 Field Notes, June 20, 2012.

126 Field Notes, May 23, 2012.

127 Field Notes, May 30, 2012.

128 Field Notes, May 30, 2012.

129 Field Notes, June 13, 2012.

130 Field Notes, May 23, 2012.

131 Ostermann, 2011; Pew Charitable Trusts, 2014.

132 "Without paper" refers to individuals who max out by serving their entire criminal sentence; prisoners who max out and leave prison "without paper" go from the highly controlled environment of prison to a social environment with no externally imposed rules or schedules. The number of individuals maxing out and leaving prison "without paper" is growing.

133 Holl & Kolovich, 2007; Ostermann, 2011; Petersilia, 2003, 2007.

134 Brantingham & Brantingham, 1981.

135 Field Notes, May 30, 2012.

136 Field Notes, June 27, 2012.

137 Field Notes, January 30, 2013.

CHAPTER 3. DENYING ACCESS TO PUBLIC HOUSING

1 Field Notes, May 30, 2012.

2 Ibid.

3 Interview with Janaye on April 19, 2011.

4 Field Notes, January 30, 2013.

5 Field Notes, several days.

6 Field Notes, several days.

7 Field Notes, January 30, 2013.

8 Ibid.

9 Field Notes, February 6, 2013. Parole makes reintegration difficult because it requires getting permission to travel (e.g., leaving the state or going to work), 100 percent disclosure of family financial assets (e.g., income, bank records, expenses), as well as reporting to a parole officer on a regular basis and reporting any contact with government agents (i.e., the police), and other rules and regulations.

10 Field Notes, February 6, 2013. It is possible to have one's parole jurisdiction transferred to another state through the Interstate Commission for Adult Offender Supervision (ICAOS; www.interstatecompact.org); however, it is not a simple process. Parolees must be able to access the required documentation and finances to pay any fees, provide a "good" reason for the transfer that demonstrates that it will increase the likelihood of successful reentry, and have the receiving jurisdiction accept the transfer and the original jurisdiction release them.

11 Interview with Rich on May 23, 2011.

12 Interview with Huxley on April 18, 2011.

13 Interview with Alyssa on May 9, 2011.

14 If someone with a drug conviction can obtain a Section 8 voucher, he or she is able to secure housing where the voucher is accepted; however, more private landlords use a background check to determine whether they will rent to a tenant or not.

15 See Carey, 2005; Holzman, 1996; Conley, 2001; Hellegers, 1999; Lamb, 2005; Landau, 2002; Newman & Harkness, 2002; M. Schneider, 2010; Somerville, 1998.

16 Caves, 1989.

17 Conley, 2001.

18 Haber & Toro, 2004; Goodman, Saxe & Harvey, 1991.

19 Gothman, 2000.

20 Rosenbaum, 1995; Henretta, 1979; Conley, 2001.

21 See Conley, 2001.

22 Jencks & Mayer, 1990; see Parcel & Dufur, 2001.

23 Guzman, Bahtia & Durazo, 2005; Kappel Ramji Consulting Group, 2002; Bartlett, 1997.

24 U.S. Code Title 42, Chapter 119, Subchapter I, § 11302, contains the federal definition of homelessness. Federal law states that anyone who is imprisoned or detained pursuant to an act of Congress or state law is *not* homeless.

25 Donovan, 2010.

26 Schill, 1993; Carey, 2005; Donovan, 2010; Caves, 1989; Williams, 2004.

27 The six programs include (1) federal housing; (2) community planning and development; (3) public and Native American housing; (4) policy development and research; (5) fair housing and equal opportunity; and (6) national mortgage assistance (HUD Organizational and Reporting Structure Chart, March 15, 2010, available at www.hud.gov).

28 See 42 U.S.C. § 1437a(b)(2) 2002.

29 Caves, 1989.

30 See Caves, 1989. Trickle-down policies have failed under every Republican president.

31 Caves, 1989.

32 VonHoffman, 2000.

33 Martinez, 2000; Caves, 1989; Donovan, 2010; Carey, 2005; Department of Housing and Urban Development Act of 1965, Pub L. No. 89–174, § 3, 79 Stat. 667 (1965) codified at 42 U.S.C. § 3531 (2000).

34 342 U.S.C. § 3301 (1970).

35 Donovan, 2010; Carey, 2005; Caves, 1989; Department of Housing and Urban Development Act of 1965, Pub L. No. 89–174, § 3, 79 Stat. 667 (1965) codified at 42 U.S.C. § 3531 (2000).

36 Schill, 1993; Housing Act of 1937, Public Law No. 75–412, 50 Statute 888 (1937), 42 U.S.C. 1437 2000.

37 12 U.S.C. 1701u (P.L. 90–448); Martinez, 2000; and Schafer & Field, 1968. The Housing and Urban Development Act of 1968 provided the legislative framework for comprehensive housing and community development programs, breaking from traditional patterns of law.

38 42 U.S.C.A. §§ 3601–3631; the 1968 Fair Housing Act, also known as Title VIII of the Civil Rights Act of 1968, was hailed as a comprehensive solution to housing discrimination based on race, color, sex, national origin, or religion, and expanded the Department of Justice's jurisdiction to bring suit on behalf of victims of housing discrimination (Fair Housing and Equal Opportunity Programs (FHEO), available at www.hud.gov).

39 Gothman, 2000; Lamb, 2005. The National Housing Act of 1968 addressed racial segregation in housing by shifting federal housing support away from PHAs and

directing it to residents in the form of direct subsidies that could be used on the private market.

40 Landers & Worsnop, 1970; Martinez, 2000; see McDougall, 1987. The Federal Housing Administration (FHA) administered most of these programs.

41 Massey & Denton, 1993; Martinez, 2000.

42 VonHoffman, 2000; Williams, 2004; Reiman, 1995.

43 Gothman, 2000; Schafer & Field, 1968. In the 1950s, private building contractors pocketed millions of dollars in profit from federally backed mortgage loans because the loans frequently exceeded the cost of construction. Known as the "windfall scandals," Section 235 of the Housing Act of 1968 had similar problems of fraud in the 1970s.

44 Tucker, 1990; Caves, 1989.

45 Caves, 1989.

46 Kerekes, 1994; Carey, 2005; Caves, 1989; Williams, 2004; Perl, 2010. The Housing and Community Development Act of 1974, Pub. L. No. 93–383, § 201(a), 88 Stat. 662 (1974), codified as amended as 42 U.S.C. § 1437f (2000). Major changes included a public-private partnership insuring mortgages for the construction or rehabilitation of dilapidated housing, the distribution of rent subsidies to low-income households, and government-subsidized mortgage support for housing developments.

47 Caves, 1989; Model Cities (1968) was replaced with block grants that communities could use for local development and redevelopment projects.

48 Michigan Advisory Committee to the United States Commission on Civil Rights, June 1976, page 1 (http://www.law.umaryland.edu).

49 Project-based subsidies offered rental assistance to families who lived in a designated public housing development; they were required to pay 30 percent of income towards rent and the federal program paid the remainder.

50 The tenant-based subsidy or voucher is for a family to rent a unit on the private market from any owner willing to participate in the program. If the tenant moves out, the contract with the owner of the unit ends, and the tenant can use the voucher to move to another housing unit. The voucher covers a portion of rent, which usually falls between 30 percent and 40 percent of the household's income. HUD pays a subsidy to the property owner to make up the difference between the tenant's payment and the market rent.

51 Donovan, 2010.

52 Nadasen, 2007, 52; see Middlemass, 2014b.

53 Levin, 2013; see Barak, 1994.

54 See Hancock, 1994.

55 Levin, 2013; see Hancock, 1994; Murray, 2000; Gilens, 1999.

56 Middlemass, 2014b.

57 Donovan, 2010; the Housing and Community Development Act of 1987 (P.L. No. 100–242, February 5, 1988), passed in Congress in 1987 and signed into law by President Reagan in 1988. The literature and press accounts use both the year 1987

and the year 1988 to refer to the same act. The law was renamed the Emergency Low-Income Housing Preservation Act of 1987.

58 President Reagan, comments on February 5, 1988, in the Roosevelt Room at the White House, just before signing the bill into law. Retrieved from the speech archives at www.reagan.utexas.edu.

59 Stuntz, 2001; Chambliss, 2001.

60 Renzetti, 2001; Hellegers, 1999; Holzman, 1996. Criminal activity does exist in public housing; however, the percentage of criminals is small in comparison to the sizable majority of noncriminal residents living in public housing.

61 See Renzetti, 2001; Hellegers, 1999; Holzman, 1996; Stuntz, 2001; Chambliss, 2001; Jordan, 2004; Reiman, 1995.

62 Brownstein, 1996; Chambliss, 2001. The rate of violent crime in 1995 was 685 violent crimes per 100,000 people, and in 1989 it was 663 violent crimes per 100,000. Violent crime increased by 126 percent from 1960 to 1970 and 23 percent from 1980 to 1990 (Brownstein, 1996).

63 Brownstein, 1996; Chin, 2002.

64 Chin, 2002; Musto, 1999; Auerhahn, 1999a, 1999b; Chambliss, 2001; Ramaswamy & Freudenberg, 2012.

65 Brownstein, 1996; Chin, 2002; Chambliss, 2001; Lum et al., 2014; see Stuntz, 2001.

66 Coyle, 2003; Auerhahn, 1999a; Chin, 2002; Musto, 1999.

67 Chin, 2002; Brownstein, 1996; Chambliss, 2001; Barnett, 2003.

68 King, 2008.

69 Ibid.

70 See Lum et al., 2014.

71 See Chambliss, 2001.

72 Middlemass, 2014b.

73 Brownstein, 1996.

74 Ibid.; U.S. Sentencing Commission, 1995.

75 Brownstein, 1996, 2000; Clear, 2009.

76 The Final Report of the National Commission on Severely Distressed Public Housing, chapter 1, p. 36, www.hud.gov.

77 The Final Report of the National Commission on Severely Distressed Public Housing, chapter 1, pp. 37–38, www.hud.gov.

78 Brownstein, 2000; Gilliam & Iyengar, 2000. "Super-predators" is a term used to categorize and marginalize minority offenders who are under the age of eighteen and deemed to be a threat to the public's safety. The term also relates to whites' fear of certain violent criminals and their related support for punitive criminal justice policies (Gilliam & Iyengar, 2000).

79 Brownstein, 1996; Chin, 2002; Chambliss, 2001; see Schmidt, 1971. The phrase "War on Drugs" is attributed to President Nixon. In 1969, President Nixon, in a special message to Congress, identified drug abuse as a "serious national threat." Two years later, in June 1971, Nixon created the Special Action Office for Drug

Abuse Prevention, declaring a "War on Drugs" because drug abuse was "public enemy number one." Retrieved from www.npr.org.

80 Pursuant to Public Law 101–235, the Final Report of the National Commission on Severely Distressed Public Housing, chapter 1, p. 36, www.hud.gov.

81 Public & Indian Housing, HOPE VI, www.hud.gov.

82 The Final Report of the National Commission on Severely Distressed Public Housing, chapter 1, pp. 3, 5, www.hud.gov.

83 Ibid., chapter 1, pp. 2, 4.

84 Ibid., chapter 1, p. 4.

85 Ibid., chapter 1, p. 38.

86 Ibid., chapter 1, p. 39; Nussbaum, 1982.

87 The Final Report of the National Commission on Severely Distressed Public Housing, chapter 1, pp. 4, 5, www.hud.gov.

88 Nussbaum, 1982.

89 See Hancock, 2004.

90 The Final Report of the National Commission on Severely Distressed Public Housing, chapter 2, p. 48, www.hud.gov.

91 Ibid.; see Northam, 1971.

92 Wilson, 1987; Marks, 1991; Oreopoulos, 2003; Williams, 2004; Oliver & Shapiro, 1997; see Jordan, 2004.

93 The Final Report of the National Commission on Severely Distressed Public Housing, chapter 2, p. 47, www.hud.gov.

94 See Northam, 1971.

95 Holzman, 1996; Hellegers, 1999; Renzetti, 2001.

96 P.L. 104–120, March 28, 1996.

97 Stuntz, 2001; see Reiman, 1995.

98 See Nussbaum, 1982.

99 P.L. 104–120, "Screening and Eviction Guidelines for Public Housing Authorities," Memorandum to state and area coordinators, public housing directors, and public housing agencies, April 12, 1996.

100 Public Law 104–120 (1996) 110 STAT 837 Section 9 Safety and Security in Public and Assisted Housing 9(a)(q)(1A,B) and 24 C.F.R. § 960.203(3i) Standards for PHA Tenant Selection Criteria.

101 Section 9(b) provides an opportunity to challenge an adverse action, receive a copy of their criminal record, and dispute the accuracy and relevance of that record.

102 Renzetti, 2001. NCIC and criminal background checks are explored further in chapter 5.

103 Nussbaum, 1982. See *City of South San Francisco Housing Authority v. Guillory*, 49 Cal Rptr. 2d 367 (Cal. App. Dep't Super Ct. 1995); *Housing Authority of New Orleans v. Green*, 657 So. 2d 552 (La. Ct. App. 1995); *Syracuse Housing Authority v. Boule*, 265 A.D. 2d 832, 701 N.Y.S. 2d 541 (N.Y. App. Div. 1999); and *Department of Housing & Urban Development v. Rucker*, 535 U.S. 125, 2002.

104 24 C.F.R. § 960.206(a) Waiting List: Local Preferences in Admission to Public Housing Program.

105 24 C.F.R. § 960.203(1–3) Standards for PHA Tenant Selection Criteria. The law does not include a comprehensive list of "unfavorable criminal histories," which means that PHAs have the discretion to determine who is allowed to reside in public housing.

106 24 C.F.R. § 960.204(a) Denial of Admission for Criminal Activity or Drug Abuse by Household Members.

107 Interview with Janaye on April 19, 2011.

108 24 C.F.R. § 960.203(d1i-ii) Standards for PHA Tenant Selection Criteria and (d2) Standards for PHA Tenant Selection Criteria.

109 Public Law 104–120 (1996) 110 STAT 837 Section 9 Safety and Security in Public and Assisted Housing 9(c) Ineligibility Because of Eviction for Drug-Related Activity (42 USC 1437d).

110 24 C.F.R. § 960.206 Waiting List: Local Preferences in Admission to Public Housing Program.

111 24 C.F.R. § 960.203(d) Standards for PHA Tenant Selection Criteria.

112 Interview with Janaye on April 19, 2011.

113 Carey, 2005; 24 C.F.R. § 960.203(3ii) Standards for PHA Tenant Selection Criteria.

114 24 C.F.R. § 960.202 Tenant Selection Policies.

115 Interview with Janaye on April 29, 2011.

116 Interview with Huxley on April 18, 2011.

117 See Goodman, Saxe & Harvey, 1991.

118 Interview with Gavin on April 11, 2011.

119 Ibid.

120 Ibid.

121 Field Notes, February 22, 2012.

122 Goodman, Saxe & Harvey, 1991.

123 Interview with Maurice on April 11, 2011.

124 Temporary Rental Assistance (TRA) in New Jersey is one benefit individuals who are homeless, are at risk of being homeless, or have experienced a substantial loss of housing, food, clothing, or household furnishings due to fire or flood, are eligible for after they provide documentary evidence. Most former prisoners are eligible if they are able to provide a letter from their probation officer explaining why the applicant went to prison and why he or she cannot go back to his or her original home. Participants said it was nearly impossible to get a letter for these benefits.

125 Interview with Maurice on April 11, 2011.

126 Ibid.

127 Interview with Tony on April 25, 2011.

128 Interview with Craig on April 19, 2011.

129 Interview with Lamar on April 18, 2011.

130 Field Notes, several days.

131 Field Notes, several days.

132 Field Notes, February 6, 2013.

133 Interview with Jesus on May 9, 2011.

134 Interview with Gavin on April 11, 2011.

135 See Baumeister et al., 2005; Russell-Brown, 2004; Russell & Milovanovic, 2001.

136 Ewald, 2002; Damaska, 1968.

137 Demleitner, 1999; see Manza & Uggen, 2006.

138 See Olson, 2007.

139 Donovan, 2010, 203; Archer & Williams, 2006; Venkatesh, 2002; Reentry Policy Council of the Council of State Governments Justice Center, a national nonprofit organization that serves policymakers at the local, state, and federal levels from all branches of government. Retrieved from reentrypolicy.org.

140 Ingebretsen, 1998.

141 Stuntz, 2001; Carey, 2005; Goff et al., 2008.

142 Interview with Janaye on April 29, 2011.

CHAPTER 4. EDUCATION'S FAILED PROMISE

1 See Bushway & Apel, 2012.

2 Bushway & Apel, 2012; Parcel & Dufur, 2001.

3 Bushway & Apel, 2012.

4 Pager, 2007.

5 Owens, 2009.

6 Interview with Darren on August 15, 2011.

7 Field Notes, August 1, 2012.

8 Field Notes, several days.

9 Child support orders often go unpaid while a parent is incarcerated, so the debt, fees, and interest accumulates to untenable levels (Turetsky, 2007). Debt is discussed further in chapter 5.

10 See Pager, 2007.

11 Except for Clear (2009), most studies offer top-down advice without incorporating firsthand accounts in the analysis or analyzing secondary data (Beck, 2000; Burke & Tonry, 2006; Draine & Herman, 2007; Freeman, 2003; Lynch & Sabol, 2001; Petersilia, 2004, 2003; Thompson, 2008; and Travis, 2005).

12 Interview with Huxley on April 18, 2011. The notion of more educational degrees removing the background check is unfounded; more and more universities conduct background checks on new faculty hires, and have the right to withdraw any job offer if the background check comes back "negative."

13 Parcel & Dufur, 2001.

14 Ainsworth & Roscigno, 2005.

15 Ibid.

16 The postrecession economy, however, is challenging these traditional notions and beliefs about the important role of education in advancing through life.

17 Field Notes, several days.

18 Blackburn, 1981; Burke & James, 2001; Burke & Tonry, 2006; Chappell, 2004; Vacca, 2004; Ward, 2009.
19 Lynch & Sabol, 2001; Mallach, 2010; Wilson, 1980, 1987; Marks, 1991.
20 Wilson, 1980, 1987; Marks, 1991; Oreopoulos, 2003; see Whiteford, 2001.
21 Buysse, 1997.
22 Baumeister et al., 2005.
23 Thomson, 1997; Murphy, 1990.
24 Field Notes, May 9, 2012.
25 Ibid.
26 Page et al., 2007.
27 The Higher Education Act of 1965 (HEA) Pub. L. No. 89–329.
28 The HEA's major components are outreach and community service for continuing educational programs; library assistance; accreditation, support for faculty exchanges, development of training programs and faculties for emerging institutions (e.g., historically black colleges, universities in the South, and two-year college and technical institutions); grants, loans, and work-study programs for students in financial need; teacher fellowships and training for the teaching corps; support for undergraduate instruction and scholarship; and funds for institutions to meet increased demands.
29 Stoll, 2006.
30 Title IV: Student Assistance, Section 401 20 U.S.C. 1070, Federal Pell Grants: Amount and Determinations; Applications.
31 Cervantes et al., 2005; Crayton & Neusteter, 2008.
32 The three oldest prison college programs include the Inside Out Center (Temple University), the Prison University Project at San Quentin State Prison, and Boston University's Prison Education Program, which started in 1972. Another well-known program is the Bard Prison Initiative at Bard College; other "Inside-Out" prison programs are found at universities and colleges across the country.
33 Ryan & McCabe, 1994, 451.
34 Informal conversations with professors teaching "Inside-Out" courses in New York and Pennsylvania.
35 Fine et al., 2001; see Blackburn, 1981.
36 Now, most prison education programs (PEPs) are funded through voluntary commitments supported by institutions of higher learning.
37 Crayton & Neusteter, 2008.
38 Ibid. at 4.
39 See Burke & James, 2001; Burke & Tonry, 2006; see Chappell, 2004.
40 Senate Amendment No. 1158 was offered on November 10, 1993, and reads as follows: "No basic grant shall be awarded under this subpart to any individual who is incarcerated in any Federal, State or local penal institution" (20 U.S. Code § 1070a—Federal Pell Grants: amount and determinations; applications). It was an amendment to the Violent Crime Control and Law Enforcement Act of 1994 and

the Higher Education Act of 1965 [1994—Subsec. (b)(8). Pub. L. 103-322 amended par. (8)(A)].

41 Hutchison, 1993.

42 Fine et al., 2001, 5.

43 A Pell grant does not have to be repaid, and is awarded to students pursuing undergraduate or professional degrees. Maximum lifetime Pell grant is $5,815 (2016–2017), and is paid out over a maximum of twelve semesters (six years).

44 See Batiuk et al., 2005.

45 Coley & Barton, 2006; Nally et al., 2012; Gehring, 1997.

46 Blackburn, 1981; see Coley & Barton, 2006.

47 Foley & Gao, 2004; see Batiuk et al., 2005.

48 L. Davis et al., 2013.

49 Coley & Barton, 2006; L. Davis et al., 2013; Harlow, Jenkins & Steurer, 2010.

50 L. Davis et al., 2013, 8; Batiuk et al., 2005; Chappell, 2004; Mercer, 2009; Owens, 2009; Lochner & Moretti, 2004.

51 Stephan, 2008 (table 18).

52 Lochner & Moretti, 2004.

53 Vacca, 2004; Ward, 2009; see Chappell, 2004.

54 Mauer, 2006.

55 N.J. Division of Programs & Community Services, About Office of Educational Services www.state.nj.us.

56 New Jersey Department of Corrections, Division of Programs & Community Services, Office of Educational Services (retrieved from www.state.nj.us/corrections).

57 Harlow, Jenkins & Steurer, 2010.

58 L. Davis et al., 2013.

59 Interview with Jermaine on May 2, 2011.

60 Interview with Huxley on April 18, 2011.

61 Field Notes, June 20, 2012.

62 Field Notes, several days. If prisoners' ingenuity comes to the attention of guards, the response from guards may come in the form of cell searches, restricted yard time, or lock-down.

63 See Middlemass & Smiley, 2016.

64 Field Notes, several days.

65 Travis, 2005.

66 Allen, 2006; Archer & Williams, 2006; see D. Roberts, 2004.

67 Field Notes, June 6, 2012.

68 As of January 1, 2014, the new GED format is an exclusively computer-based exam, and requires higher literacy and math skills. This will ultimately make it harder to obtain a GED diploma for former inmates because of their limited access to computers; the increased need for adequate typing skills to complete the exam in the designated time; the increased cost of the exam; and the lack of teachers trained on the new test components.

69 Moran, 2012a and 2012b. Being incarcerated for long periods of time is said to add ten years to a person's physical age; older prisoners have different needs and vulnerabilities than younger prisoners inside and outside of prison (Human Rights Watch, 2012).

70 Parole is not an integral part of this study, but some parolees were in group sessions and were observed during my fieldwork.

71 Field Notes, several days. If a participant's whereabouts was not known, he or she could be "violated" and sent back to prison.

72 Field Notes, several days. For participants on parole, it was understandable when they asked permission to go to the bathroom, but it was unsettling to watch grown men and women ask to go pee.

73 Field Notes, several days.

74 Cose, 2002.

75 Durose, Cooper & Snyder, 2014; Langan & Levin, 2002; Harrison & Beck, 2003.

76 Lochner & Moretti, 2004.

77 Nally et al., 2012.

78 Field Notes, June 27, 2012.

79 Interview with Tyrone on February 27, 2012.

80 Field Notes, June 27, 2012.

81 Nellis, 2013; Scherker, 2014.

82 Nellis, 2013. In 2012, 159,520 people were serving life sentences in the United States, and tens of thousands of individuals in state and federal prisons are currently serving life without the possibility of parole for nonviolent crimes (ACLU, 2013).

83 Field Notes, several days; Nellis, 2013; Scherker, 2014; Human Rights Watch, 2012.

84 Field Notes, March 21, 2012.

85 Interview with Tyrone on February 27, 2012. "Fifty with twenty" means that Tyrone was sentenced to serve fifty years, and he had to be incarcerated for a minimum of twenty years before being eligible for parole.

86 Ibid.

87 Field Notes, June 27, 2012.

88 A "shank" is the generic term for a prison weapon made from any hard material, such as plastic from a toothbrush or metal wire, where one end is filed down to a sharp point and the opposing end is wrapped in tape or cloth to form a handle/grip.

89 Field Notes, June 27, 2012.

90 The "No Early Release Act" (N.J.S.A. 2C:43–7.2), June 7, 1997.

91 Field Notes, June 27, 2012.

92 Innes, 1986; James et al., 1997; Gibbons & Katzenbach, 2006.

93 Skarbek, 2012.

94 Prior to the "War on Drugs," the national standard for prison cell space mandated at least sixty square feet per inmate; however, as overcrowding forces inmates to share a cell involuntarily with another inmate not of their choosing, the square feet per inmate is halved (Innes, 1986; see James et al., 1997; DeVeaux, 2013; Binnall, 2008).

95 Interview with Huxley on April 18, 2011.

96 Field Notes, May 16, 2012.

97 Field Notes, June 6, 2012.

98 Interview with Ryan on August 22, 2011.

99 Interview with Maurice on April 11, 2011.

100 "The Big Book" is the informal name for *Alcoholics Anonymous: The Story of How More Than One Hundred Men Have Recovered from Alcoholism*, which details the twelve-step program and guides those attempting to recover from alcoholism through a series of prayers and meditation.

101 Interview with Maurice on April 11, 2011.

102 Field Notes, May 30, 2012.

103 Ibid.

104 Ibid.

105 Field Notes, March 5, 2012.

106 Field Notes, May 30, 2012.

107 Field Notes, July 11, 2012.

108 Ibid.

109 Interview with Tyrone on February 27, 2012.

110 Interview with Alton on August 22, 2011.

111 Field Notes, several days.

112 "Good time credits" are credits earned by prisoners for good behavior—exemplary compliance with the institutional rules and regulations—and are used to reduce a prisoner's actual time incarcerated. Prior to 1997, New Jersey prisoners could earn good time credits four ways: for good behavior, work, minimum custody credits, and parole contact credits (New Jersey Parole Book, 2012).

113 The "No Early Release Act" (N.J.S.A. 2C:43–7.2).

114 Field Notes, July 11, 2012.

115 Methodological Appendix, table A.2, "Interviewed Participants & Their Criminal Charges."

116 Field Notes, March 5, 2012.

117 Field Notes, May 30, 2012.

118 Interview with Tony on April 25, 2011.

119 Harlow, Jenkins & Steurer, 2010.

120 Field Notes, March 5, 2012.

121 Pager, 2007.

122 Interview with Maurice on April 11, 2011.

123 Interview with Darius on May 23, 2011.

124 See Dance, 2002.

125 Interview with Duncan on January 30, 2012.

126 Allen, 2006; Batiuk et al., 2005; Blackburn, 1981; Burke & James, 2001; Chappell, 2004; Coley & Barton, 2006; Crayton & Neusteter, 2008; L. Davis et al., 2013; Vacca, 2004.

127 Middlemass, 2014a; see Allen, 2006.

128 Interview with George on April 25, 2011.

129 Interview with Walter on February 20, 2013.

130 Field Notes, March 5, 2012.

131 Field Notes, July 11, 2012.

132 Field Notes, January 30, 2013.

CHAPTER 5. NOT WORKING AND UNABLE TO WORK

1 Interview with Darren on August 15, 2011.

2 Participants used "hustling" and "banging" as generic terms to refer to a wide range of criminal behavior. "Hustling" refers to drug dealing activities, including manufacturing and distribution, as well as criminal activities that could involve theft, robbery, and distribution of stolen goods. "Banging" refers to gang activity but can also include "knocking heads" as a strong arm man or criminal activity that includes violence or threats of violence to support hustling.

3 For approximately forty years, recidivism rates have remained at approximately 67 percent, which indicates that about 33 percent of adults released from prison successfully reenter society (see Freeman, 2003; Langan & Levin, 2002; Harrison & Beck, 2003; Durose, Cooper & Snyder, 2014).

4 Smiley & Middlemass, 2016.

5 Bushway & Apel, 2012; Pager, 2007.

6 Petersilia, 2003; Travis, 2005; 42 U.S.C. § 17501(b)(18), Second Chance Act findings.

7 Field Notes, several days; see Martin, 2011.

8 Human Rights Watch, "Profiting from Probation: America's 'Offender-Funded' Probation Industry," retrieved from www.hrw.org.

9 Field Notes, several days.

10 Interview with Brandon on May 23, 2011.

11 Interview with Elton on March 12, 2012.

12 Cammett, 2011; Turetsky, 2007; Peffley, Hurwitz & Sniderman, 1997. PRWORA instituted TANF, and became effective July 1, 1997, replacing Aid to Families with Dependent Children (AFDC).

13 A study of 350 parolees in Colorado demonstrated that they had an average balance of $16,651 due in child support arrears (Pearson & Davis, 2001; Pearson, 2004). A study of 650 inmates in Massachusetts found that the parents entered prison with an average of $10,543 in unpaid child support, and that this figure would double by the time they were released, plus interest and late penalty charges (Peffley, Hurwitz & Sniderman, 1997).

14 Child-support orders are not automatically suspended, so the arrears accumulate while a parent is incarcerated unless the prison can interact with the child support division or go to court to have the payments suspended via state court order (Pearson, 2004).

15 Incarcerated parents, in most states, can request the court or child support agency to reduce an existing child support order as incarceration is considered voluntary

unemployment, but the process is cumbersome, lengthy, and requires knowledge of how to access it, usually through legal representation (Pearson, 2004; see Turetsky, 2007).

16 Pearson, 2004. Common judicial approaches to assessing the effects of incarceration and standing child support orders fall into three categories: No Justification approach (twenty-one states treat incarceration as insufficient to justify the elimination or reduction of an existing child support order); Complete Justification Approach (thirteen states and the District of Columbia treat incarceration as sufficient to justify elimination or reduction of an existing child support order); One Factor Approach (eleven states deem that incarceration is one factor of many to take into account when considering whether to eliminate or reduce an open support obligation); and a case-by-case analysis (the remaining five states).

17 *Mooney v. Brennan*, 848 P.2d 1020, 1023 (Montana, 1993).

18 Pearson, 2004.

19 Many state courts only consider a request to modify after a prisoner files a case, which means the debt can grow rapidly (Pearson, 2004).

20 Turetsky, 2007.

21 P.L. 104-193, the Personal Responsibility and Work Opportunity Act of 1996 (PRWORA), Section 369.

22 Child Support Recovery Act of 1992, 18 U.S.C. § 228.

23 The severity of punishments differs in each state, and ranges from a misdemeanor with small fines to a felony with a prison term and thousands of dollars in fines.

24 Field Notes, May 23, 2012.

25 Field Notes, June 6, 2012.

26 461 U.S. 660 (1983).

27 See "Fines and Fees" at the Southern Center for Human Rights. Retrieved from www.schr.org.

28 Examples from Ferguson, Missouri, of the excessive fees implemented by local jurisdictions.

29 Private probation companies, such as Sentinel Offender Services, use perverse techniques to charge fees, and then have the poor people jailed after failure to keep up with the mounting fees on offenses such as public drunkenness, rolling through a stop sign, and failure to wear a seatbelt. Sentinel is notorious for overcharging probationers and lying about paperwork "not in the system" yet. See ThinkProgress.org for examples.

30 Field Notes, several days.

31 Field Notes, June 6, 2012.

32 Nilsen, 2007, 138; Field Notes, several days.

33 Tyler, Casper & Fisher, 1989.

34 Field Notes, June 20, 2012.

35 Field Notes, March 28, 2012.

36 Federal Parole, U.S. Department of Justice. To understand parole violations and the revocation process, it is necessary to unpack the "black box" of the decision-

making process, which is beyond the scope of this study (see Grattet et al., 2009 for an example).

37 Interview with Alyssa on May 9, 2011.

38 Ibid.

39 Interview with Tyrone on February 27, 2012.

40 Field Notes, June 27, 2012.

41 Interview with Brandon on May 23, 2011.

42 Field Notes, March 28, 2012.

43 Field Notes, April 2, 2012.

44 Interview with Walter on February 20, 2013.

45 Field Notes, several days.

46 Interview with Bishop on April 2, 2012.

47 Field Notes, May 1, 2013.

48 Ibid.

49 Interview with Tyrone on February 27, 2012.

50 See Pager, 2007.

51 Interview with Brandon on May 23, 2011.

52 DSM-5, 2013. The clinical behaviors associated with catatonia are varied, but can include holding oneself motionless in a rigid pose; looking as if one is in a lethargic stupor, oblivious to nearby people and the environment; speaking very little and exhibiting a negative attitude when speaking; exhibiting visible agitation displayed with repetitive movement; or constant frowning or sneering (DSM-5, Section II, Diagnostic Criteria and Codes, Catatonia Associated with Another Mental Disorder, Catatonia Specifier).

53 Interview with Gavin on April 11, 2011.

54 Schneider, 2010; Aukerman, 2005; Stacy, 1973; Sabol & Lynch, 2003.

55 Interview with Jermaine on May 2, 2011.

56 Public Law 103–159.

57 See the National Instant Criminal Background Check System Regulation, 63 Fed. Reg 58, on implementing the NICS pursuant to the Brady Act.

58 The Federal Bureau of Investigation's (FBI) Criminal Justice Information Services Division operates NICS. Criminal records of state arrests and convictions are maintained in state repositories, and each state has passed its own laws regarding who has access to maintain the database.

59 Balko, 2013. Example: In Ferguson, Missouri, in August 2014, in the aftermath of college-bound black teenager Michael Brown being shot and killed by a white police officer, mostly peaceful community protests were met by a militarized police force that included stun grenades, rubber bullets, riot gear, teargas, smoke bombs, SWAT teams, armored vehicles, and mine-resistant vehicles in the suburbs of St. Louis. The *Huffington Post* headline the day after the aggressive police response read, "Baghdad, USA."

60 Pursuant to 28 U.S.C. § 534, the FBI collects fingerprints and criminal histories, and the information is entered into the Integrated Automated Fingerprint

Identification System (IAFIS); information is entered into the National Criminal History Record File, which becomes the master file of state and federal subjects' fingerprints and criminal histories. Retrieved from www.fbi.gov.

61 Rodriguez & Emsellem, 2011.

62 Private companies conducting background checks tend to look at criminal history, civil history (e.g., if applicant has been a plaintiff or defendant in civil court), warrants (e.g., to see if the applicant is "wanted" by law enforcement), credit report, Social Security reports, previous employer verification, drug tests (usually for individuals who will be operating machinery or a motor vehicle), reference verification, verification of education (e.g., attendance dates, and major, degrees, and certificates earned), and driving history (e.g., license status, violations or suspensions).

63 Omnibus Crime Control and Safe Streets Act of 1968, Public Law 105–251; 42 U.S.C. 3760, as amended; Bureau of Justice Statistics, National Criminal History Improvement Program (NCHIP).

64 Harvey, 1994; Demleitner, 1999, 2000; Ewald, 2002, 2005; Hench, 1998; Karlan, 2004; Manza & Uggen, 2006; Pettus, 2005.

65 Commercial driver's licenses (CDL) are required to transport hazardous materials, vehicles designed to transport sixteen or more passengers, tow truck drivers, and vehicles weighing more than twenty-six thousand pounds. Commercial motor vehicle (CMV) licenses are required for drivers of tractor trailers, tanker truck vehicles that carry liquefied loads (milk, water, gasoline, diesel, chemicals, concrete), long combination vehicles, and buses, limousines, or large passenger vans for hire.

66 See Holzer, Raphael & Stoll, 2006.

67 According to the 2012 guidelines issued by the Equal Employment Opportunity Commission (EEOC), the EEOC is trying to make it harder for employers to use blanket exclusion policies to automatically deny all applicants with an arrest or conviction record. The EEOC is calling on employers to conduct individualized assessments that examine the nature and gravity of the offense, the time passed since the conviction, and the nature of the job (www.eeoc.gov).

68 If someone robs a bank, that person has shown a propensity to steal money, so it may not be wise to have a former bank robber employed in a position handling money, but that doesn't mean such a person is not capable of doing an assortment of other tasks, including landscaping or construction work or work as a machinist, as a cook, or in food prep.

69 Field Notes, June 6, 2012.

70 Ibid.

71 Data from "Background Checking: The Use of Criminal Background Checks in Hiring Decisions," June 19, 2012 (retrieved from www.shrm.org).

72 Interview with Max on May 30, 2012.

73 Data from "Background Checking: The Use of Criminal Background Checks in Hiring Decisions," June 19, 2012 (retrieved from www.shrm.org). The data does

not provide the percentage of companies that extend a job offer after a candidate explains the results of his or her criminal background check.

74 See Aukerman, 2005.

75 Hurwitz & Peffley, 1997; Demleitner, 1999.

76 Pager, 2007; Travis, Solomon & Waul, 2001; see also the National Employment Law Project (2005) for a detailed discussion of the use of background checks, and the "Employment Screening for Criminal Records: Attorney General's Recommendations to Congress: Comments of the National Employment Law Project to the U.S. Attorney General Office of Legal Policy."

77 See Holzer, Raphael & Stoll, 2006; National Employment Law Project, 2005.

78 Interview with Bailey on August 15, 2011.

79 Field Notes, June 6, 2012.

80 May, 1995.

81 Examples of professions in New Jersey requiring a license to legally work in the profession include plumbers, barbers/cosmetologists, physical therapists, assisted living attendants and home nursing care providers, boxing promoters, acupuncturists, massage therapists, pest exterminators, and commercial truck drivers.

82 Examples in New Jersey of revenue-raising licensing fees are new businesses that must obtain an occupational license to conduct business in a particular jurisdiction (e.g. state, county, parish, and city). The business licenses are for home-based businesses, retail and commercial businesses and stores, wholesale dealers, lending businesses, apartment complexes, and limited liability companies.

83 May, 1995.

84 Ibid.; Peffley, Hurwitz & Sniderman, 1997.

85 Freeman, 2003; see Justice Douglas's dissenting opinion in *Barsky v. Board of Regents*, 347 U.S. 442 (1954).

86 See Ramaswamy & Freudenberg, 2012.

87 Love, 2011; see Cohen & Rivkin, 1971.

88 In November 2012, the American Bar Association released a list identifying more than thirty-eight thousand punitive provisions that apply to convicted felons (American Bar Association, 2012).

89 See Gellhorn, 1976.

90 Ibid.

91 Vitiello, 2008; Binnall, 2010.

92 Mossoney & Roecker, 2005.

93 Love, 2006; American Bar Association, 2002, 2003, 2004, 2012.

94 Pager, 2007; see Aukerman, 2005.

95 Love, 2006.

96 Demleitner, 1999; Sabol & Lynch, 2003.

97 Emsellem, 2005.

98 Interview with Ryan on August 22, 2011.

99 Interview with Curtis on February 13, 2012.

100 J. Roberts, 2008; Vitiello, 2008; see *Kansas v. Hendricks*, 521 U.S. 346 (1997); *Steele v. Murphy*, 365 F.3d 14 (1st Circuit, 2004).

101 See J. Roberts, 2008.

102 Vitiello, 2008; Binnall, 2008, 2009, 2010; Steinacker, 2003; May, 1995; see Martinson, 1974.

103 Yankah, 2004; Doris, 2002; Aukerman, 2005.

104 Kalt, 2003; Aukerman, 2005; Binnall, 2009.

105 See Binnall, 2010.

106 Vitiello, 2008; Binnall, 2010; Kalt, 2003; Ewald, 2002, 2005; Love, 2006; May, 1995.

107 See Stacy, 1973.

108 May, 1995.

109 May, 1995; Aukerman, 2005.

110 *Konigsberg v. State Bar of California*, 353 U.S. 252 at 263 (1957).

111 *Dandridge v. Williams*, 397 U.S. 471 at 485 (1970); see May, 1995.

112 353 U.S. 232 (1957).

113 Aukerman, 2005; 353 U.S. 232 at 239 (1957).

114 363 U.S. 144 (1960).

115 Aukerman, 2005; 363 U.S. 144 at 157–158 (1960). The United States Supreme Court found that the state of New York was not restricting felons in an arbitrary manner; rather, the state was using its legislative power to combat corruption.

116 *Butts v. Nichols*, 381 F. Supp 573 at 580 (S.D. Iowa 1974).

117 Aukerman, 2005, 38; *Butts v. Nichols*, 381 F. Supp 573 at 580–581 (S.D. Iowa 1974). In *Butts*, the court declared that it was totally irrational to restrict individuals with irrelevant felonies from employment opportunities.

118 May, 1995.

119 May, 1995; National Employment Law Project, 2005.

120 Field Notes, May 30, 2012.

121 Binnall, 2010; Baumeister et al., 2005; Holl & Kolovich, 2007.

122 Field Notes, May 9, 2012.

123 Love, 2011.

124 Field Notes, May 9, 2012.

125 Stacy, 1973.

126 Interview with Max on May 30, 2012.

127 Interview with Mahoney on May 2, 2011.

128 Interview with Brandon on May 23, 2011.

129 Interview with Gavin on April 11, 2011.

130 Interview with Bailey on August 15, 2011.

131 Ibid.

132 Interview with Gavin on April 11, 2011.

133 Field Notes, May 9, 2012.

134 Field Notes, June 6, 2012.

135 Interview with Tony on April 25, 2011.

136 Ibid.

137 Interview with Maurice on April 11, 2011.

138 Field Notes, July 11, 2012. An understudied phenomenon is "maxing out." Individuals, due to knowledge about the rules of parole and probation, and awareness of how many people fail at parole, make the rational decision to serve their entire sentence in prison instead of reentering society under the rules and restrictions of parole or probation. "I can do eighteen months inside, but three years on parole, that's a long time to be good all the time, no speeding ticket, no trouble" (Field Notes, July 11, 2012).

139 Field Notes, May 30, 2012.

140 Ibid.

141 Field Notes, February 6, 2013.

142 Field Notes, June 6, 2012.

143 Field Notes, June 6, 2012.

144 Field Notes, June 20, 2012.

145 Interview with Walter on February 20, 2013.

146 Ibid.; see Venkatesh (2008); Ragin & Amoroso (2011). Many argue that it is *not* unethical to observe illegal or abhorrent behavior as a researcher because the objective is to understand life of a subset of society (Ragin & Amoroso, 2011, 80).

147 The Ban the Box campaign continues to be successful, and more cities and states, as well as the federal government, are taking action to add antidiscrimination hiring practices to their employment policies. Go to http://bantheboxcampaign.org for up-to-date information concerning Ban the Box campaign efforts across the country.

148 See Pager, 2007.

149 Field Notes, June 6, 2012.

150 Interview with Walter on February 20, 2013.

151 Field Notes, June 6, 2012.

152 Interview with Walter on February 20, 2013.

153 Field Notes, June 6, 2012.

154 Ibid.

155 Ibid.

156 Interview with Walter on February 20, 2013.

157 Rose & Clear, 2002, 187.

158 Field Notes, June 6, 2012; see Falk, 2001, 315.

159 Uggen, 2000.

160 Saxonhouse, 2004.

161 May, 1995.

162 J. Roberts, 2008.

CONCLUSION

1 Field Notes, April 4, 2012.

2 Damaska, 1968.

3 Klimchuk, 2001; see Tonry, 1995.

NOTES | 235

4 Stuntz, 2001.
5 Tonry, 1995, 179, 180.
6 Field Notes, May 23, 2012.
7 Travis, 2005.
8 Interview with Janaye on April 29, 2011.
9 Field Notes, March 28, 2012.
10 Field Notes, May 30, 2012.
11 Field Notes, May 15 2013.
12 Field Notes, several days.
13 Durose, Cooper & Snider, 2014.
14 Maruna, 2011.
15 See Garland, 2001b; Visher & Travis, 2003; Blumstein et al., 1986; Langan & Levin, 2002; Visher, LaVigne & Castro, 2003; Wolfgang, Thornberry & Figlio, 1987.
16 Wacquant, 2010a.
17 See Phelps, 2013.
18 Field Notes, June 27, 2012.
19 Field Notes, several days.
20 See Martinson, 1974.
21 Clear, 2007, 3.
22 Field Notes, June 13, 2012.
23 See Myrdal, 1964; Du Bois, 1903.
24 Lieberman, 2005.
25 Alexander, 2010; Blumer, 1965.
26 Lum et al., 2014.
27 See Alexander, 2010.
28 See Kappeler, 2015; Butterfield, 1996.
29 Betancur & Herring, 2012; Bobo & Thompson, 2010, 2006; Burgess, 1965; Chin, 2002; Clear, 2009; Coyle, 2003; Eberhardt et al., 2004; Fields, 1982; Ghandnoosh, 2014; Gilens, 1999; Gossett, 1997; Haney-Lopez, 1996, 1994; Hurwitz & Peffley, 1997; Jordan & Freiburger, 2010; Kennedy, 1997; Langan, 1991; Lieberman, 2005; Marable, Steinberg & Middlemass, 2007; Mauer, 2006; Mauer & King, 2007; Middlemass, 2014b, 2015; Montagu, 1974, 1941; Muhammad, 2009; Pettit & Western, 2004; Thompson, 2008; Omi & Winant, 1994; Wacquant, 2010a, 2009, 2002a, 2001, 2000; West, 1993; Western, 2009; Wilson, 1980; Ladson-Billings, 1999; Aylward, 1999.
30 Alexander, 2010.
31 See Haney-Lopez, 1996.
32 Pew Research Center, in "America's New Drug Policy Landscape," explores changing public beliefs about how the government should change its policies concerning the "War on Drugs" (April 2, 2014, retrieved from www.people-press.org); see also Cardoso, Gaviria & Zedillo, 2009; Bobo & Thompson, 2010.
33 Carson, 2014.
34 Wacquant, 2001.

35 See Balko, 2013.

36 Balko, 2013.

37 #BlackLivesMatter; Marable, Steinberg & Middlemass, 2007; Kennedy, 1997.

38 Officer Betty Shelby was charged with manslaughter in the first degree for shooting and killing Terence Crutcher. She is out on a fifty-thousand-dollar bond awaiting trial.

39 Officer Michael Brelo fired 49 of the 137 shots, and 15 of the shots were fired into the windshield while he was standing on the hood of Russell's car. Brelo was found not guilty of voluntary manslaughter.

40 Dominique Mosbergen, "Death of Tanisha Anderson, Mentally Ill Woman in Police Custody, Ruled a Homicide." *Huffington Post*, January 2, 2015, www.huffingtonpost.com.

41 Six Baltimore police officers were arrested in connection with the unlawful arrest and treatment of Freddie Gray. Three of the officers were acquitted of all charges and Baltimore prosecutors dropped all charges against the three remaining officers.

42 Michael Slager, the officer, was arrested and charged with murder for shooting Mr. Scott in the back. Mr. Slager's trial started in November 2016, and had not concluded at the time the manuscript went to press. Police officers charged with murder or manslaughter are rarely found guilty in a court of law for killing unarmed black men, women, and children.

43 See Mariko Gaines writing for the Racial Justice Project at New York Law School, February 25, 2011 (www.racialjusticeproject.com).

44 "Chicago Police Officer Dante Servin Charged in 2012 Shooting Death of Unarmed Rekia Boyd." *Huffington Post*, November 25, 2013, www.huffingtonpost.com.

45 Defense Logistics Agency, Disposition Services, 1033 Program.

46 See Balko, 2013.

47 Field Notes, several days.

48 Thomson, 1997, 33.

49 See Phelps, 2013.

50 In *Kimbrough v. United States* (552 U.S. 85, 2007), the Supreme Court confirmed that federal judges could use discretion to impose sentences involving the possession, distribution, and manufacture of crack cocaine that are outside the range dictated by federal sentencing guidelines.

51 Tonry & Lynch, 1996.

52 Maruna, 2011.

53 S. 2567—REDEEM Act—113th Congress (2013–2014), introduced to the U.S. Senate Judiciary Committee. S. 675—REDEEM Act—114th Congress (2015-2016), reintroduced to the U.S. Senate Judiciary Committee.

54 New Jersey Statutes, N.J.S. § 2C:12–3. Terroristic Threats.

55 L. Davis, et al., 2013.

56 "Pell Grants for Prisoners Moves Forward," *Politico*, June 24, 2016, describes the Obama administration's efforts to extend Pell grants to current prisoners and the political resistance from Republicans (retrieved from www.politico.com/story).

57 H.R. 3327—the "Kids before Cons Act"—was introduced by Representative Chris Collins on July 29, 2015, and is an amendment to the Higher Education Act of 1965 designed to uphold the ban on Pell grants for anyone who is incarcerated, and to prohibit any institution of higher learning from awarding Pell grants to incarcerated individuals or convicted felons.

58 "Pell Grants for Prisoners," *USA Today*, June 24, 2016, describes the Obama administration's efforts to provide Pell grants to prisoners and explains why the pilot program requires Congress to pass legislation to make the pilot program permanent (retrieved from www.usatoday.com).

59 Martin, 2011; Pettus, 2005.

60 Field Notes, several days.

61 Field Notes, June 6, 2012.

62 See Smiley & Middlemass, 2016.

63 Foucault, 1979.

64 Clear, 2009.

65 Kleiman, 2009.

66 Foucault, 1979; see Damaska, 1968.

67 Foucault, 1982.

68 Field Notes, August 1, 2012.

METHODOLOGICAL APPENDIX

1 See DiCicco-Bloom & Crabtree, 2006.

2 Sutton 2011.

3 See DiCicco-Bloom & Crabtree, 2006.

BIBLIOGRAPHY

Abberley, Paul. 1987. "The Concepts of Oppression and the Development of a Social Theory of Disability." *Disability, Handicap & Society* 2(1):5–19.

ACLU. 2013. "A Living Death: Life without Parole for Nonviolent Offenses." www.aclu.org.

Ainsworth, James, and Vincent Roscigno. 2005. "Stratification, School-Work Linkages, and Vocational Education." *Social Forces* 84(1):257–84.

Alexander, Michelle. 2010. *The New Jim Crow: Mass Incarceration in the Age of Colorblindness*. New York: New Press.

Allen, Robert. 2006. "An Economic Analysis of Prison Education Programs and Recidivism." Emory University, Atlanta, GA. www.economics.emory.edu.

Aluwihare-Samaranayake, Dilmi. 2012. "Ethics in Qualitative Research: A View of the Participants' and Researchers' World from a Critical Standpoint." *International Journal of Qualitative Methods* 11(2):64–81.

American Bar Association. 2012. *National Inventory of the Collateral Consequences of Convictions*. Washington, DC: American Bar Association. www.abacollateral consequences.org.

———. 2004. "Collateral Sanctions and Discretionary Disqualification of Convicted Persons." *ABA Standards for Criminal Justice*, 3rd ed. Washington, DC: American Bar Association.

———. 2003. "Collateral Sanctions and Discretionary Disqualification of Convicted Persons." *ABA Standards for Criminal Justice*, 2nd ed. Washington, DC: Criminal Justice Section, American Bar Association.

———. 2002. "Collateral Sanctions and Discretionary Disqualification of Convicted Persons." *ABA Standards for Criminal Justice*, 1st ed. Washington, DC: Criminal Justice Section, American Bar Association.

Anderson, David. 1995. *Crime and the Politics of Hysteria: How the Willie Horton Story Changed American Justice*. New York: Time Books (Crown Publishing Group).

Anderson, Elijah. 2003. *A Place on the Corner: A Study of Black Street Corner Men*, 2nd ed. Chicago: University of Chicago Press.

———. 1999. *Code of the Street: Decency, Violence, and the Moral Life of the Inner City*. New York: Norton.

Angei, David H. 1997. "A 'Second Look' at Crack Cocaine Sentencing Policies: One More Try for Federal Equal Protection." *American Criminal Law Review* 34:1211–41.

Archer, Deborah, and Kele Williams. 2006. "Restoring Socioeconomic Rights for Ex-Offenders." *New York University Review of Law & Social Change* 30:527–83.

Armour, Jody. 1997. *Negrophobia and Reasonable Racism: The Hidden Costs of Being Black in America*. New York: New York University Press.

Atkinson, Rob. 2000. "Narratives of Policy: The Construction of Urban Problems and Urban Policy in the Official Discourse of British Government, 1968–1998." *Critical Social Policy* 20(2):211–32.

Auerhahn, Kathleen. 1999a. "Selective Incapacitation and the Problem of Prediction Criminology." *Criminology* 37:703–34.

———. 1999b. "The Split Labor Market and the Origins of Anti-Drug Legislation in the United States." *Law & Society Inquiry* 24(2):411–40.

Aukerman, Miriam. 2005. "The Somewhat Suspect Class: Towards a Constitutional Framework for Evaluating Occupational Restrictions Affecting People with Criminal Records." *Journal of Law in Society* 7:18–87.

Austin, James, and Barry Krisberg. 1981. "Wider, Stronger, and Different Nets: The Dialectics of Criminal Justice Reform." *Journal of Research in Crime and Delinquency* 18(1):165–96.

Aylward, Carol. 1999. *Canadian Critical Race Theory: Racism and the Law*. Halifax, NS: Fernwood.

Baker, John. 2002. *An Introduction to English Legal History*, 4th ed. New York: Oxford University Press.

Bal, Mieke. 2004. *Narrative Theory*. Volume 1, *Major Issues in Narrative Theory: Critical Concepts in Literary and Cultural Studies*. New York: Routledge.

Balko, Radley. 2013. *Rise of the Warrior Cop: The Militarization of America's Police Forces*. Philadelphia: PublicAffairs (Perseus Books Group).

Banner, Stuart. 2002. *The Death Penalty: An American History*. Cambridge, MA: Harvard University Press.

Barak, Gregg. 1994. "Newsmaking Criminology: Reflections on the Media, Intellectuals, and Crime." In *Media, Process, and the Social Construction of Crime: Studies in Newsmaking Criminology*, edited by Gregg Barak, 237–64. New York: Routledge.

Barkan, Elazar. 1992. *The Retreat of Scientific Racism*. Cambridge, MA: Cambridge University Press.

Barnett, Brooke. 2003. "Guilty and Threatening: Visual Bias in Television News Crime Stories." *Journalism & Communication Monographs* 5(3):104–55.

Bartlett, Sheridan. 1997. "The Significance of Relocation for Chronically Poor Families in the USA." *Environment and Urbanization* 9(1):121–32.

Batiuk, Mary, Karen Lahm, Matthew McKeever, Norma Wilcox, and Pamela Wilcox. 2005. "Disentangling the Effects of Correctional Education." *Criminology & Criminal Justice* 5(1):55–74.

Baumeister, Roy, Nathan DeWall, Natalie Ciarocco, and Jean Twenge. 2005. "Social Exclusion Impairs Self-Regulation." *Journal of Personality and Social Psychology* 88(4):589–604.

Beck, Allen. 2000. *State and Federal Prisoners Returning to the Community: Findings from the Bureau of Justice Statistics*. Office of Justice Programs. Presented at First

Reentry Courts Initiative Cluster Meeting, Washington, DC: U.S. Department of Justice. bjs.ojp.us doj.gov.

Beckett, Katherine, and Theodore Sasson. 2004. *The Politics of Injustice: Crime and Punishment in America*, 2nd ed. Thousand Oaks, CA: Sage.

Beer, Amanda, Robert D. Morgan, John T. Garland, and Lisa B. Spanierman. 2007. "The Role of Romantic/Intimate Relationships in the Well-Being of Incarcerated Females." *Psychological Services* 4(4):250–61.

Behrens, Angela, Christopher Uggen, and Jeff Manza. 2003. "Ballot Manipulation and the 'Menace of Negro Domination': Racial Threat and Felon Disenfranchisement in the United States, 1850–2002." *American Journal of Sociology* 109(3):559–605.

Bell, Derrick. 1992. *Faces at the Bottom of the Well: The Permanence of Racism*. New York: Basic Books.

———. 1988. "Property Rights in Whiteness: Their Legal Legacy, Their Economic Costs." *Villanova Law Review* 33(5):767–79.

———. 1980. "*Brown* and the Interest Convergence Dilemma." In *Shades of "Brown": New Perspectives on School Desegregation*, edited by Derrick Bell, 90–106. New York: Teachers College Press.

Betancur, John, and Cedric Herring. 2012. "Reinventing Race, Reinventing Racism: An Introduction." In *Reinventing Race, Reinventing Racism*, edited by John Betancur and Cedric Herring, 1–22. Leiden, Netherlands: Brill.

Binnall, James. 2010. "A Felon Deliberates: Policy Implications of the Michigan Supreme Court's Holding in *People v. Miller*." *University of Detroit Mercy Law Review* 87(2):59–81.

———. 2009. "Sixteen Million Angry Men: Reviving a Dead Doctrine to Challenge the Constitutionality of Excluding Felons from Jury Service." *Virginia Journal of Society Policy and the Law* 17(1):1–42.

———. 2008. "EG1900 . . . the Number They Gave Me When They Revoked My Citizenship: Perverse Consequences of Ex-Felon Civic Exile." *Willamette Law Review* 44:667–97.

Blackburn, F. S. 1981. "The Relationship between Recidivism and Participation in a Community College Program for Incarcerated Offenders." *Journal of Correctional Education* 32(3):23–25.

Blumenbach, Johann Friedrich. 2000. "On the Natural Variety of Mankind." In *The Idea of Race,* edited by Robert Bernasconi and Tommy Lee Lott, 27–37. Cambridge, MA: Hackett.

Blumer, Herbert. 1965. "The Future of the Color Line." In *The South in Continuity and Change*, edited by John McKinney and Edgar Thompson, 322–36. Durham, NC: Duke University Press.

Blumstein, Alfred, Jacqueline Cohen, Jeffrey Roth, and Christy Visher. 1986. *Criminal Careers and "Career Criminals."* Washington, DC: National Academy Press.

Bobo, Lawrence, and Victor Thompson. 2010. "Racialized Mass Incarceration: African Americans and the Criminal Justice System." In *Doing Race: 21 Essays for the 21st Century*, edited by Hazel Markus and Paula Moya, 322–55. New York: Norton.

———. 2006. "Unfair by Design: The War on Drugs, Race, and the Legitimacy of the Criminal Justice System." *Social Research* 73(2):445–72.

Bogdan, Robert, and Sari Biklen. 1998. *Qualitative Research for Education: An Introduction to Theory and Methods*, 3rd ed. Boston: Allyn & Bacon

Bond, Charles, and Bella DePaulo. 2006. "Accuracy of Deception Judgments." *Personality and Social Psychology Review* 10:214–34.

Bosk, Charles, and Raymond DeVries. 2004. "Bureaucracies of Mass Deception: Institutional Review Boards and the Ethics of Ethnographic Research." *Annals of the American Academy of Political and Social Science* 595(1):249–63.

Bouie, Jamelle. 2014. "The New Racism: First You Deny Racism Exists, Then You Smear the Reputation of Any Black Man Who Appears to Be a Victim." *Slate.com* (Sept. 5).

Boxer, Paul, Keesha Middlemass, and Tahlia Delorenzo. 2009. "Exposure to Violent Crime during Incarceration: Effects on Psychological Adjustment Following Release." *Criminal Justice and Behavior* 36:793–807.

Boxer, Paul, Ashley Schappell, Keesha Middlemass, Tahlia DeLorenzo, and Ignacio Mercado. 2011. "Cognitive and Emotional Covariates of Violence Exposure among Former Prisoners: Links to Antisocial Behavior and Emotional Distress and Implications for Theory." *Aggressive Behavior* 37(5):465–75.

Brantingham, Paul, and Patricia Brantingham. 1981. "Notes on the Geometry of Crime." In *Environmental Criminology*, edited by Paul Brantingham and Patricia Brantingham, 27–54. Beverly Hills, CA: Sage.

Briggs, Charles. 1986. *Learning How to Ask: A Sociolinguistic Appraisal of the Role of the Interview in Social Science Research*. New York: Cambridge University Press.

Brownstein, Henry. 2000. *Social Reality of Violence and Violent Crime*. Needham, MA: Allyn & Bacon.

———. 1996. *The Rise and Fall of a Violent Crime Wave: Crack Cocaine and the Social Construction of a Crime Problem*. Albany, NY: Harrow and Heston.

Bureau of Justice Statistics. 2008. *Slower Growth in the Nation's Prison and Jail Populations*. Washington, DC: U.S. Department of Justice, Office of Justice Programs, Bureau of Justice Statistics. www.bjs.gov.

Burgess, Elaine. 1965. "Race Relations and Social Change." In *The South in Continuity and Change*, edited by John McKinney and Edgar Thompson, 337–58. Durham, NC: Duke University Press.

Burgess, Robert. 1981. "Keeping a Research Diary." *Cambridge Journal of Education* 11(1):75–83.

Burke, Lisa, and Vivian James. 2001. "The Effect of College Programming on Recidivism Rates at the Hampden County House of Correction: A 5-Year Study." *Journal of Correctional Education* 52(4):160–62.

Burke, Peggy, and Michael Tonry. 2006. *Successful Transition and Reentry for Safer Communities: A Call to Action for Parole*. Silver Spring, MD: JEHT Foundation & Center for Effective Public Policy. www.cepp.com.

Bushway, Shawn, and Robert Apel. 2012. "A Signaling Perspective on Employment-Based Reentry Programming: Training Completion as a Desistance Signal." *Criminology and Public Policy* 11(1):21–50.

Butterfield, Fox. 1996. *All God's Children: The Bosket Family and the American Tradition of Violence*. New York: First Vintage Books.

Buysse, W. H. 1997. "Behavior Problems and Relationships with Family and Peers during Adolescence." *Journal of Adolescence* 20(6):645–59.

Calavera, Manny. 2008. *The Importance of Narrative Stories in Public Policy Analysis*. www.associatedcontent.com.

Cammett, Ann. 2011. "Deadbeats, Deadbrokes, and Prisoners." *Georgetown Journal on Poverty Law & Policy* 18(2):127–68.

Cardoso, Fernando, Cesar Gaviria, and Ernesto Zedillo. 2009. "The War on Drugs Is a Failure: We Should Focus Instead on Reducing Harm to Users and on Tackling Organized Crime." *Wall Street Journal* (Feb. 23). online.wsj.com.

Carey, Corinne. 2005. "No Second Chance: People with Criminal Records Denied Access to Public Housing." *University of Toledo Law Review* 36(3):545–94.

Carpenter, Catherine. 2010. "Legislative Epidemics: A Cautionary Tale of Criminal Laws That Have Swept the Country." *Buffalo Law Review* 58(1):1–67.

Carson, E. Ann. 2014. *Prisoners in 2013* (NCJ 247282). Washington, DC: U.S. Department of Justice, Office of Justice Programs, Bureau of Justice Statistics. www.bjs.gov.

Cavanaugh, Jillian. 2011. "Helping Those Who Serve: Veterans Treatment Courts Foster Rehabilitation and Reduce Recidivism for Offending Combat Veterans." *New England Law Review* 45(2):463–87.

Caves, Roger. 1989. "An Historical Analysis of Federal Housing Policy from the Presidential Perspective: An Intergovernmental Focus." *Urban Studies* 26(1):59–76.

Cervantes, Angelica, Marlena Creusere, Robin McMillion, Carla McQueen, Matt Short, Matt Steiner, and Jeff Webster. 2005. *Opening the Doors to Higher Education: Perspectives on Higher Education Act 40 Years Later*. Round Rock, TX: TG Research and Analytical Services. www.tgslc.org.

Chambliss, William. 2001. *Power, Politics, and Crime*. Boulder, CO: Westview.

Chappell, Cathryn. 2004. "Post-Secondary Correctional Education and Recidivism: A Meta-Analysis of Research Conducted, 1990–1999." *Journal of Correctional Education* 55(2):148–69.

Chin, Gabriel. 2002. "Race, the War on Drugs, and the Collateral Consequences of Criminal Conviction." *Journal of Gender, Race & Justice* 6:253–96.

Chin, Gabriel, and Richard Holmes. 2002. "Effective Assistance of Counsel and the Consequences of Guilty Pleas." *Cornell Law Review* 87(3):697–742.

Chiseri-Strater, Elizabeth, and Bonnie Sunstein. 1997. *Fieldworking: Reading and Writing Research*. Upper Saddle River, NJ: Blair Press.

Christie, Nils. 1986. "Ideal Victim: From Crime Policy to Victim Policy." In *From Crime Policy to Victim Policy: Reorienting the Justice System*, edited by Ezzat Fattah, 17–30. New York: Macmillan.

Clear, Todd. 2009. *Imprisoning Communities: How Mass Incarceration Makes Disadvantaged Neighborhoods Worse*. New York: Oxford University Press.

———. 2007. "The Impacts of Incarceration on Public Safety." *Social Research: An International Quarterly of the Social Sciences* 74(2):613–30.

Clemens, Franziska. 2013. *Detecting Lies about Past and Future Actions: The Strategic Use of Evidence (SUE) Technique and Suspects' Strategies*. Gothenburg, Sweden: University of Gothenburg.

Cobbina, Jennifer. 2010. "Reintegration Success and Failure: Factors Impacting Reintegration among Incarcerated and Formerly Incarcerated Women." *Journal of Offender Rehabilitation* 49:210–32.

Cohen, Neil, and Dean Rivkin. 1971. "Civil Disabilities: The Forgotten Punishment." *Federal Probation* 35(2):19–25.

Cohen, Stan. 1972. *Folk Devils and Moral Panics: The Creation of the Mods and Rockers*. St. Albans, UK: Paladin.

Coley, Richard, and Paul Barton. 2006. *Locked Up and Locked Out: An Educational Perspective on the U.S. Prison Population*. Princeton, NJ: Educational Testing Service.

Conley, Dalton. 2001. "A Room with a View or a Room of One's Own? Housing and Social Stratification." *Sociological Forum* 16(2):263–80.

Cook, Robert. 1941. "The Concept of Race in the Human Species in the Light of Genetics." *Journal of Heredity* 32:243–47.

Corry, Nida, Brendan Klick, and James Fauerbach. 2010. "Posttraumatic Stress Disorder and Pain Impact Functioning and Disability after Major Burn Injury." *Journal of Burn Care & Research* 31(1):13–25.

Cose, Ellis. 2002. *The Envy of the World: On Being a Black Man in America*. New York: Washington Square Park Press.

Coyle, Michael. 2003. "Race and Class Penalties in Crack Cocaine Sentencing." Paper presented at the annual meeting for the American Sociological Association, Atlanta, Georgia, August 16–19. http://iamsaam.org.

Crayton, Anna, and Suzanne Neusteter. 2008. "The Current State of Correctional Education." Paper presented at the meeting for the Reentry Roundtable on Education. Urban Institute, Washington, DC. http://www.urban.org.

Critcher, Clayton, and Jane Risen. 2014. "If He Can Do It, So Can They: Exposure to Counterstereotypically Successful Exemplars Prompts Automatic Inferences." *Journal of Personality and Social Psychology* 106(3):359–79.

Cronkite, Walter. 2006. "Telling the Truth about the War on Drugs." *HuffingtonPost.com* (March 1). www.huffingtonpost.com.

Damaska, Mirjan. 1968. "Adverse Legal Consequences of Conviction and Their Removal: A Comparative Study." *Journal of Criminal Law, Criminology, & Police Science* 59:347–52.

Dance, Janelle. 2002. *Tough Fronts: The Impact of Street Culture on Schooling*. New York: RoutledgeFalmer.

Davidson, Randy. 2008. "Resources on Collateral Consequences of Criminal Convictions." *Michigan Bar Journal* 87:52–53.

Davis, Angela. 2003. *Are Prisons Obsolete?* New York: Seven Stories Press.

———. 2002. "Incarceration and the Imbalance of Power." In *Invisible Punishment: The Collateral Consequences of Mass Imprisonment*, edited by Marc Mauer and Meda Chesney-Lind, 61–78. New York: Norton.

Davis, David. 1966. *The Problem of Slavery in Western Culture*. New York: Oxford University Press.

———. 1984. *Slavery and Human Progress*. New York: Oxford University Press.

Davis, F. James. 1991. *Who Is Black? One Nation's Definition*. University, PA: Pennsylvania State University Press.

———. 1978. *Minority-Dominant Relations*. Arlington Heights, IL: AHM Publishing.

Davis, Lois, Robert Bozick, Jennifer Steele, Jessica Saunders, and Jeremy Miles. 2013. *Evaluating the Effectiveness of Correctional Education: A Meta-Analysis of Programs That Provide Education to Incarcerated Adults*. Washington, DC: Rand Corporation.

Dekel, Sharon, Tamar Peleg, and Zahava Solomon. 2013. "The Relationship of PTSD to Negative Cognitions: A 17-Year Longitudinal Study." *Psychiatry* 76(3):241–55.

Demleitner, Nora. 2000. "Continuing Payment on One's Debt to Society: The German Model of Felon Disenfranchisement as an Alternative." *Minnesota Law Review* 84(4):753–804.

———. 1999. "Preventing Internal Exile: The Need for Restrictions on Collateral Sentencing Consequences." *Stanford Law & Policy Review* 11(1):153–71.

DeSouza, Eros. 2008. "Workplace Incivility, Sexual Harassment, and Racial Micro-Aggression: The Interface of Three Literatures." In *The Psychology of Women at Work: Challenges and Solutions for Our Female Workforce*, edited by Michele Paludi, 65–84. Westport, CT: Praeger.

DeVeaux, Mika'il. 2013. "The Trauma of the Incarcerated Experience." *Harvard Civil Rights–Civil Liberties Law Review* 48(1):257–77.

Devlin, Richard, and Dianne Pothier. 2006. "Toward a Critical Theory of Dis-Citizenship." In *Critical Disability Theory: Essays in Philosophy, Politics, Policy, and Law*, edited by Dianne Pothier and Richard Devlin, 1–22. Vancouver, Canada: University of British Columbia Press.

DiCicco-Bloom, Barbara, and Benjamin F. Crabtree. 2006. "The Qualitative Research Interview." *Medical Education* 40:314–21.

Dolovich, Sharon. 2012. "Two Models of the Prison: Accidental Humanity and Hypermasculinity in the L.A. County Jail." *Journal of Criminal Law & Criminology* 102(4):965–1117.

Dominguez, Virginia. 1986. *White by Definition*. New Brunswick, NJ: Rutgers University Press.

Donovan, Kathleen. 2010. "No Hope for Redemption: The False Choice between Safety and Justice in Hope VI Ex-Offender Admissions Policies." *DePaul Journal for Social Justice* 3(2):173–212.

Doris, John. 2002. *Lack of Character: Personality and Moral Behavior*. New York: Cambridge University Press.

Dowler, Kenneth. 2003. "Media Consumption and Public Attitudes toward Crime and Justice: The Relationship between Fear of Crime, Punitive Attitudes, and Perceived Police Effectiveness." *Journal of Criminal Justice and Popular Culture* 10(2):109–26.

Draine, Jeffrey, and Daniel Herman. 2007. "Critical Time Intervention for Reentry from Prison for Persons with Mental Illness." *Psychiatric Services* 58(12):1577–81.

Du Bois, William Edward Burghardt. 1903. *The Souls of Black Folk*. Cambridge, MA: University Press John Wilson and Son.

———. 1901. "The Spawn of Slavery: The Convict Lease System in the South." *Missionary Review of the World* 14:737–45.

———. 1900. *Address to the Nations of the World*. Speech to the First Pan-African Conference. London, England (July).

Durose, Matthew, Alexia Cooper, and Howard Snyder. 2014. *Recidivism of Prisoners Released in 30 States in 2005: Patterns from 2005 to 2010* (NCJ 244205). Washington, DC: U.S. Department of Justice, Office of Justice Programs, Bureau of Justice Statistics. www.bjs.gov.

Dye, Thomas. 1972. *Understanding Public Policy*. Englewood Cliffs, CA: Prentice Hall.

———. 1971. *The Politics of Equality*. New York: Bobbs-Merrill.

Eagleton, Terry. 1979. "Ideology, Fiction, Narrative." *Social Text* 2:62–80.

Easton, David. 1978. *A Framework for Political Analysis*. Chicago: University of Chicago Press.

Eberhardt, Jennifer, Phillip Goff, Valerie Purdie, and Paul Davies. 2004. "Seeing Black: Race, Crime, and Visual Processing." *Journal of Personality and Social Psychology* 87(6):876–93.

Edgell, Penny, Joseph Gerteis, and Douglas Hartmann. 2006. "Atheists as 'Other': Moral Boundaries and Cultural Membership in American Society." *American Sociological Review* 71(April):211–34.

Edsall, Thomas B., and Mary D. Edsall. 1991. *Chain Reaction: The Impact of Race, Rights, and Taxes on American Politics*. New York: Norton.

Eisen, Lauren-Brooke. 2014. "Paying for Your Time: How Charging Inmates Fees behind Bars May Violate the Excessive Fines Clause." *Loyola Journal of Public Interest Law* 15(2):319–41.

Emerson, Robert, Rachel Fretz, and Linda Shaw. 1995. *Writing Ethnographic Fieldnotes*. Chicago: University of Chicago Press.

Emirbayer, Mustafa, and Ann Mische. 1998. "What Is Agency?" *American Journal of Sociology* 103(4):962–1023.

Emsellem, Maurice. 2005. *Smart on Crime: Agenda to Promote Public Safety while Addressing Occupational Barriers for People with Criminal Records*. Washington, DC: CRS Report for Congress (RL33415, June 9).

Estrada, Felipe. 2004. "The Transformation of the Politics of Crime in High Crime Societies." *European Journal of Criminology* 1(4):419–43.

Ewald, Alec. 2005. *A "Crazy-Quilt" of Tiny Pieces: State and Local Administration of American Criminal Disenfranchisement Law*. Washington, DC: Sentencing Project.

———. 2002. "'Civil Death': The Ideological Paradox of Criminal Disenfranchisement Law in the United States." *Wisconsin Law Review* 5:1045–1137.

Falk, Gerhard. 2001. *Stigma: How We Treat Outsiders*. Amherst, NY: Prometheus.

FBI Domestic Investigations and Operations Guide. 2013 (retrieved from https://vault. fbi.gov).

Feldman, Lisa, Vincent Schiraldi, and Jason Ziedenberg. 2001. "Too Little Too Late: President Clinton's Prison Legacy." Washington, DC: Justice Policy Institute. www. justicepolicy.org.

Fenno, Richard. 1986. "Observation, Context, and Sequence in the Study of Politics." *American Political Science Review* 80(1):3–15.

———. 1978. *Home Style: Representatives in Their Districts*. Boston: Little, Brown.

Fetterman, David. 1989. *Ethnography: Step by Step*. Newbury Park, CA: Sage.

Fields, Barbara. 1982. "Ideology and Race in American History." In *Region, Race, and Reconstruction*, edited by Morgan Kousser and James McPherson, 143–77. New York: Oxford University Press.

Fine, Michelle, et al. 2001. *Changing Minds: The Impact of College in a Maximum-Security Prison*. Bedford Hills: New York Department of Correctional Services.

Finkelman, Paul. 2000. *An Imperfect Union: Slavery, Federalism, and Comity*. Chapel Hill: University of North Carolina Press.

———. 1993. "The Crime of Color." *Tulane Law Review* 67:2063–2112.

Fischman, Joshua, and Max M. Schanzenbach. 2012. "Racial Disparities under the Federal Sentencing Guidelines: The Role of Judicial Discretion and Mandatory Minimums." *Journal of Empirical Legal Studies* 9(4):729–64.

Foley, Regina, and Jing Gao. 2004. "Correctional Education: Characteristics of Academic Programs Serving Incarcerated Adults." *Journal of Correctional Education* 55(1):6–21.

Ford, Larry R. 2001. "Alleys and Urban Form: Testing the Tenets of New Urbanism." *Urban Geography* 22(3):268–86.

Forsyth, Craig, and Rhonda Evans. 2003. "Reconsidering the Pseudo-Family/Gang Gender Distinction in Prison Research." *Journal of Police & Criminal Psychology* 18(1):15–23.

Foucault, Michel. 2003. *Abnormal: Lectures at the Collège de France, 1974–1975* (translation). London: Verso.

———. 1982. "The Subject of Power." *Critical Inquiry* 8(4):777–95.

———. 1980. *Power/Knowledge: Selected Interviews and Other Writings*. New York: Pantheon.

———. 1979. *Discipline and Punish: The Birth of the Prison*. New York: Vintage.

———. 1969. *The Archaeology of Knowledge* (translation). New York: Pantheon.

———. 1967. *Madness and Civilization: A History of Insanity in the Age of Reason* (translation). London: Tavistock.

Frazee, Catherine, Joan Gilmour, and Roxanne Mykitiuk. 2006. "Now You See Her, Now You Don't: How Law Shapes Disabled Women's Experience of Exposure, Surveillance, and Assessment in the Clinical Encounter." In *Critical Disability Theory:*

Essays in Philosophy, Politics, Policy, and Law, edited by Dianne Pothier and Richard Devlin, 223–47. Vancouver, Canada: University of British Columbia Press.

Freeman, Richard. 2003. "Can We Close the Revolving Door? Recidivism vs. Employment of Ex-Offenders in the U.S." Urban Institute Reentry Roundtable, New York University Law School. http://www.urban.org.

Garfinkel, Harold. 1956. "Conditions of Successful Degradation Ceremonies." *American Journal of Sociology* 61(5):420–24.

Garland, David. 2001a. *Mass Imprisonment: Social Causes and Consequences*. London: Sage.

———. 2001b. *The Culture of Control: Crime and Social Order in Contemporary Society*. Chicago: University of Chicago Press.

———. 1991. "Sociological Perspectives on Punishment." In *Crime and Criminal Justice: A Review of Research*, edited by Michael Tonry, 115–66. Chicago: University of Chicago Press.

Gates, Nathaniel. 1997a. *Racial Classification and History*. New York: Garland.

———. 1997b. *The Concept of "Race" in Natural and Social Science*. New York: Garland.

Geertz, Clifford. 1973. *The Interpretation of Cultures*. New York: Basic Books.

Gehring, Thom. 1997. "Post-Secondary Education for Inmates: An Historical Inquiry." *Journal of Correctional Education* 48(2):46–55.

Gellhorn, Walter. 1976. "The Abuse of Occupational Licensing." *University of Chicago Law Review* 44(1):6–27.

Georges-Abeyie, Daniel. 1990. "The Myth of a Racist Criminal Justice System?" *Racism, Empiricism, and Criminal Justice*, edited by Brian D. MacLean and Dragan Milovanovic, 11–14. Vancouver, Canada: Collective Press.

Gerschick, Thomas. 2000. "Toward a Theory of Disability and Gender." *Signs: Journal of Women in Culture and Society* 25(4):1263–68.

Ghandnoosh, Nazgol. 2014. *Race and Punishment: Racial Perceptions of Crime and Support for Punitive Policies*. Washington, DC: Sentencing Project.

Gibbons, John, and Nicholas Katzenbach. 2006. "Confronting Confinement: A Report of the Commission on Safety and Abuse in America's Prisons." *Journal of Law & Policy* 22:385–562.

Gilens, Martin. 1999. *Why Americans Hate Welfare: Race, Media, and the Politics of Anti-Poverty Policy*. Chicago: University of Chicago Press.

Gilliam, Franklin, Jr., and Shanto Iyengar. 2000. "Prime Suspects: The Impact of Local Television News on the Viewing Public." *American Journal of Political Science* 44(3):560–73.

———. 1998. "The Super-Predator Script." *Nieman Reports* 52(4):45–49.

Glaser, Barney, and Anselm Strauss. 1967. *The Discovery of Grounded Theory: Strategies for Qualitative Research*. Chicago: Aldine.

Glassford, Jeremiah. 2013. "In War, There Are No Unwounded Soldiers: The Emergence of Veterans Treatment Courts in Alabama." *Alabama Law Review* 65(1):239–67.

Glaze, Lauren, and Laura Maruschak. 2008. *Parents in Prison and Their Minor Children* (NCJ 222984). Washington, DC: U.S. Department of Justice, Office of Justice Programs, Bureau of Justice Statistics. www.bjs.gov.

Glaze, Lauren E., and Erika Parks. 2012. *Correctional Populations in the United States, 2011* (NCJ 239972). Washington, DC: U.S. Department of Justice, Office of Justice Programs, Bureau of Justice Statistics. www.bjs.gov.

Gleeson, Brendan. 1996. "A Geography for Disabled People?" *Transactions of the Institute of British Geographers*, New Series 21(2):387–96.

Goebel, Julius. 1976. *Felony and Misdemeanor: A Study of the History of Criminal Law.* Philadelphia: University of Pennsylvania Press.

Goff, Ashley, Emmeline Rose, Suzanna Rose, and David Purves. 2007. "Does PTSD Occur in Sentenced Prison Populations? A Systematic Literature Review." *Criminal Behavior and Mental Health* 17:152–62.

Goff, Phillip, Jennifer Eberhardt, Melissa Williams, and Matthew Jackson. 2008. "Not Yet Human: Implicit Knowledge, Historical Dehumanization, and Contemporary Consequences." *Journal of Personality and Social Psychology* 94(2):292–306.

Goff, Phillip, Matthew Jackson, Brooke DiLeone, Carmen Culotta, Natalie DiTomasso. 2014. "The Essence of Innocence: Consequences of Dehumanizing Black Children." *Journal of Personality and Social Psychology* 106(4):526–45.

Goffman, Erving. 1963. *Stigma: Notes on the Management of Spoiled Identity.* Englewood Cliffs, NJ: Prentice Hall.

———. 1961. *Asylums: Essays on the Social Situation of Mental Patients and Other Inmates.* Garden City, NY: Doubleday.

———. 1959. *The Presentation of Self in Everyday Life.* New York: Doubleday.

———. 1957. "The Characteristics of Total Institutions." *Symposium on Preventive and Social Psychiatry,* April 15–17, Walter Reed Army Institute of Research, Washington, D.C.

Gold, Raymond. 1997. "The Ethnographic Method in Sociology." *Qualitative Enquiry* 3(4):388–402.

Goldfield, Michael. 1991. "The Color of Politics in the United States: White Supremacy as the Main Explanation for the Peculiarities of American Politics from Colonial Times to the Present." In *The Bounds of Race: Perspectives on Hegemony and Resistance*, edited by Dominick LaCapra, 104–33. Ithaca, NY: Cornell University Press.

Golledge, Reginald. 1993. "Geography and the Disabled: A Survey with Special Reference to Vision-Impaired and Blind Populations." *Transactions of the Institute of British Geographers* 18(1):63–85.

Goodman, Lisa, Leonard Saxe, and Mary Harvey. 1991. "Homelessness as Psychological Trauma." *American Psychologist* 46(11):1219–25.

Gossett, Thomas. 1997. *Race: The History of an Idea in America.* New York: Oxford University Press.

Gotanda, Neil. 1991. "A Critique of 'Our Constitution Is Color-Blind.'" *Stanford Law Review* 44(1):1–68.

Gothman, Kevin. 2000. "Separate and Unequal: The Housing Act of 1968 and the Section 235 Program." *Sociological Forum* 15(1):13–37.

Gottschalk, Marie. 2006. *The Prison and the Gallows: The Politics of Mass Incarceration in America.* New York: Cambridge University Press.

Gould, Stephen. 1994. "The Geometer of Race." *Discover* 15(November):65–69.

Granucci, Anthony. 1969. "Nor Cruel and Unusual Punishment Inflicted: The Original Meaning." *California Law Review* 57(4):839–65.

Grattet, Ryken, Joan Petersilia, Jeffrey Lin, and Marlene Beckman. 2009. "Parole Violations and Revocations in California: Analysis and Suggestions for Action." *Federal Probation* 73(1):2–11.

Greenridge, Abel. 1894. *Infamia: Its Place in Roman Public and Private Law.* London: Clarendon.

Greer, Chris. 2007. "News Media, Victim, and Crime." In *Victims, Crime, and Society,* edited by Pamela Davies, Peter Francis and Chris Greer, 20–49. New York: Sage.

Greer, Kimberly. 2000. "The Changing Nature of Interpersonal Relationships in a Women's Prison." *Prison Journal* 80(4):442–68.

Grinstead, Olga, Bonnie Faigeles, Carrie Bancroft, and Barry Zack. 2001. "The Financial Cost of Maintaining Relationships with Incarcerated African American Men: A Survey of Women Prison Visitors." *Journal of African American Men* 6(1):59–69.

Grossberg, Michael, and Christopher Tomlins. 2008. *The Cambridge History of Law in America,* volume I. Cambridge, MA: Cambridge University Press.

Gurney, Joan. 1985. "Not One of the Guys: The Female Researcher in a Male-Dominated Setting." *Qualitative Sociology* 8(1):42–62.

Gusfield, Joseph. 1996. *Contested Meanings: The Construction of Alcohol Problems.* Madison: University of Wisconsin Press.

Guzman, Carolina, Rajiv Bhatia, and Chris Durazo. 2005. *Anticipated Effects of Residential Displacement on Health: Results from Qualitative Research.* San Francisco Department of Public Health & South of Market Community Action Network. www.sfphes.org.

Haber, Mason, and Paul Toro. 2004. "Homelessness among Families, Children, and Adolescents: An Ecological-Developmental Perspective." *Clinical Child and Family Psychology Review* 7(3):123–64.

Hagan, John. 1992. "The Poverty of a Classless Criminology: The American Society of Criminology 1991 Presidential Address." *Criminology* 30(1):1–19.

Hagan, John, John Hewitt, and Duane Alwin. 1979. "Ceremonial Justice: Crime and Punishment in a Loosely Coupled System." *Social Forces* 58(2):506–27.

Hammersley, Martyn, and Paul Atkinson. 2007. *Ethnography: Principles in Practice,* 3rd ed. New York: Routledge.

Hancock, Ange-Marie. 2004. *The Politics of Disgust and the Public Identity of the "Welfare Queen."* New York: New York University Press.

Haney-Lopez, Ian. 1996. *White by Law: The Legal Construction of Race.* New York: New York University Press.

———. 1994. "The Social Construction of Race: Some Observations on Illusion, Fabrication, and Choice." *Harvard Civil Rights–Civil Liberties Law Review* 29(4):1–62.

Harlow, Caroline, David Jenkins, and Stephen Steurer. 2010. "GED Holders in Prison Read Better Than Those in the Household Population: Why?" *Journal of Correctional Education* 61(1):68–92.

Harrison, Paige M., and Allen J. Beck. 2003. *Prisoners in 2003* (NCJ 205335). Washington, DC: U.S. Department of Justice, Office of Justice Programs, Bureau of Justice Statistics. www.bjs.gov.

Hartnett, Stephen, Jennifer Wood, and Bryan McCann. 2011. "Turning Silence into Speech and Action: Prison Activism and the Pedagogy of Empowered Citizenship." *Communication and Critical/Cultural Studies* 8(4):331–52.

Harvard Law Review. 2000. "Winning the War on Drugs: A 'Second Chance' for Nonviolent Drug Offenders." *Harvard Law Review* 113(6):1485–1502.

Harvey, Alice. 1994. "Ex-Felon Disenfranchisement and Its Influence on the Black Vote: The Need for a Second Look." *University of Pennsylvania Law Review* 142(3):1145–89.

Hatsukami, Dorothy, and Marian Fischman. 1996. "Crack Cocaine and Cocaine Hydrochloride: Are the Differences Myth or Reality?" *Journal of American Medical Association* 276(19):1580–88.

Hedges, Chris. 2013. "The Business of Mass Incarceration." www.truthdig.com.

Heffernan, Esther. 1972. *Making It in Prison: The Square, the Cool, and the Life.* New York: Wiley.

Hellegers, Adam. 1999. "Reforming HUD's 'One Strike' Public Housing Evictions through Tenant Participation." *Journal of Criminal Law and Criminology* 90:323–61.

Hench, Virginia. 1998. "The Death of Voting Rights: The Legal Disenfranchisement of Minority Voters." *Case Western Law Review* 48(4):727–98.

Hening, William. 1809. *Statutes at Large: Being a Collection of All the Laws of Virginia, from the First Session of the Legislature, in the Year 1619.* Richmond, VA: Samuel Pleasants.

Henretta, John. 1979. "Racial Differences in Middle-Class Lifestyle: The Role of Home Ownership." *Social Science Research* 8(1):63–78.

Henry, Charles. 1990. *Culture and African American Politics.* Bloomington: Indiana University Press.

Hetey, Rebecca, and Jennifer Eberhardt. 2014. "Racial Disparities in Incarceration Increase Acceptance of Punitive Policies. "*Psychological Science* 1–6. doi: 10.1177/09567976145 40307.

Higginbotham, Leon, Jr. 1996. *Shades of Freedom: Racial Politics and Presumptions of the American Legal Process*, volume 2. New York: Oxford University Press.

Hill, Gerald, and Kathleen Hill. 2002. *The People's Law Dictionary: Taking the Mystery out of Legal Language.* New York: MJF Books.

Holian, David. 2004. "He's Stealing My Issues! Clinton's Crime Rhetoric and the Dynamics of Issue Ownership." *Political Behavior* 26(2):95–124.

Holl, Douglas, and Lisa Kolovich. 2007. *Evaluation of the Prisoner Re-Entry Initiative: Interim Report.* U.S. Department of Labor, Employment and Training Administration. Bethesda, MD.

Holzer, Harry, Steven Raphael, and Michael Stoll. 2006. "Perceived Criminality, Criminal Background Checks, and the Racial Hiring Practices of Employers." *Journal of Law and Economics* 49(2):451–80.

Holzman, Harold. 1996. "Criminology Research on Public Housing: Toward a Better Understanding of People, Places, and Spaces." *Crime & Delinquency* 42:107–26.

Hu, Jianting, Kajal Lahiri, Denton Vaughan, and Bernard Wixon. 2001. "A Structural Model of Social Security's Disability Determination Process." *Review of Economics and Statistics* 83(2):348–61.

Human Rights Watch. 2012. *Old Behind Bars: The Aging Prison Population in the United States*. New York: Human Rights Watch. www.hrw.org.

Hurwitz, Jon, and Mark Peffley. 1997. "Public Perceptions of Race and Crime: The Role of Racial Stereotypes." *American Journal of Political Science* 41(2):375–401.

Hussein, Ashatu. 2009. "The Use of Triangulation in Social Sciences Research: Can Qualitative and Quantitative Methods Be Combined?" *Journal of Comparative Social Work* 1:1–12.

Hutchison, Kay Bailey. 1993. "Violent Crime Control and Law Enforcement Act, Amendment No. 1158." *Congressional Record*, 103rd Congress (1993–1994), 1st session, Senate, November 16, p. S15746. Retrieved from: http://webarchive.loc.gov.

Hylton, John. 1982. "Rhetoric and Reality: A Critical Appraisal of Community Correctional Programs." *Crime & Delinquency* 28(3):341–73.

Immerwahr, John, and Jean Johnson. 2002. *The Revolving Door: Exploring Public Attitudes toward Prisoner Reentry*. Washington, DC: Urban Institute. www.urban.org.

Ingebretsen, Edward. 1998. "Staking the Monster: A Politics of Remonstrance." *Religion and American Culture: A Journal of Interpretation* 8(1):91–116.

Innes, Christopher. 1986. *Population Density in State Prisons* (NCJ 103204). Washington, DC: U.S. Department of Justice, Office of Justice Programs, Bureau of Justice Statistics. www.ncjrs.gov.

Itzkowitz, Howard, and Lauren Oldak. 1973. "Restoring the Ex-Offender's Right to Vote: Background and Developments." *American Criminal Law Review* 11(3):721–70.

Jacobson, Michael. 2005. *Downsizing Prisons: How to Reduce Crime and End Mass Incarceration*. New York: New York University Press.

James, Adrian, Keith Bottomley, Alison Liebling, and Emma Clare. 1997. *Privatizing Prisons: Rhetoric and Reality*. Thousand Oaks, CA: Sage.

Janoff-Bulman, Ronnie. 1992. *Shattered Assumptions: Towards a New Psychology of Trauma*. New York: Free Press.

Jencks, Christopher, and Susan Mayer. 1990. "The Social Consequences of Growing Up in a Poor Neighborhood." In *Inner-City Poverty in the United States*, edited by Lawrence Lynn Jr. and Michael McGeary, 111–86. Washington, DC: National Academy Press.

Jenkins, Richard. 1991. "Disability and Social Stratification." *British Journal of Sociology* 42(4):557–80.

Jick, Todd. 1979. "Mixing Qualitative and Quantitative Methods: Triangulation in Action." *Administrative Science Quarterly* 24(4):602–11.

Jordan, Gregory. 2004. "The Causes of Poverty: Cultural vs. Structural: Can There Be a Synthesis?" *Perspectives in Public Affairs* 1:18–34.

Jordan, Kareem, and Tina Freiburger. 2010. "Examining the Impact of Race and Ethnicity on the Sentencing of Juveniles in the Adult Court." *Criminal Justice Policy Review* 21(2):185–201.

Jordan, Winthrop. 1968. *White over Black: American Attitudes toward the Negro, 1550–1812.* Chapel Hill: University of North Carolina Press.

Kalt, Brian. 2003. "The Exclusion of Felons from Jury Service." *American University Law Review* 53:65–189.

Kanigel, Rachele. 2008. "Where You Live Determines Your Quality of Care: What to Know before You Schedule a Surgery or Fill a Prescription." *NBC News* (July 1). www.nbcnews.com.

Kappel Ramji Consulting Group. 2002. *Common Occurrence: The Impact of Homelessness on Women's Health. Phase II: Community Based Action Research. Final Report.* Toronto: Brown Books.

Kappeler, Victor E. 2015. *Community Policing: A Contemporary Perspective.* New York: Routledge.

Karlan, Pamela. 2004. "Conviction and Doubts: Retribution, Representation, and the Debate over Felon Disenfranchisement." *Stanford Law Review* 56(5):1147–70.

Kellaway, Jean. 2003. *The History of Torture and Execution: From Early Civilization through Medieval Times to the Present.* Guilford, CT: Lyons Press.

Kennedy, Randall. 1997. *Race, Crime, and the Law.* New York: Pantheon.

Kerekes, John. 1994. "The Housing and Community Development Act of 1992: Affordable Housing Initiatives May Have Found a Home." *Seton Hall Legislative Journal* 18(2):683–727.

Keyssar, Alexander. 2000. *The Right to Vote: The Contested History of Democracy in the United States.* New York: Basic Books.

King, Ryan. 2008. *Disparity by Geography: The War on Drugs in America's Cities.* Washington, DC: Sentencing Project.

Kleiman, Mark. 2009. *When Brute Force Fails: How to Have Less Crime and Less Punishment.* Princeton, NJ: Princeton University Press.

Klimchuk, Dennis. 2001. "Retribution, Restitution, and Revenge." *Law and Philosophy* 20:81–101.

Koch, Tom. 2001. "Disability and Difference: Balancing Social and Physical Constructions." *Journal of Medical Ethics* 27:370–76.

Kornblum, William. 1988. *Sociology in a Changing World,* 8th ed. New York: Holt, Rinehart & Winston.

Kosygina, Larisa. 2005. "Doing Gender in Research: Reflection on Experience in the Field." *Qualitative Report* 10(1):87–95.

Kupers, Terry. 2005. "Toxic Masculinity as a Barrier to Mental Health Treatment in Prison." *Journal of Clinical Psychology* 61(6):713–24.

Kushnick, Louis. 1998. *Race, Class, and Struggle: Essays on Racism and Inequality in Britain, the U.S., and Western Europe.* New York: Rivers Oram Press.

Kyckelhahn, Tracey. 2014. *State Corrections Expenditures, FY 1982–2010* (NCJ 239672). Washington, DC: U.S. Department of Justice, Office of Justice Programs, Bureau of Justice Statistics. www.bjs.gov.

Ladson-Billings, Gloria. 1999. "Just What Is Critical Race Theory, and What's It Doing in a Nice Field like Education?" In *Race Is . . . Race Isn't: Critical Race Theory and Qualitative Studies in Education*, edited by Laurence Parker, Donna Deyhle, and Sofia Villenas, 7–24. Boulder, CO: Westview.

Lamb, Charles. 2005. *Housing Segregation in Suburban America since 1960*. New York: Cambridge University Press.

Landau, Rue. 2002. "Criminal Records and Subsidized Housing: Families Losing the Opportunity for Decent Shelter." In *Every Door Closed: Barriers Facing Parents with Criminal Records*, edited by Amy Hirsh, Sharon Dietrich, Rue Landau, Peter Schneider, and Irv Ackelsberg, 45–55. Washington, DC: Center for Law and Social Policy & Community Legal Services.

Landers, Robert, and Richard Worsnop. 1970. "Low-Income Housing." *CQ Researcher*, October 28.

Langan, Patrick. 1991. *Race of Prisoners Admitted to State and Federal Institutions, 1926–86* (NCJ 125618). Washington, DC: U.S. Department of Justice, Office of Justice Programs, Bureau of Justice Statistics. www.ncjrs.gov.

Langan, Patrick, and David Levin. 2002. *Recidivism of Prisoners Released in 1994* (NCJ 193427). Washington, DC: U.S. Department of Justice, Office of Justice Programs, Bureau of Justice Statistics.

Law Enforcement Against Prohibition (LEAP). 2011. *Ending the Drug War: A Dream Deferred*. Medford, MA: Law Enforcement Against Prohibition.

Law, John. 2004. *After Method: Mess in Social Science Research*. New York: Routledge.

Lee, Jayne Chong-Soon. 1995. "Navigating the Topology of Race." In *Critical Race Theory: The Key Writings That Formed the Movement*, edited by Kimberlé Crenshaw, Neil Gotanda, Gary Peller, and Kendall Thomas, 441–49. New York: New Press.

Leone, Matthew C. 2002. "Net Widening." In *Encyclopedia of Crime and Punishment*, edited by David Levinson, 1088–89. Thousand, Oaks, CA: Sage.

Leverentz, Andrea. 2014. *The Ex-Prisoner's Dilemma: How Women Negotiate Competing Narratives of Reentry and Desistance*. New Brunswick, NJ: Rutgers University Press.

Levin, Josh. 2013. "The Real Story of Linda Taylor, America's Original Welfare Queen." *Slate Magazine* (December 19). www.slate.com.

Levitas, Ruth. 2000. "What Is Social Exclusion?" *Breadline Europe: The Measurement of Poverty*, edited by David Gordon and Peter Townsend, 357–84. Bristol, England: Policy Press.

Lewis, Kevin. 2013. "The Limits of Racial Prejudice." *Proceedings of the National Academy of Sciences of the United States of America* 110(47):18814–19.

Lichtenstein, Alex. 1996. *Twice the Work of Free Labour: The Political Economy of Convict Labour in the New South*. New York: Verso.

Lieberman, Robert. 2005. *Shaping Race Policy: The United States in Comparative Perspective*. Princeton, NJ: Princeton University Press.

Lippman, Matthew. 2006. *Contemporary Criminal Law: Concepts, Cases, and Controversies*. New York: Sage.

Lochner, Lance, and Enrico Moretti. 2004. "The Effect of Education on Crime: Evidence from Prison Inmates, Arrests, and Self-Reports." *American Economic Review* 94(1):155–89.

Lorber, Judith. 1994. *Paradoxes of Gender*. New Haven, CT: Yale University Press.

Lord, Elaine. 1995. "A Prison's Superintendent's Perspective on Women in Prison." *Prison Journal* 75(2):257–69.

Love, Margaret Colgate. 2011. "Paying Their Debt to Society: Forgiveness, Redemption, and the Uniform Collateral Consequences of Conviction Act." *Howard Law Journal* 54(3):753–94.

———. 2006. *Relief from the Collateral Consequences of a Criminal Conviction: A State-by-State Resource Guide*. New York: Hein.

Luckermann, Fred E. 1964. "Geography as a Formal Intellectual Discipline." *Canadian Geographer* 8(4):162–72.

Lum, Kristian, Samarth Swarup, Stephen Eubank, and James Hawdon. 2014. "The Contagious Nature of Imprisonment: An Agent-Based Model to Explain Racial Disparities in Incarceration Rates." *Journal of the Royal Society Interface* 11(98):20140409. doi:10.1098/rsif.2014.0409.

Lynch, John, and William Sabol. 2001. *Prisoner Reentry in Perspective* (Crime Policy Report 3). Washington, DC: Urban Institute. www.urban.org.

Lynch, Shannon, Dana DeHart, Joanne Belknap, and Bonnie Green. 2012. *Women's Pathways to Jail: The Roles and Intersections of Serious Mental Illness and Trauma* (Grant No. 2010-DB-BX-K048). Washington, DC: U.S. Department of Justice, Office of Justice Programs, Bureau of Justice Statistics. www.bja.gov.

Mallach, Alan. 2010. *Facing the Urban Challenge: The Federal Government and America's Older Distressed Cities*. Washington, DC: Urban Institute.

Manza, Jeff, and Christopher Uggen. 2006. *Locked Out: Felon Disenfranchisement and American Democracy*. New York: Oxford University Press.

Marable, Manning, Ian Steinberg, and Keesha Middlemass. 2007. *Racializing Justice, Disenfranchising Lives: The Racism, Criminal Justice, and Law Reader*. New York: Palgrave Macmillan.

Marks, Carole. 1991. "The Urban Underclass." *Annual Review of Sociology* 17:445–66.

Martin, Lori. 2011. "Debt to Society: Asset Poverty and Prisoner Reentry." *Review of Black Political Economy* 38:131–43.

Martin, Patricia Yancey. 2004. "Gender as a Social Institution." *Social Forces* 82(4):1249–73.

Martinez, Sylvia. 2000. "The Housing Act of 1949: Its Place in the Realization of the American Dream of Homeownership." *Housing Policy Debate* 11(2):467–87.

Martinson, Robert. 1974. "What Works? Questions and Answers about Prison Reform." *Public Interest* 35:22–54.

Maruna, Shadd. 2011. "Reentry as a Rite of Passage." *Punishment & Society* 13(1):3–28.

Mason, Cody. 2012. *Too Good to Be True: Private Prisons in America*. Washington, DC: Sentencing Project.

Massey, Alexander. 1998. "The Way We Do Things around Here: The Culture of Ethnography." Paper presented at the Ethnography and Education Conference. Oxford University, England.

Massey, Alexander, and Geoffrey Walford. 1999. *Explorations in Methodology*: [Studies in Educational Ethnography, Volume 2]. Stamford, CT: JAI Press.

Massey, Douglas, and Nancy Denton. 1993. *American Apartheid: Segregation and the Making of the Underclass*. Cambridge, MA: Harvard University Press.

Matsuda, Mari. 1996. *Where Is Your Body? And Other Essays on Race, Gender, and the Law*. Boston: Beacon.

Mauer, Marc. 2006. *Race to Incarcerate*, 2nd ed. Washington, DC: Sentencing Project.

Mauer, Marc, and Meda Chesney-Lind. 2002. *Invisible Punishment: The Collateral Consequences of Mass Imprisonment*. New York: Norton.

Mauer, Marc, and Ryan King. 2007. *Uneven Justice: State Rates of Incarceration by Race and Ethnicity*. Washington, DC: Sentencing Project.

Maxeiner, James. 1977. "Bane of American Forfeiture Law: Banished at Last?" *Cornell Law Review* 62(4):768–802.

May, Bruce. 1995. "The Character Component of Occupational Licensing Laws: A Continuing Barrier to the Ex-Felon's Employment Opportunities." *North Dakota Law Review* 71:187–210.

Mayhew, David. 1974. *Congress: The Electoral Connection*. New Haven, CT: Yale University Press.

McDougall, Harold. 1987. "Affordable Housing for the 1990s." *University of Michigan Journal of Law Reform* 20:727–88.

McKinney, John, and Edgar Thompson. 1965. *The South in Continuity and Change*. Durham, NC: Duke University Press.

McRoy, Ruth, and Edith Freeman. 1986. "Racial-Identity Issues among Mixed-Race Children." *Children & Schools* 8(3):164–74.

McWhirter, Robert. 2009. "Baby, Don't Be Cruel: What's So 'Cruel & Unusual' about the Eighth Amendment? Part 1." *Arizona Attorney* 46:13–28.

Meltzer, Milton. 1993. *Slavery: A World History*, updated edition. Cambridge, MA: DaCapo.

Mercer, Kerri. 2009. "The Importance of Funding Post-Secondary Correctional Educational Programs." *Community College Review* 37(2):153–64.

Messerschmidt, James. 1993. *Masculinities and Crime: Critique and Reconceptualization of Theory*. Lanham, MD: Rowman & Littlefield.

Middlemass, Keesha. 2015. "The Belly of the Beast." In *Organic Globalizer*, edited by Christopher Malone and George Martinez, 213–32. New York: Bloomsbury.

———. 2014a. "I Ain't Going Back: Prisoner Reentry and the Gray Area between Success and Failure." Presented at the American Political Science Association, Washington, DC, August 20. doi 10.2139/ssrn 2452092.

———. 2014b. "War as Metaphor: The Convergence of the War on Poverty and the War on Drugs." In *The War on Poverty: A Retrospective*, edited by Kyle Farmbry, 85–104. Lanham, MD: Lexington Books.

———. 2007. "The Carceral States of America." In *Racializing Justice, Disenfranchising Lives: The Racism, Criminal Justice, and Law Reader*, edited by Manning Marable, Ian Steinberg, and Keesha Middlemass, 373–80. New York: Palgrave Macmillan.

———. 2006. "Rehabilitated but Not Fit to Vote: A Comparative Racial Analysis of Disenfranchisement Laws." *SOULS* 8(2):22–39.

Middlemass, Keesha, and CalvinJohn Smiley. 2016. "Doing a Bid: The Construction of Time as Punishment." *Prison Journal* 96(6):793–813. doi 10.1177/0032885516671872 .

Miles, Robert. 1988. "Beyond the 'Race' Concept: The Reproduction of Racism in England." In *The Cultural Construction of Race*, edited by Marie de Lepervanche and Gillian Bottomley, 7–31. Sydney, Australia: Sydney Association for Studies of Society & Culture.

Mills, Nicolaus. 2006. "Hurricane Katrina and Robert Kennedy." *Dissent Magazine* 53(2):5–6.

Miranda, Joseph. N.d. "War or Pseudo-War?" home.earthlink.net.

Montagu, Ashley. 1974. *Man's Most Dangerous Myth: The Fallacy of Race*, 5th ed. New York: Oxford University Press.

———. 1941. "The Concept of Race in the Human Species in the Light of Genetics." *Journal of Heredity* 32:243–47.

Moran, Dominique. 2013. "Between Outside and Inside? Prison Visiting Rooms as Liminal Carceral Spaces." *GeoJournal* 78(2):339–51.

———. 2012a. "'Doing Time' in Carceral Space: Timespace and Carceral Geography." *Geografiska Annaler: Series B, Human Geography* 94(4):305–16.

———. 2012b. "Prisoner Reintegration and the Stigma of Prison Time Inscribed on the Body." *Punishment & Society* 14(5):564–83.

Morgan, Edmund. 1975. *American Slavery, American Freedom: The Ordeal of Colonial Virginia*. New York: Norton.

Morris, Thomas. 1988. "The Problem of the 'Sources' of Southern Slave Law." *American Journal of Legal History* 32(95):125–27.

Mossoney, Kimberly R., and Cara A. Roecker. 2005. "Ohio Collateral Consequences Project, Executive Summary." *University of Toledo Law Review* 36:611–750.

Muhammad, Khalil. 2009. *The Condemnation of Blackness: Race, Crime, and the Making of Modern Urban America*. Cambridge, MA: Harvard University Press.

Muir, Donal. 1993. "Race: The Mythic Root of Racism." *Sociological Inquiry* 63(3):339–50.

Mukamal, Debbie. 2001. *From Hard Time to Full Time: Strategies to Help Move Ex-Offenders from Welfare to Work*. U.S. Department of Labor, Employment and Training Administration, Division of Welfare-to-Work.

Murphy, Robert. 1990. *The Body Silent*. New York: Norton.

Murray, Harry. 2000. "Deniable Degradation: The Finger-Imaging of Welfare Recipients." *Sociological Forum* 15(1):39–63.

Musto, David. 1999. *The American Disease: Origins of Narcotic Control*, 3rd ed. New York: Oxford University Press.

Myrdal, Gunnar. 1964. *An American Dilemma*. New York: McGraw-Hill.

Nadasen, Premilla. 2007. "From Widow to 'Welfare Queen.'" *Black Women, Gender & Families* 1(2):52–77.

Nally, John, Susan Lockwood, Katie Knutson, and Taiping Ho. 2012. "An Evaluation of the Effect of Correctional Education Programs on Post-Release Recidivism and Employment: An Empirical Study in Indiana." *Journal of Correctional Education* 63(1):69–89.

National Employment Law Project. 2005. *Employment Screening for Criminal Records: Attorney General's Recommendations to Congress, August 5.* Oakland, CA: National Employment Law Project.

Nellis, Ashley. 2013. *Life Goes On: The Historic Rise in Life Sentences in America.* Washington, DC: Sentencing Project.

Newell, Christopher. 1999. "Critical Reflections on Disability, Difference, and Genetic Testing." In *Goodbye Normal Gene*, edited by Gabrielle O'Sullivan, Evelyn Sharman, and Stephanie Short, 58–71. Sydney, Australia: Pluto Press

New Jersey Parole Book. 2012. *A Handbook on Parole Procedures for Adult and Young Adult Inmates,* 5th ed. Trenton: New Jersey State Parole Board.

Newman, Sandra, and Joseph Harkness. 2002. "The Long-Term Effects of Public Housing on Self-Sufficiency." *Journal of Policy Analysis and Management* 21(1):21–43.

Nilsen, Eva. 2007. "Decency, Dignity, and Desert: Restoring Ideals of Humane Punishment to Constitutional Discourse." *University of California–Davis Law Review* 41(1):111–75.

Nordgren, Loran, Kasia Banas, and Geoff MacDonald. 2011. "Empathy Gaps for Social Pain: Why People Underestimate the Pain of Social Suffering." *Journal of Personality and Social Psychology* 100(1):120–28.

Northam, Ray M. 1971. "Vacant Urban Land in the American City." *Land Economics* 47(4):345–55.

Nussbaum, William. 1982. "Public Housing: Choosing among Families in Need of Housing." *Northwest Urban Law Review* 77(5):700–770.

Oliver, Melvin, and Thomas Shapiro. 1997. *Black Wealth/White Wealth: A New Perspective on Racial Inequality.* New York: Routledge.

Oliver, Michael. 1990. *The Politics of Disablement.* London: Macmillan.

Olsen, Wendy. 2004. "Triangulation in Social Research: Qualitative and Quantitative Method Can Really Be Mixed." In *Developments in Sociology*, volume 20, edited by Martin Holborn and Michael Haralambos, 103–18. Ormskirk, England: Causeway Press.

Olson, Trisha. 2007. "The Medieval Blood Sanction and the Divine Beneficence of Pain: 1100–1450." *Journal of Law and Religion* 22(1):63–129.

Omi, Michael, and Howard Winant. 1994. *Racial Formation in the United States: From the 1960s to the 1990s,* 2nd ed. New York: Routledge.

Orelus, Pierre. 2013. "The Institutional Cost of Being a Professor of Color: Unveiling Micro-Aggression, Racial [In]Visibility, and Racial Profiling through the Lens of Critical Race Theory." *Current Issues in Education* 16(2):1–9.

Oreopoulos, Philip. 2003. "The Long-Run Consequences of Living in a Poor Neighborhood." *Quarterly Journal of Economics* 118(4):1533–75.

Ostermann, Michael. 2011. "Parole? Nope, Not for Me: Voluntarily Maxing out of Prison." *Crime & Delinquency* 57(5):686–708.

Owens, Carl. 2009. "Social Symbols, Stigma, and the Labor Market Experiences of Former Prisoners." *Journal of Correctional Education* 60(4):316–42.

Page, Ava, Amanda Petteruti, Nastassia Walsh, and Jason Ziedenberg. 2007. *Education and Public Safety*. Washington, DC: Justice Policy Institute.

Pager, Devah. 2007. *Marked: Race, Crime, and Finding Work in an Era of Mass Incarceration*. Chicago: University of Chicago Press.

Pager, Devah, and Bruce Western. 2009. *Investigating Prisoner Reentry: The Impact of Conviction Status on Employment Prospects of Young Men* (NCJ 228584). Rockville, MD: U.S. Department of Justice. National Institute of Justice. www.ncjrs.gov.

Parcel, Toby, and Mikaela Dufur. 2001. "Capital at Home and at School: Effects on Child Social Adjustment." *Journal of Marriage and Family* 63(1):32–47.

Pearson, Jessica. 2004. "Building Debt while Doing Time: Child Support and Incarceration." *American Bar Association 5 Judges' Journal* 43(1):5–12.

Pearson, Jessica, and Lanae Davis. 2001. *Serving Parents Who Leave Prison: Final Report on the Work and Family Center*. Denver, CO: Center for Policy Research.

Peffley, Mark, Jon Hurwitz, and Paul M. Sniderman. 1997. "Racial Stereotypes and Whites' Political Views of Blacks in the Context of Welfare and Crime." *American Journal of Political Science* 41(1):30–60.

Perl, Libby. 2010. *Section 202 and Other HUD Rental Housing Programs for Low-Income Elderly Residents*. Washington, DC: CRS Report for Congress (RL-33508, January 13).

Petersilia, Joan. 2007. "Employ Behavioral Contracting for 'Earned Discharge' Parole." *Criminology & Public Policy* 6(4):807–14.

———. 2004. "What Works in Prisoner Reentry? Reviewing and Questioning the Evidence." *Federal Probation* 68(2):4–8.

———. 2003. *When Prisoners Come Home: Parole and Prisoner Reentry*. New York: Oxford University Press.

———. 2001. "Prisoner Reentry: Public Safety and Reintegration Challenges." *Prison Journal* 81(3):360–75.

———. 1999. "A Decade of Experimenting with Intermediate Sanctions: What Have We Learned?" *Justice Research and Policy* 1:9–23.

Pettit, Becky, and Bruce Western. 2004. "Mass Imprisonment and the Life Course: Race and Class Inequality in U.S. Incarceration." *American Sociological Review* 69(2):151–69.

Pettus, Katherine. 2005. *Felony Disenfranchisement in America: Historical Origins, Institutional Racism, and Modern Consequences*. Albany: State University of New York Press.

Pew Center on the States. 2009. *One in 31: The Long Reach of American Corrections*. Washington, DC: Pew Center on the States.

Pew Charitable Trusts. 2014. *Max Out: The Rise in Prison Inmates Released without Supervision*. Washington, DC: Pew Charitable Trusts.

Phelps, Michelle S. 2013. "The Paradox of Probation: Community Supervision in the Age of Mass Incarceration." *Law & Policy* 35(1–2):51–80.

Pinard, Michael. 2007. "Reentry-Centered Vision of Criminal Justice." *Federal Sentencing Reporter* 20(2):103–9.

———. 2006. "An Integrated Perspective on the Collateral Consequences of Criminal Convictions and Reentry Issues Faced by Formerly Incarcerated Individuals." *Boston University Law Review* 86:623–90.

———. 2004. "Broadening the Holistic Mindset: Incorporating Collateral Consequences and Reentry into Criminal Defense Lawyering." *Fordham Urban Law Journal* 31(4):1067–95.

Prokos, Anastasia, and Irene Padavic. 2002. "'There Oughtta Be a Law against Bitches': Masculinity Lessons in Police Academy Training." *Gender, Work, and Organization* 9(4):439–59.

Pyrczak, Fred, and Randall Bruce. 2005. *Writing Empirical Research Reports: A Basic Guide for Students of the Social and Behavioral Sciences*, 5th ed. Glendale, CA: Pyrczak Publishing.

Rabinow, Paul. 1991. *The Foucault Reader: An Introduction to Foucault's Thoughts*. London: Penguin.

Ragin, Charles, and Lisa Amoroso. 2011. *Constructing Social Research*, 2nd ed. Thousand Oaks, CA: Pine Forge Press.

Ramaswamy, Megha, and Nicholas Freudenberg. 2012. "The Cycle of Social Exclusion for Urban, Young Men of Color in the United States: What Is the Role of Incarceration?" *Journal of Poverty* 16:119–46.

Rattan, Aneeta, Cynthia Levine, Carol Dweck, and Jennifer Eberhardt. 2012. "Race and the Fragility of the Legal Distinction between Juveniles and Adults." *PLoS ONE* 7:5:e36680. www.plosone.org.

Reiman, Jeffrey 1995. *The Rich Get Richer and the Poor Get Prison: Ideology, Class, and Criminal Justice*. Boston: Allyn & Bacon.

Reitz, Kevin. 1996. "The Federal Role in Sentencing Law and Policy." *Annals of the American Academy of Political and Social Science* 543:116–29.

Renzetti, Claire. 2001. "One Strike and You're Out: Implications of a Federal Crime Control Policy for Battered Women." *Violence Against Women* 7(6):685–98.

Rich, Adrienne. 1971. *The Will to Change: Poems, 1968–1970*. New York: Norton.

Richardson, Laurel. 2000. "Evaluating Ethnography." *Qualitative Inquiry* 6(2):253–55.

Rips, Lance J. 2002. "Circular Reasoning." *Cognitive Sentence* 26:767–95.

Risman, Barbara. 2004. "Gender as a Social Structure: Theory Wrestling with Activism." *Gender & Society* 18(4):429–50.

Roberts, Dorothy. 2004. "The Social and Moral Cost of Mass Incarceration in African American Communities." *Stanford Law Review* 56(5):1271–1305.

Roberts, Jenny. 2008. "The Mythical Divide between Collateral and Direct Consequences of Criminal Convictions: Involuntary Commitment of 'Sexually Violent Predators.'" *Minnesota Law Review* 93:670–740.

Roberts, Julian. 1992. "Public Opinion, Crime, and Criminal Justice." *Crime and Justice* 16:99–180.

Robertson, James. 2012. "The Prison Litigation Reform Act as Sex Legislation: (Imagining) a Punk's Perspective of the Act." *Federal Sentencing Reporters* 24(4):276–86.

Robinson, Russell. 2008. "Perceptual Segregation." *Columbia Law Review* 108(5):1093–1180.

Rodriguez, Michelle, and Maurice Emsellem. 2011. *65 Million Need Not Apply: The Case for Reforming Criminal Background Checks for Employment*. New York: National Employment Law Project. www.nelp.org.

Ronay, Kate. 2011. "The Visit: Observing Children's Experience of Visiting a Relative in Prison." *Infant Observation* 14(2):191–202.

Rose, Dina, and Todd Clear. 2002. "Incarceration, Reentry, and Social Capital: Social Networks in the Balance." Presented at the U.S. Department of Health and Human Services Meeting (December 1). http://aspe.hhs.gov.

Rosenbaum, Emily. 1995. "Racial/Ethnic Differences in Home Ownership and Housing Quality, 1991." *Social Problems* 43(4):403–26.

Rosenberg, Irene Merker, and Yale Rosenberg. 1998. "Lone Star Liberal Musings on 'Eye for Eye' and the Death Penalty." *Utah Law Review* 1998(4):505–41.

Rosenmerkel, Sean, Matthew Durose, and Donald Farole Jr. 2009. *Felony Sentences in State Courts, 2006: Statistical Tables* (NCJ 226846). Washington, DC: U.S. Department of Justice, Office of Justice Programs, Bureau of Justice Statistics. bjs.ojp.usdoj.gov.

Ross, Robert, and Graham Staines. 1973. "The Politics of Analyzing Social Problems." *Social Problems* 20(18):18–40.

Rudstein, David. 2005. "A Brief History of the Fifth Amendment Guarantee against Double Jeopardy." *William & Mary Bill of Rights Journal* 14(1):193–242.

Russell, Katheryn, and Dragan Milovanovic. 2001. *Petit Apartheid in the U.S. Criminal Justice System: The Dark Figure of Racism*. Durham, NC: Carolina Academic Press.

Russell-Brown, Katheryn. 2004. *Underground Codes: Race, Crime, and Related Fires*. New York: New York University Press.

Ryan, Tracey, and Kimberly McCabe. 1994. "Mandatory vs. Voluntary Prison Education and Academic Achievement." *Prison Journal* 74(4):450–61.

Sabol, William, and James Lynch. 2003. "Assessing the Longer-Run Consequences of Incarceration: Effects on Families and Employment." In *Crime Control and Social Justice: The Delicate Balance*, edited by Darnell Hawkins, Samuel Myers, and Randolph Stone, 3–28. Westport, CT: Greenwood.

Sacco, Vincent F. 1995. "Media Constructions of Crime." *Annals of the American Academy of Political and Social Science* 539(Reactions to Crime & Violence):141–54.

Sampson, Robert, and John Laub. 1990. "Crime and Deviance over the Life Course: The Salience of Adult Social Bonds." *American Sociological Review* 55(5):609–27.

Sangoi, Lisa, and Lorie Goshin. 2013. "Women and Girls' Experiences Before, During, and After Incarceration: A Narrative of Gender-Based Violence, and an Analysis of the Criminal Justice Laws and Policies That Perpetuate This Narrative." *UCLA Women's Law Journal* 20(2):137–68.

Saxonhouse, Elena. 2004. "Unequal Protection: Comparing Former Felons' Challenges to Disenfranchisement and Employment Discrimination." *Stanford Law Review* 56:1597–1639.

Saxton, Alexander. 1990. "Introduction: Historical Explanations of Racial Inequality." In *The Rise and Fall of the White Republic: Class Politics and Mass Culture in Nineteenth-Century America*, edited by Alexander Saxton and David Roediger, 1–20. London: Verso.

Schafer, Robert, and Charles Field. 1968. "Section 235 of the National Housing Act: Homeownership for Low-Income Families." *Journal of Urban Law* 46:667–86.

Scherker, Amanda. 2014. "The 14 Most F#$%ed Up Things about America's Obsession with Putting People behind Bars." *HuffingtonPost.com* (June 14). www.huffingtonpost.com.

Schill, Michael. 1993. "Distressed Public Housing: Where Do We Go from Here?" *University of Chicago Law Review* 60(2):497–554.

Schmidt, Dana. 1971. "President Orders Wider Drug Fight: Asks $155 Million." *New York Times* (June 18). www.nytimes.com.

Schneider, Anne. 2006. "Patterns of Change in the Use of Imprisonment in the American States: An Integration of Path Dependence, Punctuated Equilibrium, and Policy Design Approaches." *Political Research Quarterly* 59(3):457–70.

Schneider, Anne, and Helen Ingram. 1997. *Policy Design for Democracy*. Lawrence: University of Kansas Press.

———. 1993a. "How the Social Construction of Target Populations Contributes to Problems in Policy Design." *Policy Currents* 3:1–4.

———. 1993b. "Social Construction of Target Populations: Implications for Politics and Policy." *American Political Science Review* 87(2):334–47.

Schneider, Meghan. 2010. "From Criminal Confinement to Social Confinement: Helping Ex-Offenders Obtain Public Housing with a Certificate of Rehabilitation." *New England Journal on Criminal and Civil Confinement* 36(2):335–58.

Schnitzer, Phoebe. 1993. "Tales of the Absent Father: Applying the 'Story' Metaphor in Family Therapy." *Family Process* 32(4):441–58.

Schur, Edwin. 1984. *Labeling Women Deviant: Gender, Stigma, and Social Control*. New York: McGraw-Hill.

Schutt, Russell K. 2012. *Investigating the Social World: The Process and Practice of Research*, 7th ed. Thousand Oaks, CA: Sage.

Scott, Charles, and Joan Gerbasi. 2005. *Handbook of Correctional Mental Health*. Arlington, VA: American Psychiatric Publishers.

Scott, James. 1998. *Seeing like a State: How Certain Schemes to Improve the Human Condition Have Failed*. New Haven, CT: Yale University Press.

Seddon, Toby. 2006. "Drugs, Crime, and Social Exclusion: Social Context and Social Theory in British Drugs-Crime Research." *British Journal of Criminology* 46(4):680–703.

Segal, Daniel. 1992. "Race and Colour in Pre-Independence Trinidad and Tobago." In *Trinidad Ethnicity*, edited by Kevin Yelvington, 81–115. Knoxville: University of Tennessee Press.

———. 1991. "The European: Allegories of Racial Purity." *Anthropology Today* 7(5):7–9.

Selling, Lowell. 1931. "The Pseudo-Family." *American Journal of Sociology* 37(2):247–53.

Shalev, Arieh. 2009. "Posttraumatic Stress Disorder (PTSD) and Stress-Related Disorders." *Psychiatric Clinics of North America* 32(3):687–704.

Shapiro, Andrew. 1993. "Challenging Criminal Disenfranchisement under the Voting Rights Act: A New Strategy." *Yale Law Journal* 103(2):537–66.

Sider, Gerald. 1993. *Lumbee Indian Histories: Race, Ethnicity, and Indian Identity in the Southern United States.* New York: Cambridge University Press.

Siebers, Tobin. 2011. *Disability Theory.* Ann Arbor: University of Michigan Press.

———. 2001. "Disability in Theory: From Social Constructionism to the New Realism of the Body." *American Literary History* 13(4):737–54.

Silverstein, Robert. 2000. "Emerging Disability Framework: A Guidepost for Analyzing Public Policy." *Iowa Law Review* 85:1691–1796.

Simon, Jonathan. 2007. *Governing through Crime: How the War on Crime Transformed American Democracy and Created a Culture of Fear.* New York: Oxford University Press.

Simpson, George, and Simpson Yinger. 1972. *Racial and Cultural Minorities: An Analysis of Prejudice and Discrimination,* 4th ed. New York: Harper & Row.

Skarbek, David. 2012. "Prison Gangs, Norms, and Organizations." *Journal of Economic Behavior & Organization* 82(1):96–109.

Smiley, CalvinJohn, and Keesha Middlemass. 2016. "Clothing Makes the Man: Impression Management and Prisoner Reentry." *Punishment & Society* 18(2):220–43.

Somerville, Peter. 1998. "Explanations of Social Exclusion: Where Does Housing Fit In?" *Housing Studies* 13(6):761–80.

Spindler, George, and Louise Spindler. 1992. "Cultural Process and Ethnography: An Anthropological Perspective." In *The Handbook of Qualitative Research in Education,* edited by Margaret LeCompte, Judith Goetz, Judith Preissle, and Wendy Millroy, 53–92. New York: Academic Press.

Spradley, James. 1979. *The Ethnographic Interview.* Fort Worth, TX: Holt, Rinehart, and Winston.

Srivastava, Prachi, and Nick Hopwood. 2009. "A Practical Iterative Framework for Qualitative Data Analysis." *International Journal of Qualitative Methods* 8(1):76–84.

Stacy, Donald. 1973. "Limitations on Denying Licensure to Ex-Offenders." *Capital University Law Review* 2(1):1–22.

Steinacker, Andrea. 2003. "The Prisoner's Campaign: Felony Disenfranchisement Laws and the Right to Hold Public Office." *Brigham Young University Law Review* 801–28.

Stephan, James. 2008. *Census of State and Federal Correctional Facilities, 2005* (NCJ 222182). Washington, DC: U.S. Department of Justice, Office of Justice Programs, Bureau of Justice Statistics. www.bjs.gov.

Stephenson, Gilbert. 1910. *Race Distinctions in American Law.* New York: Association Press (Appleton).

Stoll, Adam. 2006. *Higher Education Act Reauthorization: A Comparison of Current Law and Major Proposals.* Washington, DC: CRS Report for Congress (RL33415, May 2). www.finaid.org.

Stone, Emma, and Mark Priestley. 1996. "Parasites, Pawns, and Partners: Disability Research and the Role of Non-Disabled Researchers." *British Journal of Sociology* 47(4):699–716.

Strömwall, Leif, and Rebecca Willén. 2011. "Inside Criminal Minds: Offenders' Strategies When Lying." *Journal of Investigative Psychology and Offender Profiling* 8:271–81.

Stuntz, William. 2001. "The Pathological Politics of Criminal Law." *Michigan Law Review* 100:505–600.

Sutton, James. 2011. "An Ethnographic Account of Doing Survey Research in Prison: Descriptions, Reflections, and Suggestions from the Field." *Qualitative Sociology Review* 7(2):45–63.

Telles, Edward. 2004. *Race in Another America: The Significance of Skin Color in Brazil.* Princeton, NJ: Princeton University Press.

Thompson, Anthony. 2008. *Releasing Prisoners, Redeeming Communities: Reentry, Race, and Politics.* New York: New York University Press.

———. 2004. "Navigating the Hidden Obstacles to Ex-Offender Reentry." *Boston College Law Review* 45(2):255–306.

Thompson, Mark. 2002. "Don't Do the Crime If You Ever Intend to Vote Again: Challenging the Disenfranchisement of Ex-Felons as Cruel and Unusual Punishment." *Seton Hall Law Review* 33(1):167–205.

Thomson, Rosemarie. 1997. *Extraordinary Bodies: Figuring Physical Disability in American Culture and Literature.* New York: Columbia University Press.

Thorpe, Reuben. 2012. "Often Fun, Usually Messy: Fieldwork, Recording, and the Higher Order of Things." In *Reconsidering Archaeological Fieldwork: Exploring On-Site Relationships between Theory and Practice,* edited by Hannah Cobb, Oliver Harris, Cara Jones, and Philip Richardson, 31–52. New York: Springer.

Tirado, Linda. 2014. *Hand to Mouth: Living in Bootstrap America.* New York: Putnam.

Tolnay, Stewart, and E. M. Beck. 1992. "Racial Violence and Black Migration in the American South, 1910 to 1930." *American Sociological Review* 57(1):103–16.

Tonry, Michael. 1995. *Malign Neglect: Race, Crime, and Punishment in America.* New York: Oxford University Press.

———. 1994. "Proportionality, Parsimony, and Interchangeability of Punishments." In *A Reader on Punishment,* edited by Antony Duff and David Garland, 133–60. Oxford, England: Oxford University Press.

Tonry, Michael, and Mary Lynch. 1996. "Intermediate Sanctions." *Crime and Justice* 20:99–144.

Travis, Jeremy. 2005. *But They All Come Back: Facing the Challenges of Prisoner Reentry.* Washington, DC: Urban Institute.

———. 2002. "Invisible Punishment: An Instrument of Social Exclusion." *Invisible Punishment: The Collateral Consequences of Mass Imprisonment,* edited by Marc Mauer and Meda Chesney-Lind, 15–36. New York: Norton.

Travis, Jeremy, Amy Solomon, and Michelle Waul. 2001. *From Prison to Home: The Dimensions and Consequences of Prisoner Reentry.* Washington, DC: Justice Policy Center of the Urban Institute. www.urban.org.

Tress, Will. 2009. "Unintended Collateral Consequences: Defining Felony in the Early American Republic." *Cleveland State University Law Review* 57(3):461–91.

Truman, Jennifer, Lynn Langton, and Michael Planty. 2013. *Criminal Victimization, 2012* (NCJ 243389). Washington, DC: U.S. Department of Justice, Office of Justice Programs, Bureau of Justice Statistics. www.bjs.gov.

Tuan, Yi-Fu. 1977. *Space and Place: The Perspective of Experience.* Minneapolis: University of Minnesota Press.

Tucker, William. 1990. *The Source of America's Housing Problem: Look in Your Own Back Yard* (Policy Analysis No. 127). Washington, DC: Cato Institute. www.cato.org.

Turetsky, Vicki. 2007. *Staying in Jobs and out of the Underground: Child Support Policies That Encourage Legitimate Work* (Policy Brief 2). Washington, DC: Center for Law and Social Policy. research.policyarchive.org.

Twenge, Jean, Roy Baumeister, Dianne Tice, and Tanja Stucke. 2001. "If You Can't Join Them, Beat Them: Effects of Social Exclusion on Aggressive Behavior." *Journal of Personality and Social Psychology* 81(6):1058–69.

Twenge, Jean, Kathleen Catanese, and Roy Baumeister. 2002. "Social Exclusion Causes Self-Defeating Behavior." *Journal of Personality and Social Psychology* 83(3):606–15.

Tyler, Tom, Jonathan Casper, and Bonnie Fisher. 1989. "Maintaining Allegiance toward Political Authorities: The Role of Prior Attitudes and the Use of Fair Procedures." *American Journal of Political Science* 33(3):629–52.

Uggen, Christopher. 2000. "Work as a Turning Point in the Life Course of Criminals: A Duration Model of Age, Employment, and Recidivism." *American Sociological Review* 65(4):529–46.

Uggen, Christopher, Jeff Manza, and Melissa Thompson. 2006. "Citizenship, Democracy, and the Civic Reintegration of Criminal Offenders." *The Annals of the American Academy* 605:281–310.

United States Department of Health and Human Services. 2003. *Results from the 2004 National Survey on Drug Use and Health: Detailed Tables.* Washington, DC: U.S. Department of Justice, Office of Applied Studies, Bureau of Justice Statistics, Substance Abuse and Mental Health Services Administration. www.oas.samhsa.gov.

United States Department of Justice. 2013. *Prisoners and Prisoner Re-Entry.* Washington, DC: U.S. Department of Justice, Office of Justice Programs. www.justice.gov.

United States Sentencing Commission. 2013. *Annual Report.* Washington, DC: Office of Public Affairs. www.ussc.gov.

———. 2010. *Demographic Differences in Federal Sentencing Practices: An Update of the Booker Report's Multivariate Regression Analysis.* Washington, DC: Office of Public Affairs. www.ussc.gov.

———. 1995. *Special Report to Congress: Cocaine and Federal Sentencing Policy.* Washington, DC: Office of Public Affairs. www.ussc.gov.

Urban Institute. 2009. *Prisoner Reentry.* Washington, DC: Urban Institute. www.urban.org.

Vacca, James. 2004. "Educated Prisoners Are Less Likely to Return to Prison." *Journal of Correctional Education* 55(4):297–305.

Venkatesh, Sudhir. 2008. *Gang Leader for a Day: A Rogue Sociologist Takes to the Streets*. New York: Penguin.

———. 2002. *The Robert Taylor Homes Relocation Study*. New York: Center for Urban Research & Policy, Columbia University. www.curp.columbia.edu.

Viglione, Jill, Lance Hannon, and Robert DeFina. 2011. "The Impact of Light Skin on Prison Time for Black Female Offenders." *Social Science Quarterly* 48(1):258–50.

Visher, Christy, Nancy LaVigne, and Jennifer Castro. 2003. "Returning Home: Preliminary Findings from a Pilot Study of Soon-to-Be-Released Prisoners in Maryland." *Justice Research and Policy* 5(2):55–74.

Visher, Christy, and Jeremy Travis. 2003. "Transitions from Prison to Community: Understanding Individual Pathways." *Annual Review of Sociology* 29:89–113.

Vitiello, Michael. 2008. "Punishing Sex Offenders: When Good Intentions Go Bad." *Arizona State Law Journal* 40:651–90.

Volbert, Renate, and Max Steller. 2014. "Is This Testimony Truthful, Fabricated, or Based on False Memory?" *European Psychologist* 19(3):207–20.

VonHirsch, Andrew. 1998. "Penal Theories." In *The Handbook of Crime & Punishment*, edited by Michael Tonry, 659–82. New York: Oxford University Press.

———. 1976. *Doing Justice: The Choice of Punishments* (NCJ 031685). New York: Farrar, Strauss & Giroux.

VonHoffman, Alexander. 2000. "A Study in Contradictions: The Origins and Legacy of the Housing Act of 1949." *Housing Policy Debate* 11(2):299–326.

Votey, Harold. 1991. "Employment, Age, Race, and Crime: A Labor Theoretic Investigation." *Journal of Quantitative Criminology* 7(2):123–53.

Vrij, Aldert. 2008. *Detecting Lies and Deceit: Pitfalls and Opportunities*, 2nd ed. Chichester, England: Wiley.

Wachtler, Sol, and Keri Bagala. 2014. "From the Asylum to Solitary: Transinstitutionalization." *Albany Law Review* 77(3):915–30.

Wacquant, Loïc. 2010a. "Class, Race, and Hyperincarceration in Revanchist America." *Daedalus* 139(3):74–90.

———. 2010b. "Prisoner Reentry as Myth and Ceremony." *Dialectical Anthropology* 34(4):605–20.

———. 2009. *Punishing the Poor: The Neoliberal Government of Social Insecurity*. Durham, NC: Duke University Press.

———. 2002a. "From Slavery to Mass Incarceration: Rethinking the Race Question in the U.S." *New Left Review* 13(Jan.–Feb.):41–60.

———. 2002b. "The Curious Eclipse of Prison Ethnography in the Age of Mass Incarceration." *Ethnography* 3(4):371–97.

———. 2001. "Deadly Symbiosis: When Ghetto and Prison Meet and Merge." *Punishment & Society* 3(1):95–134.

———. 2000. "The New Peculiar Institution: On the Prison as Surrogate Ghetto." *Theoretical Criminology* 4(3):377–89.

Wahidin, Azrini. 2004. "Reclaiming Agency: Managing Aging Bodies in Prison." In *Old Age and Human Agency*, edited by Emmanuelle Tulle, 69–86. New York: Nova Science Publishers.

———. 2002. "Reconfiguring Older Bodies in the Prison Time Machine." *Journal of Aging and Identity* 7(3):177–93.

Wahidin, Azrini, and Shirley Tate. 2005. "Prison (E)scapes and Body Tropes: Older Women in the Prison Time Machine." *Journal of Body and Society* 11(2):59–79.

Walmsley, Roy. 2009. *World Prison Population List*, 8th ed. London: International Centre for Prison Studies.

Ward, David, and Gene Kassebaum. 2007. *Women's Prison: Sex and Social Structure*. Chicago: Aldine Transaction.

Ward, Shakoor. 2009. "Career and Technical Education in United States Prisons: What Have We Learned?" *Journal of Correctional Education* 60(3):191–200.

Warren, Carol, and Tracy Karner. 2005. *Discovering Qualitative Methods: Field Research, Interviews and Analysis*. Los Angeles: Roxbury.

Warren, Jennifer. 2008. *One in 100: Behind Bars in America, 2008*. Washington, DC: Pew Charitable Trusts.

Watts, Elizabeth. 1981. "The Biological Race Concept and Diseases of Modern Man." In *Biocultural Aspects of Disease*, edited by Henry Rothschild, 3–23. New York: Academic Press.

Weinberg, Kirson. 1942. "Aspects of the Prison's Social Structure." *American Journal of Sociology* 47(5):717–26.

West, Candace, and Don Zimmerman. 1987. "Doing Gender." *Gender & Society* 1(2):125–51.

West, Cornel. 1993. *Race Matters*. Boston: Beacon.

West, Heather, and William Sabol. 2011. *Prisoners in 2009* (NCJ 231675). Washington, DC: U.S. Department of Justice, Office of Justice Programs, Bureau of Justice Statistics. www.bjs.gov.

Western, Bruce. 2009. "Race, Crime, and Punishment." *Cato Unbound: A Journal of Debate*. Washington, DC: Cato Institute. www.cato-unbound.org.

———. 2006. *Punishment and Inequality in America*. New York: Russell Sage Foundation.

White, Hayden. 1980. "The Value of Narrativity in the Representation of Reality." *Critical Inquiry* 7(1):5–27.

Whiteford, Peter. 2001. "Understanding Poverty and Social Exclusion: Situating Australia Internationally." In *Creating Unequal Futures? Rethinking Poverty, Inequality, and Disadvantage*, edited by Ruth Fincher and Peter Saunders, 38–69. Sydney, Australia: Allen & Unwin.

Whitehead, Tony. 2005. "Basic Classical Ethnographic Research Methods: Secondary Data Analysis, Fieldwork, Observation/Participant Observation, and Informal and Semi-Structured Interviewing." EICCARS Working Paper, University of Maryland. www.cusag.umd.edu.

Whiting, Jason, and Robert Lee, III. 2003. "Voices from the System: A Qualitative Study of Foster Children's Stories." *Family Relations* 52(3):288–95.

Wiecek, William. 1977. "The Statutory Law of Slavery and Race in the Thirteen Mainland Colonies of British America." *William & Mary Quarterly,* Third Series 34(2):258–80.

Williams, David, Risa Lavizzo-Mourey, and Rueben Warren. 1994. "The Concept of Race and Health Status in America." *Public Health Reports* 109(1):26–41.

Williams, Paulette. 2004. "The Continuing Crisis in Affordable Housing: Systemic Issues Requiring Systemic Solutions." *Fordham Urban Law Journal* 31(2):413–78.

Willingham, Breea. 2011. "Black Women's Prison Narratives and the Intersection of Race, Gender, and Sexuality in U.S. Prisons." *Critical Survey* 23(3):55–66.

Wilson, William Julius. 1987. *The Truly Disadvantaged: The Inner City, the Underclass, and Public Policy.* Chicago: University of Chicago Press.

———. 1980. *The Declining Significance of Race: Blacks and Changing American Institutions,* 2nd ed. Chicago: University of Chicago Press.

Wolfgang, Marvin, Terence Thornberry, and Robert Figlio. 1987. *From Boy to Man: From Delinquency to Crime.* Chicago: University of Chicago Press.

Wolfinger, Nicholas. 2002. "On Writing Fieldnotes: Collection Strategies and Background Expectancies." *Qualitative Research* 2(1):85–95.

Wood, Peter. 1974. *Black Majority: Negroes in Colonial South Carolina from 1670 through the Stono Rebellion.* New York: Norton.

Woods, Peter. 1994. "Collaborating in Historical Ethnography: Researching Critical Events in Education." *International Journal of Qualitative Studies in Education* 7(4):309–21.

X, Malcolm. 1970. *By Any Means Necessary: Speeches, Interviews, and a Letter by Malcolm X.* New York: Pathfinder Press.

———. 1965. *Malcolm X Speaks: Selected Speeches and Statements.* New York: Grove Press.

Yankah, Ekow. 2004. "Good Guys and Bad Guys: Punishing Character, Equality, and the Irrelevance of Moral Character to Criminal Punishment." *Cardozo Law Review* 25(3):1019–68.

INDEX

1829 Revised Statutes of the State of New York, 32

administrative regulations, 23, 173. *See also* civil regulations; net-widening; regulations

administrative segregation, 53

Adult Basic Education (ABE), 119–120. *See also* education; General Educational Development

affordable housing, 88–89. *See also* mixed-income housing; public housing

Aid to Families with Dependent Children (AFDC), 228n12. *See also* Temporary Aid to Needy Families

alcohol, 81, 86, 98, 100–101. *See also* Alcoholics Anonymous; drugs; drug use; Narcotics Anonymous

Alcoholics Anonymous (AA), 98, 103, 227n100. *See also* alcohol; drugs; drug use; Narcotics Anonymous

aliases, 75, 102, 199n1

Amendment No. 1158, 116–117, 224n40. *See also* Hutchison, U.S. Senator Kaye Bailey; Pell grants

Anderson, Tanisha, 180, 236n40

antebellum, 45, 216n109. *See also* South

Anti-Drug Abuse Act of 1988, 91, 96, 116, 181

archival research, 14, 198

banishment, 106. *See also* displacement; exclusion; isolation

"ban the box," 167; campaign, 234n147

Basic Education Opportunity Grants, 115. *See also* education; General Education Development; Pell grants

Bearden v. Georgia, 145. *See also* debtor's prison

"being a man," 77–78

bid, 66, 122, 132, 137, 166; defined, 125. *See also* "doing time"; "to jail"

Black Codes, 45, 73

black communities, 4–5, 179, 181

"black crimes," 46, 48; crime of "being black," 41–44, 47; criminalizing blackness, 4, 16–17, 42–44, 47–48, 175, 181; examples of, 46. *See also* blackness; fear

BlackLivesMatter, 180, 236n37

"black monster," 35. *See also* criminal monster; "felon monster"; "ideal criminal"

blackness, 4, 47, 175, 178, 180–181, 207n142, 210n216; criminality, 17–18, 42–44, 47–48; fear of, 49–50. *See also* "black crimes"; fear; "one-drop" rule; "others"

Blackstone, William, 31–32, 206n110, 206n112

blanket: assessment, 33; denial, 167; exclusion, 98, 159, 231n67; felony conviction, 118; policies, 98, 154. *See also* exclusionary laws/policies/statutes; overinclusive

Blumenbach, Johann, 40; five-race scheme, 40. *See also* Linnaeus, Carolus

Brady Handgun Violence Prevention Act of 1993 (Brady Act), 152, 181, 230n57

branding, 31, 43–44

Brown, Michael, 180–181, 211n267, 230n59. *See also* Wilson, Darren

bunk bed, 127

Bush, President George H. W., 36

cage (living in), 52–53, 57–58, 63, 67, 101, 122, 126. *See also* cell mate; lock-down/locked down; prison cell

car sick, 70

Carter, President Jimmy, 48

castration, 41, 43

cell mate, 54, 63. *See also* cage (living in); lock-down/locked down; prison cell

certificate programs, 120–121, 126, 127–130, 133, 155, 185, 231n62. *See also* facilitators; New Jersey Office of Educational Services; Pell grants; prison education programs

child-support, 19, 97, 112, 143–145, 223n9, 228n13, 228n14, 228n15, 229n16; arrears, 19, 144, 228n13, 228n14. *See also* Child Support Recovery Act of 1992; "Criminal Nonsupport" statutes

Child Support Recovery Act of 1992, 144, 229n22

Christie, Governor Chris (New Jersey), 37–39, 208n163, 208n164

churn, 45. *See also* recidivism/recidivate(ing)

civil death, 31, 106; civilly dead, 30

civil disabilities, 22–23, 27, 157. *See also* civil penalties; collateral consequences; internal exile; invisible punishments; "off-book sanctions"; post-punishment; secret sentences

civil penalties, 21, 27. *See also* civil disabilities; collateral consequences; internal exile; invisible punishments; "off-book sanctions"; post-punishment; secret sentences

civil regulations, 22. *See also* administrative regulations; net-widening; regulations

Civil War, 16, 45, 178

Clinton, President Bill, 81, 86, 93–94, 96, 97, 118; race, 94. *See also* National Commission on Severely Distressed Housing; "One Strike, You're Out"; Personal Responsibility and Work Opportunity Reconciliation Act of 1996; Temporary Assistance to Needy Families; "War on Drugs"

clothes, 19, 28, 51, 58, 69, 76–78, 111, 138, 141–142, 222n124

color line, 41–44, 45, 47, 178

collateral consequences, 22. *See also* civil disabilities; civil penalties; internal exile; invisible punishments; "off-book sanctions"; post-punishment; secret sentences

convict leasing, 46

costs: criminal justice system, 113, 145, 174; fight crime, 33; housing, 88–89; living, 111, 145; reentry, 111–112; societal, 175; "tough on crime," 37. *See also* education; family; finances; money

crack cocaine, 4, 49–50, 92–93, 212n279, 212n281, 236n50; crime wave, 92; defined, 49; media, 50; open-air drug markets, 4, 50, 92; race, 49–50, 92–93; racial disparity, 50, 92–93, 212n279, 212n286; sentencing, 236n50; versus powder cocaine, 49–50, 92, 182, 212n281; violence, 50. *See also* powder cocaine; "War on Drugs"

Crawford, John, III, 180, 208n152

crime wave, 91–92, 116. *See also* crack cocaine; powder cocaine; "War on Drugs"

criminal code, 4, 31–32, 42–43, 184, 199n1, 206n112

criminal enterprises, 96

criminal history background check, 18, 97, 142, 151–157, 161, 169, 181, 231n62, 231n71, 231n73, 232n76; education, 223n12; housing 217n14, 221n102; participants, 99, 112, 151, 161–162, 164–168, 171. *See also* National Criminal History Improvement Program; National Instant Criminal Background Check System

criminal justice fees, 19, 142–145, 160. *See also* debt; debtor's prison; fees

criminal justice system, 44–50, 52, 54–55, 79, 92–93, 113, 125, 134, 145, 159, 171–174, 177–179, 181–183, 186–187, 189; back-end, 19, 37, 79, 183; front end, 37, 183. *See also* sentencing court(s)

criminal monster, 35. *See also* "black monster"; blackness; "felon monster"; "ideal criminal"

"Criminal Nonsupport" statutes, 145

criminal record, 1, 45, 55, 97, 152–153, 155, 184, 185, 190, 202n83, 221n101, 230n58, 232n76. *See also* criminal resume; "face sheet"; "jacket"; "overcoat"; rap sheet

criminal resume, 53, 55. See also criminal record; "face sheet"; "jacket"; "over-coat"; rap sheet

criminal: bankers, 149; corrupt bloodline, 30; corrupt mind, 32; corrupt soul, 28–30, 32; depraved, 32–33, 206n122; media, 91; permanent criminality, 21; status, 24, 177. *See also* demon

death penalty, 32, 125

debt, 18–19, 26, 41, 97, 142–146, 223n9, 229n19; participants, 138, 142, 145, 168, 172–173, 187. *See also* debt to society

debtor's prison, 145. See also *Bearden v. Georgia*

debt to society, 155, 173, 187

decriminalization of marijuana, 48. *See also* Carter, President Jimmy

degradation, 24, 31; ritual, 52. *See also* "social dirt"; stigma; total institution

demon, 34, 43, 181. See also criminal

Department of Corrections (DOC), 3, 15, 21–22, 23, 54–55, 72–73, 79, 83–84, 102, 126, 189–190; custody or property of, 72–73, 79, 189, 198, 192, 225n56; power, 123. *See also* New Jersey Department of Corrections

Department of Education (DOE), 185

Department of Housing and Urban Development (HUD), 87, 218n27; cabinet-level department, 89; guidelines, regulations, rules, 95, 96, 98–99, 219n50; homelessness defined, 87; Fair Housing Act, 89, 218n38; pur-pose, 88. *See also* "One Strike, You're Out"

disability studies, 2, 24, 199n2. *See also* social disability theory

discourse, 16, 29; of illegality, 16, 174; insidious, 172; political, 33, 91, 179; reentry, 17

displacement, 94. *See also* banishment; exclusion; isolation

"doing dirt," 56, 79, 107, 149

"doing time," 62, 78, 146, 155. *See also* bid; "to jail"

double consciousness, 59; level of con-sciousness, 66

"double direction," 178

Drug Enforcement Agency (DEA), 48

drugs, 5, 48–50, 56, 74, 77, 81, 86, 91–93, 96, 100–101, 103, 125, 137, 149–150, 165, 192, 196, 197, 199n15. *See also* alcohol; Alcoholics Anonymous; drug use; Narcotics Anonymous; selling drugs; "War on Drugs"

drug markets, 4, 50, 92. *See also* crack cocaine; drugs; drug use; powder cocaine; "War on Drugs"

drug use, 5, 74, 86, 102–103, 143, 213n29; racial differences, 92–93. See also crack cocaine; drugs; powder cocaine; "War on Drugs"

Dukakis, Governor Michael (Massa-chusetts), 36–37, 173. *See also* "soft on crime"

ear cropping, 31, 205n102
early release: date, 132; parole, 132, 208n163; program, 37–38. *See also* "good time credits"; No Early Release Act of 1997
earned privilege, 97
East Jersey State Prison, 116. *See also* "Inside-Out" programs
Edna Mahan Correctional Facility for Women, 57
education, 13, 16, 18, 19, 67, 104, 109–110, 114–115, 137–139, 148; certificates, 127–133; costs, 114; participants, 111; prison, 118. *See also* Adult Basic Education; educational programs; General Educational Development; Higher Education Act of 1965; Hutchison, U.S. Senator Kaye Bailey; "Inside-Out" programs; Pell grants; prison education programs
educational attainment, 67, 109, 112–113, 135
educational programs, 18, 27, 54, 112, 114, 116, 118–119, 124, 126, 139, 171, 183–185, 224n28. *See also* Adult Basic Education; certificate programs; General Educational Development; Higher Education Act of 1965; Hutchison, U.S. Senator Kaye Bailey; New Jersey Office of Educational Services; Pell grants; prison education programs
Eisenhower, President Dwight D., 88–89
empathy, 26, 106; racial empathy gap, 47–48; for victims, 128
employment policies, 13, 141–142, 151–152–153, 154, 234n147; employers, 154; parole, 147; participants, 110, 112–113, 129, 148–149, 150; public housing, 94–95, 104; reentry, 18, 29, 109, 136; slavery, 45. *See also* criminal history background check; Society for Human Resource Management
Equal Employment Opportunity Commission (EEOC), 167, 231n67

Essex County, New Jersey, 5, 120, 201n72
ethnography, 10, 200n22; ethnographic fieldwork, 2, 8, 13, 191; "pure ethnography," 10. *See also* fieldwork
exclusion, 22, 26, 157, 175, 204n67; black, 178; felons, 181; social, 22. See also banishment; displacement; isolation
exclusionary laws/policies/statutes, 86, 102, 106, 160, 169, 174
extra-legal, 3, 29, 174. *See also* felony conviction: changes legal status

Facebook, 123
"face sheet," 1, 102, 198, 199n1, 202n83. See also criminal record; criminal resume; "jacket"; "overcoat"; rap sheet
facilitators, 131–133. *See also* certificate programs
Fair Housing Act of 1968, 89–90
failure to reenter, 9, 23, 51, 173, 175, 177, 182. *See also* prisoner reentry; recidivism/recidivate(ing); reenter; reincarceration
family, 3, 6, 11, 13, 17–18, 31, 35, 51, 67, 75, 85–86, 94, 102, 112–113, 123, 128, 163–165, 172; finances, 75–78, 83, 101–102, 142, 217n9; gender, 61; housing, 27, 84, 90, 97–99, 103–104, 175, 219n50; incarceration, 12, 54, 58–60, 69–70, 138, 189–190; parents, 12, 67, 83, 114, 117, 143–145, 228n13, 228n15; parole, 83–84, 110; pseudo, 62, 215n65; support, 10, 14, 27–28, 52, 64–65, 68–69, 71, 83–84, 164–165, 186; weak bonds, 13
fear, 26, 74: 1980 presidential campaign, 90–91; blackness, 33; 35, 36–37, 39, 42–43, 47, 49–50, 178–181; crime, 116; criminality, 26; hiring felons, 155; police, 181; politics of, 34, 116–117, 173, 181; prison, 63, 67; public, 22, 33–34; reentry, 67, 148; slaves, 43–44; urban violence, 42. *See also* Brown, Michael;

language; racial fear; white fear; "Willie Horton"; Wilson, Darren

Federal Bureau of Investigation (FBI), 152, 200n18, 203n25, 207n142, 230n58, 230n60

federal firearms licensees (FFLs), 152–153

fees, 229n23, 229n27; child support orders, 143, 223n9, 228n14, 229n16, 229n19; court-mandated, 143; drug test, 143; halfway house, 112, 142–143; incarcerated parents, 143–145, 228n13, 228n15; judicial approach, 143–144, 229n16; parole, 19, 142–144, 146–148, 217n10, 229n27, 229n28; revenue source, 145–147, 229n29. *See also* criminal justice fees; debt; debtor's prison

"felon monster," 106, 177; black, 35; criminal, 35. *See also* "black monster"; blackness; criminal monster; "ideal criminal"

felony conviction: changes legal status, 3, 110; character of, 24, 27, 29, 33, 152, 172; criminal code, 31–32; defined by U.S. Supreme Court, 32, 206n119; disability, 26–29; employment, 151, 154, 233n115; "felt value," 29; history, 22–24, 30–33; housing, 82, 100, 102; insidious, 172, 177; institutional character, 24, 30, 52, 106, 186; participants, 7, 50, 65, 84, 98, 100, 136; pejorative, 33, 187; politics, 24; public hostility, 4; public record, 7, 109, 174, 182, 183; reentry, 12; slavery, 4; "special ensemble," 29, 39; unchanging, 159, 176; unnatural state of existence, 27, 182. *See also* civil disabilities; criminal record; criminal resume; "face sheet"; hostility: public; infamous crimes; "jacket"; nonfelon; "overcoat"; petite penal institution; rap sheet; social disability; stigma

feudal system, 30. *See also* forfeiture

fieldwork, 2; research context, 5–6, 8, 13, 72, 191, 226n70. See also archival research; ethnography; "magpie approach"; qualitative methods, research design and methods

finances, 75–78, 83, 101–102, 142, 217n9; family, 58, 60, 75–77, 105, 106–107; reentry, 83; while incarcerated, 77. *See also* family; money

food, 70–71

food insecurity, 3, 18, 24, 82, 105, 113; examples of, 19, 24, 82, 145, 165, 169; hungry, 24, 28, 111, 150, 164, 186; ineligible for food benefits, 94, 124. *See also* food stamps; Supplemental Nutrition Assistance program

food in prison, 58, 63, 70

food security, 76, 165

food stamps, 94, 184. *See also* food insecurity; Supplemental Nutrition Assistance program

forfeiture, 30, 206n112

Foucault, Michel, 29, 187; 201n57

"free" blacks, 42, 46, 73

furlough program, 36

gallows, 31

gang(s), 54, 56–57, 124, 126–127, 190, 213n29, 228n2

Gantt, Harvey, 36–37

gender, 14, 22, 44, 97; "doing gender," 61; gender roles, 60–61; men's prisons, 60–61; "pseudo-family," 61–62; same-sex environments, 60–63; women's prisons, 61–62, 215n65. *See also* hypermasculinity; masculinity

General Educational Development (GED), 54, 104–105, 114–115, 118, 119–121, 225n68; inside prison, 122, 124, 125–126; participants, 127–128, 129, 134–135, 136, 138. *See also* Adult Basic Education; education; Hutchison, U.S Senator Kaye Bailey; Pell grants; prison education programs

ghetto, 48

Goffman, Erving, 11–12, 26

good moral character tests, 159–161; good character, 160, 165, 169

"good prisoners," 131. *See also* inmate

"good time credits," 127, 132–133, 227n112. *See also* early release; No Early Release Act of 1997

Gore, Al, 36. *See also* Dukakis, Governor Michael

government assistance (benefits), 94. *See also* public benefits; social benefits

Gray, Freddie, 180, 236n41

gray area, 27–29, 52, 78–79, 137–138

Great Migration, 46–47

hamstringing, 44

Helms, Jesse, 36–37, 208n156. *See also* Gantt, Harvey

Higher Education Act of 1965 (HEA), 114–115, 185, 224n27, 224n28

hoax, 177. *See also* myth of reentry

homeless(ness), 3, 10, 13, 15, 18, 28, 81–84, 86–87, 97, 99–104, 106, 139, 146, 150–151, 164, 169, 171, 175, 186, 189, 218n24, 222n124; shelter, 13, 78, 81–83, 85, 100, 102–104

homophobia, 61

homosexuality, 61, 213n29

hostility, 2, 3–4, 171, 176; public, 16, 19, 30, 106, 174; towards felons, 16, 142

Housing Act of 1937, 88, 218n36

Housing and Community Development Act of 1974, 90, 219n46, 219n57. *See also* public housing; Public Housing Authorities; Section 8

Housing and Community Development Act of 1987 (Emergency Low-Income Housing and Urban Development Act of 1987), 89–90, 218n33, 218n35, 218n37

Housing and Urban Development (HUD). *See* Department of Housing and Urban Development

Housing and Urban Development Act of 1965, 89, 218n33, 218n35

Housing and Urban Development Act of 1968, 218n37

housing industry, 86, 90

Housing Opportunity Program Extension Act of 1996, 96, 218n38

Housing Preservation Act of 1987, 219n57

Hutchison, U.S. Senator Kaye Bailey, 116–118. *See also* Amendment No. 1158; Pell grants; Violent Crime Control and Law Enforcement Act

hyper-masculinity, 61, 78. *See also* gender; masculinity

"ideal criminal," 177. *See also* "black monster"; criminal monster; "felon monster"

"ideal victim," 207n141

identification, 6, 71–72, 74–75; photo, 6, 75, 128; state ID, 72–73. *See also* paperwork

illiteracy, illiterate, 91, 114, 124, 134–136; uneducated, 124, 133–139, 169, 171, 186. *See also* education; General Educational Development; National Assessment of Adult Literacy; Pell grants; prison education programs

incarceration, 37, 47, 60, 62, 105, 182–183, 185, 190; costs, 122; New Jersey, 202n73; parents, 228n15, 229n16; policies, 37, 44; race, 14, 46, 47–48, 50, 202n73; rate, 14, 37, 93, 182–183. *See also* failure to re-enter; Post-Traumatic Stress Disorder; prisoner reentry; reenter, rehabilitation; social control

indentured servants, 41–42

in-depth interviews, 2, 8, 13, 98, 191

infamous crimes, 30–32, 45, 206n119. *See also* infamy; "traditional nine crimes"

infamy, 31. *See also* infamous crimes; "traditional nine crimes"

informant(s), 7; "key informants," 201n50.
See also participants
inmate, 7, 53, 58, 69, 117, 126, 128, 131–133,
142, 200n25, 201n57, 213n13, 225n68,
226n94; "good," 131, 133. *See also* "good
prisoners"
"Inside-Out" programs, 115–116, 118,
224n32
"in situ," 8. *See also* archival research;
ethnography; fieldwork; "magpie approach"; qualitative methods; research
design and methods
institutional abandonment, 48, 92, 95–96,
113, 182, 211n270
institutionalized prisoners, 58, 68–70, 131–
132, 200n25. *See also* inmate
institutions: public, 39 113, 155; social,
113
Integrated Automated Fingerprint
Identification System (IAFIS), 203n25,
230n60
internal exile, 22, 106. *See also* civil disabilities; civil penalties; collateral consequences; invisible punishments; "off-
book sanctions"; post-punishment;
secret sentences
invisible punishments, 22–23, 26. *See also*
civil disabilities; collateral consequences; internal exile; "off-book
sanctions"; post-punishment; secret
sentences
isolation, 53, 175. See also banishment;
displacement; exclusion

"jacket," 1, 53–56, 72, 102, 146, 168, 202n83.
See also criminal record; criminal
resume; "face sheet"; "overcoat"; rap
sheet
Jim Crow, 4, 41, 45, 73
Johnson, President Lyndon, 89

Kennedy, President John, 89
"Kids before Cons Act," 185, 237n57

labor, 32, 46–47, 89, 136; black, 47; hard,
31, 206n119; force, 169; manual, 132;
market skills, 123; prison, 161; slave, 42,
45–46
language: felony conviction, 29–30; fear,
90, 181; incarceration, 54; oppressor,
29; politics, 173, 176; race, 39, 181; reentry, 8, 68, 101, 129, 187
lawless, 173
lifers, 125, 132. *See also* life sentence
life sentence, 4, 125–126, 132. *See also*
death penalty; lifers
lifetime bans, 23–24, 99, 157–158, 182,
184; Pell grants, 225n43; restrictions,
157–158
Linnaeus, Carolus, 39–40; four races of
humans, 39; taxonomy, 39. *See also*
Blumenbach, Johann
literacy, 114, 122, 136, 225n68
Livingston, Edward, 31–32, 206n112
lock-down/locked down, 121, 124–127,
225n62. *See also* locked up
locked up, 12, 36, 47, 52–53, 57–59, 63, 67,
69, 74, 76, 79, 84–85, 101–102, 132, 137,
143, 145, 171, 173–174, 205n102. *See also*
lock-down/locked down
"lost" time, 60. *See also* bid; "doing time";
reenter; "to jail"
lying, 14, 75, 134, 166–169, 175, 229n29
lynching, 206n122

macro-level policies, 9
"magpie approach," 8. *See also* "in situ";
qualitative methods; research design
and methods
mandatory minimum prison sentences,
49, 50, 125, 132–133, 178; drug sentencing laws, 49–50. *See also* parole; "Three
Strikes You're Out"; "truth in sentencing"
Martin, Trayvon, 181
masculinity, 61. *See also* gender; hyper-
masculinity

"max/ed/ing out," 3, 68–69, 72, 79, 104–
    105, 123, 146, 194, 196, 213n21, 215n100,
    217n132, 234n138. *See also* parole; "with
    papers"
media, 33–35, 37; crime, criminality, 35, 37,
    39, 91, 96, 116; crack cocaine, 50, 92–
    93; black men, 94; black women and
    children, 34, 90–91, 207n142; "miss-
    ing white women syndrome," 34–35,
    207n141; politics, 33; racial bias, 92–93,
    208n148; white women and children,
    34–35. *See also* Christie, Governor
    Chris; "felon monster"
medieval, 30, 45
menace to society, 52, 176
mental health, 11–12, 53, 58, 60, 62–64,
    71, 87, 105, 123, 151, 183, 190, 204n63,
    213n28, 230n52; mentally ill, mental
    illness, 53, 58, 213n13, 236n40. *See also*
    post-traumatic stress disorder
micro-level behaviors, 8, 10, 13, 51
misdemeanor, 32, 180–181, 213n19, 229n23;
    misdemeanor murder, 206n122
"missing white women syndrome," 34–35,
    207n141. *See also* media
mixed-income housing, 88, 95, 97. *See also*
    affordable housing; public housing
models of disability, 24–26
money, 28, 52, 56, 73, 82, 94–95, 99, 102,
    104, 111, 114, 138–139, 141, 148–149,
    154, 156, 160, 165, 167; crime, 100, 109;
    employment, 142; family, 75–78, 105,
    189; "gate money," 51; incarceration, 58;
    payroll deduction, 145–146; Pell grants,
    116–118. *See also* costs; family; finances
monster, 35, 106, 177. *See also* "black
    monster"; criminal monster; "felon
    monster"
moral failure, 91
morality, 90–91, 158–159
moral panics, 34–35
moral turpitude, 125, 160
myth of reentry, 13, 177. *See also* hoax

Narcotics Anonymous (NA), 98, 103. *See
    also* Alcoholics Anonymous; drugs;
    drug use
National Action Plan of 1992 (Housing),
    94
National Assessment of Adult Literacy
    (NAAL), 122
National Commission on Severely Dis-
    tressed Housing (1992 Commission),
    93–95, 96, 116, 220n76, 220n77, 221n80,
    221n81, 221n82, 221n87, 221n90, 221n93
National Criminal History Improvement
    Program (NCHIP), 152–153, 231n63
National Housing Act of 1968, 89–90,
    218n39
National Instant Criminal Background
    Check System (NICS), 152–153, 181,
    230n57, 230n58
Native American, 85, 198; housing, 88,
    218n27
negative externalities, 15, 34, 151, 172, 175
net-widening, 15, 27, 181, 202
net widener policies, 19, 34, 45, 172
Newark, New Jersey, 5; lack of jobs, 146;
    Public Housing Authorities (PHAs),
    98; research context, 5–6; reentry to,
    14, 52, 56, 68, 83, 182
New Deal, 88
New Jersey Department of Corrections
    (DOC), 54, 73, 120, 198, 225n56
New Jersey Office of Educational Services
    (OES), 119–120, 225n55, 225n56. *See
    also* education
New Jersey Parole Board, 37–38
New York (state), 31–32, 185, 216n109,
    224n34, 233n115
New York City, 180
night watches, 179. *See also* slave patrols,
    slavery
"Nikko," 37, 208n159. *See also* political
    commercials; "White Hands"; "Willie
    Horton"
Nixon, President Richard, 48, 90, 220n79

No Early Release Act of 1997, 132–133, 226n90, 227n113; 85 percent time, 79, 127, 132–133; "ineligibility time," 132; reformed, 37–39, 208n163. *See also* "good time credits"

nonfelon, 27, 187–188. *See also* felony conviction

nonprofit organization, 1–2; gender, 201n72; parole officers, 123, 147; participants, 11, 39, 64, 74, 76, 79, 128, 150–151, 165, 179, 191; policies, 151; research context, 5–7, 10, 13

North Carolina, 36

occupational licenses, 156–159. *See also* good moral character tests

"off-book sanctions," 23. *See also* civil disabilities; collateral consequences; internal exile; invisible punishments; post-punishment; secret sentences

Omnibus Crime Bill of 1984, 91, 181; of 1968, 231n63

"one-drop" rule, 210n216

"One Strike, You're Out," 95–97, 100, 106. *See also* Clinton, President Bill; public housing

"others," 22, 26, 35, 173. *See also* blackness; social construction

outlaw, 3, 5, 19, 28, 30, 33, 69, 106, 110, 173, 174, 187–188

"overcoat," 15, 202n83. See also criminal record; criminal resume; "face sheet"; "jacket"; rap sheet

overinclusive, 98. *See also* blanket: policies; exclusionary laws/policies/statutes

Panopticon, 187

paperwork, 71–72, 134, 163, 229n29. *See also* identification

parole: DOC property, 72; eligibility, 54, 79, 132–133; life without, 36, 117, 125; mandatory, 38; officers, 1, 39, 123, 138; 147–148; reentry on, 3, 19, 23, 39, 56, 68, 84, 123, 126, 128, 138, 147, 164–165; requirements, 14, 18, 23, 84, 105, 110, 142, 147, 167–168; private, 80, 229n29; technical violation, 147, 148. *See also* Christie, Governor Chris; early release; fees; "max/ed/ing out"; No Early Release Act of 1997; "with paper"

participants: described, 7, 13–14; "key participants," 10; marginalized population, 7; meaning of, 6–7; research, 2. *See also* informant(s); research design and methods

Pell grants, 18, 112, 115, 116–119, 171, 185, 224n30, 224n40, 236n56, 237n57, 237n58. *See also* Amendment No. 1158; Basic Education Opportunity Grants; education; Higher Education Act of 1965; Hutchison, U.S. Senator Kaye Bailey; Violent Crime Control and Law Enforcement Act of 1994

Pell Pilot Program, 185–186. *See also* Department of Education; Pell grants

Pennsylvania, 31, 41, 224n34

"perfect storm," 178

Personal Responsibility and Work Opportunity Reconciliation Act of 1996 (PRWORA), 143–144, 181, 184, 228n12, 229n21

petite penal institution, 9–10, 16, 17, 106, 142, 174, 176

pillory, 31, 205n102

pistol-whipped, 36. *See also* "Willie Horton"

police, 1, 7, 19, 60, 74, 98, 102, 137, 145, 149, 152; cocaine, 50; housing, 155; militarization of, 5, 33, 49, 153, 179, 199n13, 230n59; overpolicing, 181; police tactics, 4, 47, 179; policing, 5, 42, 44, 48, 179–180, 183; race, 45, 48, 179–181; state police, 144. *See also* police state; reenter

police state, 126

political benefit (of a felony conviction), 172

political commercials, 35–38. *See also* "Nikko"; "White Hands"; "Willie Horton"

political rhetoric, 19, 23, 90–93, 96, 106, 116, 127, 177–178. *See also* rhetoric

politics of: crime and criminality, 36, 91, 95; fear, 34, 181; poverty, 95; punishment, 19, 173, 176, 178; race, 43, 95

post-punishment, 19, 27, 172; civil penalties, 27; penalties, 172; restrictions, 186. *See also* civil disabilities; collateral consequences; internal exile; invisible punishments; "off-book sanctions"; secret sentences

Post-Traumatic Stress Disorder (PTSD), 151, 214n45; defined, 60; emotions (inside prison), 57–60, 62–63; prison, 62, 101; reentry, 62, 150–151; symptoms, 17, 62, 175

poverty, 146, 182, 187; black women, 91; concentrated, 90, 113; criminality, 91–93, 95–96; public housing, 94; participants, 82; prison population, 50; welfare queen, 91. *See also* institutional abandonment

powder cocaine, 49, 92–93, 182, 212n281; defined, 49. *See also* crack cocaine; "War on Drugs"

predators, 63, 127. *See also* super-predators

prison cell, 32, 57–60, 63–64, 66, 121–122, 124, 127, 225n62, 226n94; cell mate, 54, 63; "doubled up," 60; open bed, 54–55; searches, 225n62; size, 57, 127, 226n94. *See also* bunk bed; cage (living in); cell mate; lock-down/locked down

prison education programs (PEP), 118, 224n36. *See also* certificate programs; education; "Inside-Out" programs

prisoner reentry. *See also* reenter

prison population, 37, 47, 53, 62, 110, 118, 122, 172, 183, 202n73

prison visit, 58–59, 214n37. *See also* family, finances, money

project-based subsidy, 90, 219n49. *See also* tenant-based voucher

public assistance, 90, 135, 172, 184. *See also* government benefits, public benefits, social benefits, Temporary Assistance to Needy Families (TANF)

public benefits, 3, 7, 15, 19, 23, 28, 33, 52, 90, 92, 142–143, 152–153, 164, 173, 182, 186. *See also* government assistance, public benefits, social benefits

public fear, 22, 33–34. *See also* fear

public housing, 17–18, 27; defined, 88; felony conviction, 84; gender, 82; government program, 88–91; housing for poor, 81–83; race, 91–92; severely distressed, 93–95; tenant criteria, 96–98. *See also* affordable housing; Clinton, President Bill; crack cocaine, mixed-income housing, "One Strike and You're Out,"

Public Housing Authorities (PHAs), 17–18, 221n99; legislative power of, 89; lifetime bans, 99; Newark PHAs, 98–99; wait lists, 97–99, 222n104, 222n110

public safety, 34, 38, 153, 159, 174, 182; threat to, 38, 86, 153–154, 159, 220n78

punishment, 4, 184, 186–187, 206n112, 229n23; felony conviction, 15, 22; felt experience, 31, 39, 175; politics, 19, 22; post-punishment, 19, 186; proportionality, 30; purpose of, 199n15; race, 16–17, 49; types of, 15, 31, 43–44, 205n102. *See also* sentencing laws

Quakers, 32

qualitative methods, 93, 201n53

race, 4–5, 14, 19, 22, 35, 39–44: 1988 presidential election, 36–37; criminality, 16, 19, 37, 41–44, 49; criminal background checks, 153; criminal justice system,

44–46; drugs, 5, 49–50, 92, 179; felony conviction, 156; history, 47, 179; housing, 93, 95; institutionalized, 4, 44; media's use of, 35; participants, 13–14; prisoner reentry, 4, 17; racism, 44; "racis," 39; significance of, 16–17; slavery, 41; social construction of, 16, 22, 39–40. *See also* Blumenbach, Johann; color line; Linnaeus, Carolus

racial animus, 4, 16, 22, 37, 179, 181, 187. *See also* racial bias

racial bias, 33, 35, 40, 44–45, 47–48, 50, 175, 178; categories, 40; criminality, 41; criminal justice system, 45–46, 179; disparities, 35, 42–43, 45, 47–48, 49–50; history, 41, 47; politics, 93; prejudice, 93; taxonomies, 40; "War on Drugs," 4, 50, 92. *See also* race; racial animus

racial fear, 90. *See also* fear

racialized: crime and criminality, 22, 34, 41, 179; groups, 40; justice, 45–46; laws and policies, 4, 22, 45, 93, 179; media, 34; policing, 42, 179; politics, 93; "War on Drugs," 4, 50. *See also* "War on Drugs"

racial minorities, 5, 13–14, 40–41, 44–45, 49, 92, 155

Rahway State Prison, 56–57, 116, 192

rap sheet, 1. See also criminal record; criminal resume; "face sheet"; "jacket"; "overcoat"

rape, 30, 36, 117; black men, 41, 208n159; black women, 41–42, 210n216; trauma, 60; violent crime, 30, 60, 117, 207n144, 213n29. *See also* Pennsylvania; "Willie Horton"

Reagan, Nancy, 56

Reagan, President Ronald, 50, 90–91, 219n57, 220n58. *See also* "welfare queen"

recidivism/recidivate(ing), 19, 106, 113, 116, 122, 142, 172, 228n3; debt, 145–146; education, 119, 122, 124; employment, 161, 169; failure rate (67 percent), 9, 19, 124, 142, 160–161, 177–178, 182, 185–186, 228n3; incarceration, 172; rate, 124, 169, 177; success rate (33 percent), 142, 177, 184, 228n3. *See also* churn; prisoner reentry; reenter

Reconstruction, 45

reenter, 2–3, 9, 14, 16–17, 19, 51–5; 95 percent, 21, 122; back-end, 19, 37, 79, 183; criminal charge, 55; culture of, 4, 8, 10, 13, 29, 52, 176; defined, 28; described, 4–5; dichotomous variable, 28, 51–52; displaced people, 67; emotions, 62–63, 75–76, 83, 105, 128–129, 164; individual responsibility, 2–3, 51–52, 76, 110, 142, 160–161, 173–176; men and women, 9; messy, 9, 175; myth, 13, 177; police, 175; process, 63, 105, 116, 123; research context, 7–9. *See also* clothes; recidivism/recidivate(ing); rehabilitation; social capital; waiting

reentry narrative, 147, 174, 176. *See also* survival

regulations, 15, 22–23, 38, 94, 173; corrections, 119; housing, 94–95; licensing, 158; parole, 38. *See also* administrative regulations; civil regulations; netwidening

rehabilitation, 22–23, 80, 97–99, 115, 122, 125, 154, 158, 160, 176–178, 187, 189–190, 202n84, 219n46; drug, 86, 98; programs, 37, 50

reincarceration, 51, 144

research design and methods, 5, 7–9. See also archival research; ethnography; "in situ"; "magpie approach"; qualitative methods

retribution (retributive), 4, 27, 146, 173; debt, 146; policies, 92, 172; political, 122; post-punishment, 172; punishment, 124, 159; theories, 172–173; violent, 43

Rice, Tamir, 180, 211n267

rhetoric, 18, 34, 90–93, 118; news media, 34, 91, 93, 96; political, 19, 23, 90–93, 96, 106, 116, 127, 177–178; punitive, 118, 178. *See also* political rhetoric; "soft on crime"; "tough on crime"

Scott, Walter, 180
secret sentences, 22–23. *See also* civil disabilities; collateral consequences; internal exile; invisible punishments; "off-book sanctions"; post-punishment
Section 8, 90–91, 99, 103, 105, 107, 217n14. *See also* Housing and Community Development Act of 1974; public housing; Public Housing Authorities
segregation, 26, 90, 218n39
selling drugs, 77, 103, 165
sensory overload, 70
sentencing court(s), 15, 23, 151
sentencing laws, 19, 48–49, 119, 173, 182; guidelines, 236n50
Sentencing Project, the, 93, 208n162
Sentencing Reform Act of 1984, 157
sexual violence, 35, 60, 61, 62, 207n144, 213n28, 213n29. *See also* violence
slavery, 46, 216n109; criminality of black skin, 41–42; justification of 42; peculiar institution, 44; race relations, 16, 179; relationship to a felony conviction, 4; voting, 46 . *See also* Black Codes; "free" blacks; Jim Crow; night watches; slave patrols
slave patrols, 43, 179. *See also* night watches; slavery
slave population, 43
social benefits, 7, 16, 19, 22–23, 28, 153. *See also* government assistance; public benefits; social benefits
social capital, 3, 10, 11, 13–14, 26, 52 64–65, 84, 87, 106, 113, 142, 183, 186; financial support, 6, 19. *See also* clothes; family; finances; money
social control, 15, 50, 121, 178; racial, 181

"social dirt," 24, 27, 113, 182
social disability, 2, 10, 148; analogy to a felony conviction, 16, 22; construction of 14, 16, 29; defined, 24; felony conviction, 27; housing, 99; public policies, 174; prisoner reentry, 11, 16, 174–175. *See also* disability studies; social disability theory
social disability theory, 22–23, 24–26
social(ly) constructed, 2, 4, 5, 16, 22–23, 26, 92, 174–175; blackness, 47–48; "others," 22; poverty, 91; race, 16, 39–40, 42
socially disabling: effects, 5, 28, 81, 142, 165–166, 169, 175, 177, 181–183; employment, 151, 157, 169, 172; exclusionary laws/policies/statutes, 2, 19, 106, 146, 148, 152, 159, 187; felony conviction, 3, 16; housing, 87; public's safety, 174; sex offenders, 203n28
social model of disability, 2
social networks, 6, 96, 137–138. *See also* Facebook; social capital
Social Security, 6, 72, 74–75, 128, 168, 231n62. *See also* identification
social welfare, 90. *See also* Personal Responsibility and Work Opportunity Reconciliation Act; Temporary Assistance to Needy Families; welfare
Society for Human Resource Management (SHRM), 154–155, 231n71, 231n73
"soft on crime," 36–37, 173, 174. *See also* Dukakis, Governor Michael
South, the, 44; criminal laws, 46; southern politicians, 45–46, 49; violence, 44. *See also* "black crimes"; convict leasing; "one-drop" rule
South Carolina, 43, 180
South Woods State Prison, 57, 192
stigma, 3–4, 16, 19, 22, 24; examples, 31, 151; fear, 26, 155, 174; felony conviction, 19, 26, 31, 50, 114, 163; legal stigma, 163; social stigma, 26, 114. *See also* pillory; "social dirt"

super-predators, 94, 220n78. *See also* predators

Supplemental Nutrition Assistance program (SNAP), 184. *See also* food insecurity; food stamps

supply-side economics, 88–89

surveillance, 5, 48–49, 59, 127, 152–153, 187, 208n167, 216n101; personal, 62

survival, 17, 51, 59–60; reentry, 28, 79, 170, 176, 188; prison, 53, 56, 58–66, 123, 176; tactics, 66. *See also* gray area

technology, 28, 71, 111, 122–123; database management, 153

technological: changes, 64, 123; deficits, 123; knowledge, 122–123

Temporary Aid to Needy Families (TANF), 143, 181, 184, 228n12

Temporary Rental Assistance (TRA), 103, 222n124,

tenant-based voucher, 90–91, 219n50. *See also* project-based subsidy

tenant criteria, 96–97

terrorism, 184–185; 9/11, 5, 60, 152–153, 158, 184–185; attacks, 35, 60; terroristic threat, 184–185, 194, 196, 236n54. *See also* Post-Traumatic Stress Disorder

threat: assessment, 38, 97–98, 154; crime, 34, 50; drugs, 220n79; prison, 147; reenter, 82–83; violating parole, 142; violence, 60, 121, 127, 228n2. *See also* public safety; terrorism

"Three Strikes You're Out," 49. *See also* mandatory minimum prison sentences; "truth in sentencing"

"to jail," 58, 75, 177

total institution, 11, 52–53; autonomy, 79; dysfunction, 61, 121; madness, 58; mental harm, 60; treated like animals, 56, 57–58, 59, waiting, 121–122. *See also* caged; degradation: ritual

"tough on crime," 3–5, 49, 122, 125, 153; drugs, 91; education, 118–119; politi-cians, 18, 33–34, 36–37, 43, 115–116, 132–133, 172–173; political rhetoric, 4, 18, 33–34, 36–37, 116, 118–119, 132, 157, 173–174, 177, 179, 181, 185–186. *See also* mandatory minimum prison sentences; "Three Strikes You're Out"; "truth in sentencing"; "War on Drugs"; white supremacy; "Willie Horton"

"traditional nine crimes," 30–33

trauma, 3; prison, 62–64, 101; prison visits, 59; sexual violence, 61, 62; traumatic events, 60. *See also* post-traumatic stress disorder (PTSD)

Truman, President Harry, 88

"truth in sentencing," 49–50

Union County College, 116. *See also* "Inside-Out" programs

urban communities, 45, 47, 50, 89; core, 47; urban centers, 46–47. *See also* ghetto

urban crime, 92

U.S. Sentencing Commission, 211n258, 212n279, 212n283, 212n286, 220n74

violence: against women and children, 32, 35, 82, 153, 207n143; cocaine, 4, 50; gang, 124, 127; media attention, 92; prison, 56, 60–61, 101, 119, 121, 124, 127, 154, 213n29, 228n2; race, 43; sexual, 35, 60, 61, 62, 207n144, 213n28, 213n29; slavery, 43–44; terrorism, 184; urban, 33

violent crime, 34–35, 125, 154, 207n144, 220n62. *See also* infamy; "traditional nine crimes"; Violent Crime Control and Law Enforcement Act of 1994

Violent Crime Control and Law Enforcement Act of 1994, 116, 181, 224n40

Virginia, 31, 42

waiting, 120–124. *See also* reentry; total institution

war, 5, 33, 48–49, 60, 62, 179, 181, 199n13. *See also* police

"War on Drugs," 4–5, 18, 48–50, 91, 96, 116, 127, 157, 199n13, 220n79, 220n79, 226n94, 235n32; crack cocaine, 49; education, 116; life sentences, 127; occupational licenses, 157; politics, 33; public housing, 91, 96; race, 4–5, 48, 50, 179, 181. *See also* "tough on crime"

welfare, 90–91, 103, 143, 157, 184. *See also* Personal Responsibility and Work Opportunity Reconciliation Act; social welfare; Temporary Assistance to Needy Families

"welfare queen," 91

whipping, 31, 41, 43

white flight, 48, 89

white fear, 35, 37, 42–44, 47, 179, 208n159, 220n78. *See also* fear

"White Hands," 36. *See also* "Nikko"; political commercials; "Willie Horton"

white supremacy, 41–42, 46, 172; hegemony, 42–43

"wildin' out," 53, 56, 65, 121, 213n12, 213n26, 215n88; defined, 53. *See also* mental health

Willie Horton, 36

"Willie Horton," 36; 1988 presidential election, 36; 1990 North Carolina U.S. Senate race, 36; crime politics, 36, 174; political commercial, 36; politics, 36–37; race and crime, 37; "Willie Horton-izing," 174. *See also* "Nikko"; political commercials; "tough on crime"; "White Hands"

Wilson, Darren, 181

"without" or "off paper," 79, 213n21, 217n132. *See also* max/ed/ing out

"with paper," 3, 199n6. *See also* "max/ed/ing out"; parole

work experience, 29, 67, 86, 110, 146, 161, 163, 166, 189

ABOUT THE AUTHOR

Keesha M. Middlemass is an Associate Professor of Political Science at Trinity University (San Antonio, Texas). Her research primarily focuses on the intersection of race, inequality, public policies, politics, and institutions, and she studies these issues using interdisciplinary research designs and multiple methods. Her scholarship is published in *Punishment & Society*, the *Prison Journal*, *Aggressive Behavior*, *Criminal Justice & Behavior*, and *Social Science Quarterly*.